ADVANCE PRAISE FOR *WALKING TO THE END OF THE WORLD*

"Beth Jusino doesn't pull any punches in her vivid [...] of the pilgrimage she and her husband made, but [...] with us her small victories and the many lessons s[...] her marriage, and just plain 'life.' Perhaps most un[...] [...]ons is contained in her 'Santiago Moment' near the end of [...] book: gratitude!"
—**Kevin A. Codd**, author of *To the Field of Stars*

"Sprinkled with self-deprecating humor and life insights, *Walking to the End of World* recounts a host of colorful characters, drawing readers into the daily trials and triumphs of a challenging yet meaningful journey and break from ordinary life."
—**Anna Dintaman Landis**, author of *Camino Francés: Village to Village Guide*

"An enchanting tale of faith, friendship, and pushing your own limits. I'm probably never going to hike the Camino (who am I kidding? I'm definitely not), but Jusino's book had me looking up flights. She may be a novice pilgrim, but she is a master storyteller."
—**Geraldine DeRuiter**, author of *All Over the Place: Adventures in Travel, True Love, and Petty Theft*

"Beth Jusino has captured the essence of this ancient pilgrimage, which inspires the reader with detail, wit, and spot-on accounts of what it's really like to walk the Camino de Santiago."
—**Gabriel Schirm**, author of *Sunrises to Santiago: Searching for Purpose on the Camino de Santiago*

"This wholly fresh story enchanted me with the cultures, people, chapels, and landscape. Despite the rigors of the Way, Jusino invites us to relish the rhythm of walking and delight in convivial evenings with other pilgrims over free-flowing wine and local food. With the depth of hard-won wisdom, she asks at the end 'Who had I become?'"
—**Gail D. Storey**, author of *I Promise Not to Suffer: A Fool for Love Hikes the Pacific Crest Trail*

"This charming tale is infused with wry, self-deprecating humor and vivid descriptions of people and places that carry you along the 1000-mile trek as though you are there too."
—**Wendy Hinman**, author of *Sea Trials* and *Tightwads on the Loose*

"*Walking to the End of the World* keeps us turning its pages—an elegant story woven in the seasoned voice of writer Beth Jusino, who shares great insight into her own strengths and weaknesses, relationships of all sorts, and a world view we'd all do well to consider. Among Camino memoirs this book takes its place in the top tier."
—**Steve Watkins**, Author of *Pilgrim Strong: Rewriting My Story on the Way of St. James*

WALKING
TO THE
BETH JUSINO
END OF THE
WORLD

A THOUSAND MILES ON
THE CAMINO DE SANTIAGO

**MOUNTAINEERS
BOOKS**

MOUNTAINEERS BOOKS is the publishing division of The Mountaineers, an organization founded in 1906 and dedicated to the exploration, preservation, and enjoyment of outdoor and wilderness areas.

1001 SW Klickitat Way, Suite 201 • Seattle, WA 98134
800.553.4453 • www.mountaineersbooks.org

Printed in the United States of America
Distributed in the United Kingdom by Cordee, www.cordee.co.uk
23 22 21 20   2 3 4 5

Copyeditor: Amy Smith Bell
Design and layout: Heidi Smets Graphic Design
Cartographer: Lohnes+Wright

Library of Congress Cataloging-in-Publication Data
Names: Jusino, Beth, author.
Title: Walking to the end of the world : a thousand miles on the Camino de Santiago / by Beth Jusino.
Description: Seattle, WA : Mountaineers Books, 2018.
Identifiers: LCCN 2018007474| ISBN 9781680512038 (trade paper) | ISBN 9781680512045 (ebook)
Subjects: LCSH: Jusino, Beth—Travel—Camino de Santiago de Compostela. | Camino de Santiago de Compostela. | Spain, Northern—Description and travel. | France, Southern—Description and travel. | Christian pilgrims and pilgrimages—Spain—Santiago de Compostela.
Classification: LCC DP285 .J87 2018 | DDC 914.4/8048412—dc23
LC record available at https://lccn.loc.gov/2018007474

Mountaineers Books titles may be purchased for corporate, educational, or other promotional sales, and our authors are available for a wide range of events. For information on special discounts or booking an author, contact our customer service at 800-553-4453 or mbooks@mountaineersbooks.org.

♻ Printed on recycled paper

ISBN (paperback): 978-1-68051-203-8
ISBN (ebook): 978-1-68051-204-5

For Eric, of course

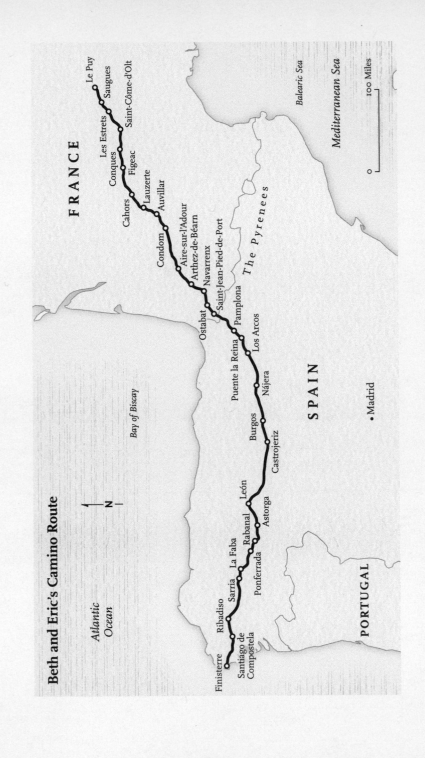

Beth and Eric's Camino Route

N

Atlantic
Ocean

Bay of Biscay

Balearic Sea

Mediterranean Sea

100 Miles

FRANCE

SPAIN

PORTUGAL

The Pyrenees

• Madrid

Le Puy
Saugues
Saint-Côme-d'Olt
Les Estrets
Conques
Figeac
Cahors
Lauzerte
Auvillar
Condom
Aire-sur-l'Adour
Arthez-de-Béarn
Navarrenx
Saint-Jean-Pied-de-Port
Ostabat
Pamplona
Puente la Reina
Los Arcos
Nájera
Burgos
Castrojeriz
León
Rabanal
Astorga
La Faba
Ponferrada
Sarria
Ribadiso
Finisterre
Santiago de
Compostela

CONTENTS

INTRODUCTION
THE TRAIN

I climbed the narrow stairs to the upper level of the train, my backpack strapped over my shoulders, a bag of sandwiches clutched in my hand, and my husband a few steps behind me. The car was empty as I settled into a forward-facing seat, feeling smug. Everything was going exactly as planned.

Eric and I had flown from Seattle to Paris the day before, breezing through a predawn customs interview during a layover in Iceland. We easily found the high-speed train that took our jet-lagged bodies directly from Charles de Gaulle Airport to Lyon, bypassing the confusion of downtown Paris. Following a map I'd printed at home, we navigated a few blocks to our Airbnb room in a private apartment, chatted with our English-speaking host, and found an open restaurant for dinner even though it was a holiday. (I didn't know that the Monday after Easter is considered a holiday in France—but then, as far as I can tell, so are most Mondays and quite a few Tuesdays.)

The next morning Eric and I wandered through Lyon's famous Les Halles market and indulged in our first *cafés* and *pain au chocolat*. We strolled along the Rhône River and were back at the station with an hour to spare before our local train departed for the two-hour ride southwest to Le Puy. So far, so good.

The monitors said that the train was on time, so I gathered my courage and stood in a food stand line to acquire, through pointing and a helpless look, *jambon* and Brie sandwiches for the road.

When the train doors opened, we were on the platform and ready to board. A man climbed into the train car right behind us. He was tall, almost gaunt, all angles and with what Eric would later describe as an epic French nose. He, too, was carrying a backpack. Eyeing our practical shoes and bulging packs, the man rattled off a string of syllables that sounded like a question.

My stomach tightened, and I responded with the sentence I'd practiced all morning: *Je ne parle pas français* (I do not speak French).

After months of sporadic online lessons, the only other sentence I felt confident with was *Le pomme est rouge* (The apple is red). If I thought carefully about the way to add a direct object, I could say, "The cat eats the apple." Not once in the six weeks we spent in France did anyone ask me about apples.

Eric, though naturally better than me at linguistics, hadn't bothered with any language lessons. He wanted to "learn French from the French," which so far meant his vocabulary was limited to what he'd picked up watching a few French movies with English subtitles.

Undeterred, our train companion pointed to our bags. "Chemin de San Jacques?"

Oui! We were here to walk the Way of Saint James.

He nodded and pointed to himself. "Jean Claude."

Well, of course he was. How very French.

Jean Claude, it turned out, knew a little Spanish, as did Eric. They pieced together that he was coming from Strasbourg, in northern France, to walk the Way. We told him we were Americans, from Seattle. That exhausted our vocabularies.

We were smiling mutely at one another, fellow travelers at the beginning of a great adventure, when a woman with a lit cigarette clattered up the metal stairs to our car, trailing smoke and perfume. She said something fast and loud. She looked angry, or maybe concerned. I let the words flow over me, distracted by the cigarette. *Could she have that on a train?*

Jean Claude, however, was suddenly all attention. He asked her something. She answered, gesturing out the window. He leapt to his feet and paused just long enough to find the words for us.

"Wrong train!"

There wasn't time to ask questions, even if I knew how. The train to Le Puy left at 11:10. It was 11:05.

We scrambled to collect backpacks, jackets, and the bag of sandwiches, then tumbled out the doors and onto the platform, sprinting for the stairs. We dodged French families, workers, and whoever else stood around a train station in the middle of the day.

I found a screen. The Le Puy train now said Track F. The monitors had originally sent us to Track B, but must have changed as soon as we were out of sight. It was 11:07.

The three of us ran across the station, up a different set of stairs, and onto another platform. The train was still there.

We dove through the first open door, into a car crowded with people. I saw backpacks, walking sticks, and solemn faces. The doors slid closed while we were still standing, panting, and the train started moving before we could sit down.

The train we'd first boarded went the opposite direction that day, to the industrial city of Grenoble. Twelve weeks later, when we were resting a thousand miles away on the Atlantic Coast, a man in Grenoble would behead his former boss, throw explosive gas canisters at a chemical factory, and raise an Islamic flag. France, already on edge after the *Charlie Hebdo* attacks, would raise the terror threat level to high.

But on that Tuesday, Eric and I were going back in time, not forward. We were bound for a thousand-year-old story full of Knights Templar and saints performing miracles.

As the train cleared the station, we collapsed into the last seats available, near the bathroom and facing backward. I get sick on moving vehicles, especially if I'm facing backward. But at least we were going to the right place. And after this, we'd be on foot. Surely it would be easier on foot.

Or maybe not. The pattern of those confusing ten minutes in the train station, I learned, would repeat itself over the next three months. I was sure that four years of reading every book, researching every item we carried, and soaking in the details of the Camino de Santiago, the Way of Saint James, would make me feel prepared. (I *really* like being prepared.)

But then, practically every day, the Camino threw me something unexpected. The train platform switch. The cow on the wrong side of the fence. The castle on the hill. The miracle sheep. The entire town that was "closed for rest." The missing woman. The river perfect for swimming. And the people . . . the many, many people.

Somewhere I read that each person who walks the Camino de Santiago experiences it in three stages. Regardless of how far they go, what shape they're in, or why they think they're there, the first third of their journey will be a test of the body, the second a test of the mind, and the final third a gift to the soul.

Seventy-nine days gave us a lot of time for tests and gifts.

When we got home, people would ask, "How was your trip?" How does a person answer that? It was beautiful. Painful. Perspective changing. It taught me that there are some things I just can't prepare myself for.

The only way to really explain it is to share it. So here we go.

PART I

A TEST OF THE BODY

A quiet moment in the cloisters of Cahors

LE PUY

The train followed a valley as it climbed into the Massif Central, the rolling high country in the middle of southern France. We left modern suburbs and then sprawling farms behind as the land grew wooded and steep.

Just across a river, on top of a hill, was a crumbling stone castle. Most of our train car companions ignored it, but Eric and I couldn't look away. You don't see many castles in the States.

We stopped in a few shabby-looking towns, where most of the people not wearing backpacks got off. There were just half a dozen of us left to hear the garbled announcement that we were arriving in Le Puy-en-Velay.

This was it. From here, we would walk.

Eric and I gathered our packs, adjusted straps that still felt awkward, and stepped into the chilly April air two thousand feet—or six hundred meters, since I had to start thinking in metric—above sea level. We exited the station onto a modern-looking street and looked blankly around.

Based on everything I'd read about Le Puy, I'd been expecting towering cathedrals and cobblestone streets. Instead, I faced a parking lot and a featureless white apartment building. I hadn't prepared for this.

The west-facing door of the Cathédrale Notre-Dame du Puy

Every year, a quarter of a million people follow some part of the Way of Saint James. They travel by foot, bicycle, or horseback toward the Spanish city of Santiago de Compostela, about sixteen hundred kilometers from where we currently stood. They come from around the world, and for a multitude of reasons. It's not uncommon for complete strangers to ask, "Why are you walking the Way?"

I never had a good answer. I certainly wasn't there for sport. In the spring of 2015, at thirty-eight years old, I didn't look like someone who could—let alone would—walk a thousand miles. I wasn't the "outdoors type." I didn't run marathons, climb mountains, or even exercise regularly. Sure, I walked almost everywhere in my urban neighborhood, but I'd never been backpacking. My idea of a hike was a three-mile stroll through well-tended, preferably flat, city parks.

Nor did I go to France looking for a miracle or pursuing an existential spiritual quest. Even the word "pilgrimage," with its religious undertones, made me uncomfortable. I'd grown up in a traditional Baptist church and was educated from kindergarten through college in Christian schools, but my relationship with the church had changed over time. Over the past decade we'd amicably gone our separate ways, and I wasn't interested in revisiting the relationship.

And no, I wasn't seeking the answer to some important question, grieving a loss, or looking for a radical change to my everyday life. Eric and I both did meaningful work that fit our personalities and passions. We had good friends, a healthy extended family, and hobbies galore. We were childless by choice, so there was no drama there. We lived in a city I loved, in a corner of the world I thought was just about perfect. But yet here I was, in a remote corner of France few Americans had ever heard of, with a plan to walk all the way to the Atlantic Ocean. Why *was* I here?

Well, because twenty years of postmodern adulting had burned me to a crisp. My life, like that of most of those in my generation, was controlled by the relentless demands of screens. I ran a publishing consulting business and spent my days, and too many nights, hunched over a laptop. Though I controlled my schedule, I had trouble believing that I could take a day off and still pay the rent. I had four separate email inboxes, all of them filled with demands on my attention. My electronic calendar was a rainbow of appointments, commitments, deadlines, and tasks—all overlapping. My social media habits had accelerated with the rest of my life's demands. I constantly checked my smartphone. Some days I couldn't get from my apartment to my car without opening Facebook. What if I missed something?

What I was missing was a life that felt real. I was here because the Camino, with its thousand years of history, felt real.

I first heard the phrase Camino de Santiago in 2010 from a fellow writer who blogged about her one-week trek along a medieval trail. She described endless rain and mud, steep climbs, physical pain, and blisters. Nothing she said should have appealed to me, sheltered and sedentary in my comfortable urban cocoon, with a cat purring on my lap. And yet, something drew me to look into it further.

I knew the wilderness called to Eric. When he was a teenager, his church youth group took him on backpacking and canoe trips through a Canadian national park. He loved it so much he went back as a college student and became a trip leader. For as long as I'd known him, he'd talked about walking the Appalachian Trail someday. For just as long, I'd told him he'd have to go alone. I don't sleep in tents, and I don't eat freeze-dried food for weeks on end.

But the way my writer friend described this Camino thing seemed different. A long trail that didn't follow a steep mountain range, but instead wound through pastoral towns and countryside? A well-marked path dotted with hostels offering affordable beds and showers and wine every evening? A historic journey that didn't require smartphones, or email, or the latest app? The Camino called to me.

I did what any self-respecting book lover would do. I went to the library and checked out everything with the words "Camino de Santiago." The first book I read set the course for everything that followed.

Conrad Rudolph's *Pilgrimage to the End of the World* is a slim memoir with grainy photographs and an emphasis on art and history. To be honest, it's not the most informative book available, but it cemented in my mind that Le Puy-en-Velay, France, was where a person went to begin their walk to Santiago de Compostela.

It would be months more before I understood that Saint-Jean-Pied-de-Port, eight hundred kilometers closer to the holy city, was the more common starting point for modern journeyers to Santiago. Of the fifteen thousand Americans who arrived at the Pilgrim's Office in Santiago in 2015, fewer than two percent started in Le Puy-en-Velay. But for me, "the Camino" was already established as a three-month, two-country, thousand-mile journey that went not just to Santiago, but all the way to the Atlantic Ocean at Finisterre.

Instinctively, I knew that a thirty-day trip wasn't enough for the extended, intense sabbatical I desperately needed.

The next question was how I could convince my husband to fly off to Europe for a quarter of a year. It's not that he's put off by new places. Between us, Eric and I have sold our belongings, packed our cars, and moved across the country half a dozen times, often without jobs or housing lined up. We've lived in every time zone in the continental United States, but international travel had never been part of our shared experience or vocabulary. Neither of us grew up in families that traveled far, and we'd both been too responsible (or cash-strapped) for gap-year adventures before or after college.

Once we were tied to traditional jobs and the ubiquitous two-week American vacation, Eric repeatedly claimed he had no interest in long plane rides followed by running from tourist site to tourist site. On top of that, the Camino de Santiago has Christian roots, and Eric's divorce from his fundamentalist church upbringing had left some strong feelings about religion. I wasn't sure how he would react to spending three months under the sign of the cross.

Still, the first time I floated the idea of a long walk along a historically Catholic path in Europe, he was on board. Clearly I wasn't the only one who needed a radical change in daily life.

After that, though, the conversation stalled. It was easy to say we wanted to do this, but the logistics were daunting. How could we take three months off in our "prime career" years? We both had jobs that we didn't want to quit. And bills. And family obligations. And an aging, high-maintenance cat.

And yet. We had a bit of money tucked away, the last remnant of a pre–Great Recession nest egg. We were responsibly saving it for that oft-predicted rainy day. Jetting off to Europe wasn't responsible.

And yet. Our daily lives continued to feel stifling and unexplored. Years passed. The Camino kept coming up. I kept bringing it up. I watched Martin Sheen in *The Way*. I read more Camino books. My computer screens kept filling faster than I could empty them. Projects and people flickered across my overcommitted life like social media streams, taking time but barely leaving ripples in my memory.

It wasn't until I started dreaming about running away from everything that I finally jumped. Late one September night, after a rough week and without much discussion, I bought two nonrefundable plane tickets for a date seven months in the future.

We were going to do this.

Offering plenty of notice and cashing in all of the goodwill he'd stocked up over years of hard work, Eric arranged for a leave of absence from his job. I stopped taking new projects and rearranged deadlines with my regular clients. My sister, fresh out of college and underemployed, agreed to move to Seattle and house-sit/cater to the difficult cat.

That's when the panic kicked in. What was I doing? I didn't know anything about backpacking. I'd never slept in a hostel. I didn't even own a sleeping bag!

I threw myself into overpreparation to make up for what I didn't know. I obsessed over my packing list, haunting Camino Facebook groups and sporting goods stores. I spent a fortune on just the right hiking shirt (and then, at the last minute, tossed in a "backup" shirt I'd owned for years, which I ended up wearing every day). I collected every suggested thing we might need, including bags of safety pins (good idea), wet wipes (bad idea), and four hundred adhesive bandages (we used three).

As the fall turned to winter and the winter to spring, I worked seven days a week to meet my obligations, arrange our absence, and make sure there were no surprises. Eric gamely ignored me. We both accept that I'm the planner in our partnership and he's the improviser. A week before we left, he made one trip to REI, came home with two merino wool T-shirts and a raincoat, and declared himself ready to go. I couldn't decide whether to be mad or jealous.

I filled the smallest cracks of time with last-minute tasks. When I had trouble sleeping because of the stress, I reminded myself that as soon as we got to Le Puy, everything would be okay. I would turn off my phone and bury it in my backpack, to be used only in dire emergencies. I would pay attention only to the trail in front of me. Surely, then, all of my anxiety would go away. I would let go, and as I'd heard time after time, the Camino would provide.

But clearly, this Le Puy train station was too early to let go. Where were the cobblestone streets? Where was the cathedral? Where were our beds?

I had the name of a pilgrim's hostel, a *gîte de pèlerin*, recommended by someone on some website, but without Google Maps, I had no idea how to find it. And I wasn't going to break my own "no phone" rule in the first five minutes. Surely we could figure this out.

I didn't see any scallop shells, the traditional symbol of the Camino, or the red-and-white–striped markers of the Chemin du Puy, the French part of the Way of Saint James as it wound from Le Puy to Saint-Jean-Pied-de-Port. And of course, I had no idea how to ask anyone.

As I stood there, not quite panicking, Eric pointed out Jean Claude's tall form striding away. He'd saved us once already, and he looked like he knew where he was going. Trying not to be obvious, we trailed him across a busy street and then up a hill. The buildings grew older, the streets grew narrower, and finally the pavement under our feet turned to cobblestone. This felt like the right direction.

At one point our guide looked back and waved, then pointed ahead and said something in French. So much for not being obvious. He led us up more steep streets until I was sweating and breathless. If I found walking in a hilly town this hard, what would happen when I got to the Pyrenees?

I distracted myself by looking around. This part of Le Puy-en-Velay felt like a movie set. Crooked houses made of black volcanic rock leaned over streets barely wide enough for the occasional car to pass. Old women in long dresses sat in doorways and watched us. I wanted to stop and soak it in but couldn't risk losing Jean Claude.

Finally, our guide turned again and waited for us to catch up. He asked, in broken Spanish, where we were going. I pointed to the name on our paper, not brave enough to try the words out loud: Gîte de pèlerin de Les Amis de Saint Jacques, 28 rue Cardinal de Polignac.

The Frenchman nodded and pointed down an angled street, then strode off in a different direction. Left on our own, Eric and I wandered up and down the narrow street three times before we noticed the engraved number 28 on a thick wooden door that led to a courtyard. Two plastic patio chairs sat incongruously against the stone walls, and a small sign on the door announced, as far as we could tell, that the gîte opened at 3:00. It was only 2:30, but we weren't sure we could find our way back if we ventured too far. We settled in to wait, feeling awkward and excited and mesmerized.

Precisely at 3:00, an older man ambled into the courtyard and unlocked the door, cheerily waving us inside. His name was Isidore, and we discovered he spoke only about ten words of English. When he realized that we spoke even less French, his smile faltered, but only for a second. It was becoming clear that our lack of basic skills in the local language was going to be a problem, yet our French host welcomed us to his country anyway. Anyone who believes the stereotype that the French are all aloof and judgmental has never met Isidore.

The gîte was run by the Amis de Saint Jacques, the Friends of Saint James, an organization of volunteers like Isidore that ran several gîtes de pèlerins, including the one where we now sat, for pilgrims walking the Way of Saint James in France. They provided beds, showers, breakfasts, and guidance for free, although guests were invited to give donations of whatever they could afford.

Isidore was joined by a second volunteer, a woman who spoke even less English than him, and together they plowed ahead to settle the unprepared American *enfants*. The woman, whose name I never caught, told us in simple words and pantomime that we were the first Americans to stay in their gîte this year. That made me a little nervous until I remembered they'd just opened for the season a few days before. Many French facilities along the Camino close from October to Easter, since winter storms in the high country can be dangerous for hikers.

Still, it was a taste of the reaction we would get almost daily for the entire time we were in France. *You are American? Here? I did not think Americans knew about the Chemin!* But here we were.

Isidore gave us a sheet printed in English with the house rules. We were to leave our backpacks in lockers in a separate room, far from our beds, out of concern for bedbugs. There was a welcome session for all new pilgrims that afternoon at 5:30. We were to be back inside the gîte before they locked the doors at 10:00. Breakfast would be at 6:00 the next morning, and there was a pilgrim mass in the cathedral at 7:00.

6:00 a.m.? I knew, in theory, that pilgrims started early, but my night-owl self still shuddered.

Isidore pulled out his ink pad and carefully placed the first stamp in our credentials, basically our pilgrimage passports. The Camino credential is a multipaneled cardboard sheet that's stamped each day by a hostel or pilgrim office in order to prove that a person is a pilgrim moving forward. The *donativo* gîtes like this one and municipally run hostels only accept guests with credentials, to prevent tourists from taking advantage of the free or well-below-market rates. Many churches and even restaurants add their own stamps, and as weeks pass, a Camino credential becomes a memento and visual story of a person's unique trip. Most pilgrims consider their tattered, colorful credentials the most important souvenirs of their experience, and so it was a big deal when Isidore signed his own name to verify our acceptance to the Way of Saint James.

Most gîtes let pilgrims stay for only one night. However, Isidore explained/pantomimed that since we had traveled so far and were still probably jet-lagged, Eric and I could spend two nights here with them.

I met Eric's eye and tried to read his mind. We weren't in a hurry. Our return flight to Seattle was three months away, which gave us

more than enough time to reach the Atlantic. But we'd been anticipating this for, literally, years. And now we were here.

Eric shook his head, just a tiny bit, at the same time I did.
After almost fourteen years of marriage, we did stuff like that.
"Non, merci," he told our hosts. We would begin our Camino the
next morning.

Isidore nodded, his expression unreadable. His partner led us
up three flights of stairs, where she assigned us each to a small
cubicle in the *dortoir*, the dormitory. The Friends of Saint Jacques
eased us into communal living by giving each person a partially
walled area with a cot, a chair, a lamp, and a wooden cupboard. The
entrances were even covered with curtains.

Eric and I unpacked and spent the next two hours wandering
through Le Puy, taking in its steep angles and red roofs and black
rock. Our meandering path brought us eventually to the Cathédrale
Notre-Dame du Puy.

The church was unlocked, dark, and mostly empty in the quiet
of midafternoon. We tiptoed through the echoing stone sanctuary and studied the elaborate altar, where the small face of the
cathedral's Black Virgin looked out from above a stiff, conical robe
of gold brocade. There were ebony statues like this of Mary and
the Christ Child scattered across central Europe. Most dated to
medieval times—the Black Virgin in Le Puy is a replica of one
given to the church by Louis IX as he returned from a Crusade in
1254—but the symbolism behind their appearance has been lost
to history.

We stopped in the cathedral gift shop to get our second credential stamps, and Eric picked out a French-language guidebook
with detailed information about gîtes and other services along
GR65, the French Grande Randonnée hiking route for the Way
of Saint James between Le Puy and Saint-Jean-Pied-de-Port. That
book, *Miam Miam Dodo* (which translates to something like baby
talk for "yum-yum sleep-sleep"), became our primary reference
all the way to the Spanish border, despite its silly name.

From the cathedral, we climbed toward the most visually
familiar icon of Le Puy, the chapel of Saint-Michel d'Aiguilhe. The
tenth-century structure rises improbably out of an almost vertical needle of volcanic rock three hundred feet—I mean, eighty

meters—high. At the base of the 268-step climb, a ticket collector warned us that the site would close in fifteen minutes. We could *probably* make the climb to the top, he said, but we wouldn't be able to linger. And yes, we'd have to pay full price for the tickets.

Eric and I thanked him, but decided to pass, a decision I've regretted ever since. Instead, figuring we needed all the help we could get on this adventure, we wound back to the pilgrim welcome center, just across the street from the cathedral, in time for the daily information session.

We found about a dozen people already there, sitting in an awkward circle in front of a fireplace. The volunteer hosts, who of course spoke only French, asked a question that set off a round of what seemed to be introductions.

When I told the group that my name was Beth, I saw a lot of furrowed brows. "Bett?" The host's mouth twisted, as if he couldn't quite get the syllable out. I remembered that Isidore, too, had trouble with my name.

"Elizabeth?" I offered.

Everyone relaxed and smiled. "Ah! Elisabet!" And just like that, I changed my name. For the next thirty-five days I was Elizabeth, a name no one but my immediate family had ever used before.

Introductions over, Eric and I smiled blankly and watched the room while others chatted. My first impression was that everyone was older than us by at least a decade. About half the group seemed to be traveling together, and one of their members, a friendly woman named Michelle, spoke enough English to introduce herself.

She asked where we were staying the next night and seemed surprised that we didn't have reservations. I was surprised that she did. The Camino literature I'd read never mentioned reservations. A person could just walk into town and trust that there would be a place to stay. Traveling with a large group must be different, I thought.

The conversation lulled, and I was starting to get antsy when a new person came in. The volunteers greeted him, and after a few seconds I saw them light up. "Canada!" I heard, and then they pointed to us: "American!" We were from the same hemisphere, so therefore they assumed we would have things to talk about.

The Canadian, who looked about our age, made his way over warily. "Hello, I am Remi." His words were hesitant, his accent strong. Remi was from a small town in Quebec, and French was his native tongue. He rarely spoke English.

Rarely was better than never, though, and we pieced together our stories. This was the first time Remi had ever left Quebec. A devout Catholic, he always dreamed of walking the pilgrimage of Saint Jacques. He'd been planning to come in five years, when his children were older and his job was more stable. He patted his belly. "And when I have time to lose this."

But then, the week before, something happened. Remi didn't go into detail, but the upshot was that he suddenly had a month off work. His wife told him it was a sign from God to begin his pilgrimage. So he bought a plane ticket and a bunch of trekking gear, and he flew to Paris.

I'd been planning this trip for years, I realized, and this man didn't know he was coming until eight days ago.

We asked if he was going to the pilgrims' mass the next morning. Remi sighed and touched his cheek. He'd cracked a tooth and had to get it fixed before he could begin walking. There were no dentists open this late in the afternoon, so he would deal with it tomorrow and start on Thursday. As we said our goodbyes, I hoped he would be a fast walker and catch up with us, but he never did.

Back on the street, Eric and I set out to find dinner. It was too early for most restaurants to be open, but we found a cheerful cafe that seemed to cater to Camino walkers. Michelle's group was already settling into a big table up front, and I also recognized the two thin, serious-looking men at the other occupied table. They'd been on our train from Lyon, and I'd spent a fair amount of time covertly studying them.

They were enigmatic. They wore jeans rather than hiking pants but carried top-of-the-line backpacks and walking sticks.

Obviously traveling together, from what I observed they barely spoke or even made eye contact with each other.

"They're brothers," I told Eric.

"They look nothing alike," he disagreed. Eric is generally more observant about physical traits than I am. He can recognize a family resemblance in the turn of a nose, and he often describes someone by the shape of their feet or the way they walk. So if he said the two men didn't look alike, he was probably right. But I'm good at watching how people interact with each other, and these two men didn't act like friends. Yet they were traveling together, so I assumed they must be related.

We continued the debate as we ate a simple dinner of lentils and sausage, the specialty of the region, filled out with fresh bread and a bottle of thick, dry local wine. When we left the restaurant, the streets were dark and quiet. We were back in the gîte well before curfew, and I fell onto my single cot in the darkness. When was the last time I'd gone to bed before 10:00?

I was asleep before I answered the question.

PILGRIMS AT LAST

Despite the wine and the jet lag, or perhaps because of them, I slept fitfully in Le Puy, waking every hour to stare into the darkness and listen to people breathing in the cubicles around me. We were so close to beginning this thing. When my digital watch finally said it was close to 6:00, I turned off the alarm and quietly packed my bag in the dark. I put on my "walking clothes"—the hiking pants, the merino wool shirt, the vest, the scarf—that I'd so carefully chosen. I could hear the sound of a dozen other people doing the same thing, but no one spoke.

Downstairs, the tables were set for breakfast. I saw a pitcher of orange juice and a basket of crusty bread. But this early in the morning, the April sky still dark outside, all I could think about was coffee. My wishes were granted when the female volunteer came over with a coffee pot.

"Café?"

"Yes, merci." My Frenglish made her smile as she waited to pour.

I looked at my place setting more carefully. There was a cereal bowl and a juice glass. No mug. Hesitantly, I reached for the glass. Maybe the French didn't drink their coffee venti-sized. *Demitasse* was a French word, wasn't it?

Her smile turned into a laugh. "Non, non." She reached past me and poured me a full *bowl* of coffee. I looked around and realized that yes, everyone had a bowl of coffee.

Well, okay. When in France. I chalked up another lesson about the change in culture. The centerpiece of our French country breakfasts was a bowl of coffee, alongside which we ate sliced bread, not toasted, with butter and/or fruit *confiture* (jam).

At 6:45, Isidore told the assembled group (while pantomiming for us) that he would take us to the cathedral, but first we should please clean our dishes. A dozen people moved to gather bowls and cups, and a line formed at the sink. Eric, whose desire to be helpful is almost pathological sometimes, settled in at the tap and washed everyone's dishes while they donned their jackets and packs.

They were, of course, charmed by him. Well, everyone but me. I was impatient with my husband's good deeds. What if they left without us? What if we were late?

But of course, we weren't late. As the first light of dawn started to break, Isidore led our group up an alley I hadn't noticed and into a side entrance of the cathedral. He took us through the main sanctuary, pausing to make the sign of the cross before the Black Virgin, and to a smaller side chapel, where a line of backpacks rested against the wall.

There were twenty or so people in the pews already, and our group filled in around them. Remi wasn't there, but I recognized the maybe-brothers from dinner. They stood, arms crossed, stiff and frowning. I mentally christened them the Brothers Grim.

The mass, of course, was in French. The words washed over me as I looked around the stone chapel. How many people had gone through these same motions in this same place before they set out in the name of Saint Jacques?

To understand the modern experience of what we now call the Camino de Santiago, it helps to look back to where it came from and why it matters. This journey is much more than a hike through the countryside.

Throughout the first millennium, as the Roman Empire spread across Europe, Christianity spread with it. As the Romans conquered and assimilated disparate peoples, the church gave them a common language and purpose—which is the nice way of saying it gave them something to focus on other than killing each other.

One of the most important unifying practices of the early church, and of most religions of the time, was pilgrimage. The physical commitment of traveling to a holy site, in a world where few people ever left the village where they were born, marked a person's piety. Pilgrimage was an act of penance, devotion, and also adventure.

There were plenty of regional pilgrimage destinations all over Europe, each claiming some holy object that could convey bless-ing or absolution. The cathedral of Le Puy, I've been told, once boasted the foreskin of Christ himself—but then again, so did a dozen other towns across Europe. If a pilgrim really wanted to show devotion, there were two Big Pilgrimage destinations: Jerusalem, where Jesus was killed, and Rome, where many of the early apostles were martyred, all by the same Roman Empire that now sponsored them. (As with most things in medieval history, it's best not to think too carefully about the details.)

As centuries passed and Christianity spread into Germany and the Low Countries, however, the distance of those big journeys became almost impossible for new converts. Enter a Spanish hermit named Pelayo, who in AD 813 reported experiencing a series of strange visions in a field in northern Spain. As the story goes, he followed a mysterious star and discovered, in an unmarked field, the body of Saint James the Greater, one of Jesus's original disciples.

How a Jewish guy from Galilee happened to wind up buried in one of the farthest corners of the known world takes some creative explaining, but first-century storytellers were well equipped for that. It seems that after Jesus's crucifixion, his followers scattered over the known world to convert others. James traveled to what is now Spain but had little success with the people there. He unwisely returned to Jerusalem, where he was arrested by Herod Agrippa, beheaded, and thrown over the city walls for the dogs to eat.

Not willing to let the brother of the apostle John become puppy chow, his disciples snuck out under the cover of night and retrieved the body (and, presumably, the head), put it on a rudder-less, unmanned stone boat guarded by an angel, and launched it into the Mediterranean. The boat miraculously traveled back

The first steps of the Chemin du Puy, looking back toward the cathedral

to the Iberian Peninsula, where, in some versions of the story, it sank just offshore, and James's body washed onto the beach, covered in scallop shells.

His Spanish disciples somehow were there to receive the gift from the sea. They secretly buried the apostle in an unmarked grave in a Galician cemetery, which was later abandoned until Pelayo found it almost eight hundred years later under the star (hence Compostela: the Field of the Star).

When the bishop of the area heard the story, he recognized the opportunity a relic of this importance offered to create a major new pilgrimage route. European penitents would have to scale mountains and cross rivers to get to the far northwest of Spain, but there was a Roman trade road that passed nearby, so the journey was not impossible. As an added benefit, the bishop and later the pope must have realized that a Christian holy site on the Iberian Peninsula would support and motivate the struggling Spanish Christians in their ongoing fight against Moorish invaders, who controlled all of southern Spain.

So the church built a cathedral worthy of the relic it protected, and just like that, Santiago de Compostela became the third most holy site of Christianity. A thriving city grew around it, and in the eleventh and twelfth centuries, when the first wave of Santiago pilgrims peaked, as many as a million people streamed across Europe to Santiago. They sought miracles, forgiveness, favors, and probably good stories to tell at their local watering holes.

Towns sprang up to support pilgrims and to profit from the commerce they brought. The church's elite military order, the Knights Templar, protected them, and dozens of church-sponsored hospitals cared for them. Still, hundreds of thousands died along the way from disease, exposure, and violent crime.

The popularity of the Santiago pilgrimage, and pilgrimage in general, dwindled in subsequent centuries due to the additional risks brought by the Black Death plague and, later, the theological shifts of the Protestant Reformation. By the twentieth century the Camino was all but forgotten. But writers can't let a good story die, and starting in the 1980s, a surge of books and articles brought it back to public attention. Not long after, in 1993, the Camino de

Santiago was named one of UNESCO's World Heritage Sites, and the popularity of the pilgrimage exploded.

In 1992 only 9,764 people received a Compostela, the church's official certificate confirming a pilgrim's arrival at the tomb of Saint James. In 2015 the number was 262,459.

A pilgrimage, of course, focuses on the destination and not the route traveled, so there is no single "starting point" for the Camino. The earliest pilgrims' journeys began wherever they lived. However, according to a twelfth-century guide for pilgrims, the *Codex Calixtinus*, there were four primary pilgrim routes that developed in France to funnel pilgrims together and guide them past other holy sites on their way to Santiago. Vía Podiensis began in Le Puy, Vía Turonensis began in Paris, Vía Lemovicensis began in Vézelay, and Vía Tolosana began in Arles. Based on those writings, UNESCO's designation recognized the trails that stretched back over the Pyrenees and across France, to those four cities. In subsequent years, the Heritage designation has expanded to include additional paths stretching to all four corners of Spain.

The most heavily traveled section of the Camino, then and now, is called the Camino Francés, which translates to "the French Camino" not because it's in France (all but twenty kilometers are in Spain), but because historically this was the path taken most often by French pilgrims. Camino Francés begins in the French border town of Saint-Jean-Pied-de-Port, at the point where three of the *Codex Calixtinus* paths converge, and goes west, crossing the Pyrenees and winding across northern Spain to Santiago. Today, this is often mistaken as the "whole" Camino rather than a single branch.

The mass ended, and the priest explained—in several languages, including English—that we would proceed to the altar of Saint Jacques for a blessing. Eric and I followed the group back across the main sanctuary to an alcove near the main doorway, where a wooden image of Jacques was dressed as a pilgrim, with a floppy hat, pilgrim shell, and staff in hand.

The priest asked each pilgrim to introduce themselves. Almost everyone was French. Eric and I were, not surprisingly, the only

Americans and English speakers, but there were also a couple of Germans and at least one woman from Belgium.

The priest read a prayer in the native language of each pilgrim, and a nun in a full habit and wimple gave us prayer cards to carry with us. One sentence in particular stood out to me: *Be for them shade in the heat of the day, light in the darkness of night, relief in tiredness, so that they may come safely, under your protection, to the end of their journey.* The spiritual and the physical worlds entwined.

After another prayer, the priest gave us each a small silver medallion the size of my thumbnail. On one side was a scallop shell, and on the other, the Black Virgin and the words "Notre Dame de Puy." I slid it onto my necklace cord and wore that medallion every day until we were back in Seattle. Eric, I noticed, also paused to attach his medallion to the cord he wears around his neck to carry his wedding ring.

There was something about that moment, in a place that had blessed people like us for a thousand years, that demanded solemnity and an act of commitment. We were joining something older than anything we'd experienced.

When we left Lyon, we were backpackers. Now, I was a pilgrim of Le Puy.

Blessed and ready to go, we filed out through the grand, west-facing cathedral entrance. My nervous energy made me feel clumsy as I descended the long flight of stairs and then an even longer hill paved with cobblestones. The sky was blue but the air was cold; there was still morning frost on the ground this early in spring.

We followed the pilgrims in front of us at first, forgetting to look for the red and white stripes that would mark our way. But the hikers spread out as we all found our own paces, and Eric and I were soon beyond the edges of Le Puy, in the middle of rolling farmland, with only the painted markers to guide us.

We climbed and descended, and climbed again. The hills weren't particularly high, but they were relentless. There didn't seem to be a square meter of flat ground anywhere. After an hour, I was sweating despite the chill in the air.

I should mention here that my overpreparation in the previous months had all been mental, not physical. I knew I was supposed to "train" for a long hike, whatever that meant, but I'd convinced myself there'd been no time. The first time I put on my full backpack was the day we left, and I'd walked only a couple of miles at a time in my new, fancy trail runners.

My plan was to keep our distance short on the first day. Most of the pilgrims at the welcome gathering told us they were going to Saint-Privat-d'Allier, which was fifteen miles—er, twenty-four kilometers—from Le Puy. But according to our guidebook, there was a small town named Montbonnet with a restaurant and accommodations just fifteen kilometers from Le Puy. That seemed like a more reasonable distance for our first day.

The kilometers slipped by slowly as I tried to see everything at once. I took photos of every horse in a field or centuries-old stone cross by the side of the road. As the hours ticked by, I regretted that I'd been too nervous to eat more than a single slice of bread at breakfast. It was close to noon, and I'd walked farther than I had in months. By the time we reached Montbonnet, I was starving and, as Eric calls it, hangry. The excitement had worn off. My feet hurt. I needed lunch.

However, the Camino had other plans. Instead of getting a sandwich, I learned a new French word: *fermé*. Closed.

Montbonnet turned out to be a single street with a few houses and a cafe, which was fermé. The adjacent gîte was also fermé. It was clearly being renovated, but there was no explanation for why the cafe was closed. We could hear people moving around inside, yet the door was locked and the lights were off. There was no other place to get food in the town, and there were no other towns nearby.

This was not my plan, and Eric will gladly tell you I'm not good when things don't go according to my plan.

Fermé or not, after fifteen kilometers without a break, I needed to stop. We sprawled on the porch of the closed establishment, and I took off my shoes and socks to rub my aching feet. It was nice to stretch my toes in the sunshine, but I was still hangry.

While I railed against the cafe and the town and everything conspiring against me, Eric gave me a leftover granola bar from his pack and waited out my sulk. These are always awkward moments for us, when I lose my shit over something that neither of us can control. He is, as I've said, an extremely helpful person. He wants to fix things. But when I'm mad at the universe, there's not much he can do.

And so he sat and waited for an hour or so, until I was done, before he pointed out the obvious. We weren't going to stay here, and the next town was still almost nine kilometers away. As annoyed as I was, I couldn't dispute his conclusion, so we walked on.

The break had refreshed me, and while my feet still ached and my right shoulder had formed a knot under the weight of the unfamiliar pack, I told myself it wasn't so bad. This was still an adventure.

We followed the red and white stripes of GR65 along a wooded trail toward Saint Privat, passing a number of French pilgrims as they rested in the shade. I noticed they were all eating the food that they'd wisely bought the day before and carried with them. Lesson learned: when in France, pack a lunch.

If entering Le Puy was a surprise for its bustling commerce, Saint Privat was the opposite. There was nothing modern about this sleepy town of listing buildings on a steep hill, and there were no people in sight.

We followed the main Camino markers until we came across Jean Claude, lounging on a bench with a few other men. The stone cottage behind them had a small vine-covered sign that said GÎTE. Since I hadn't planned to stay here, I knew almost nothing about the town or where we should go to find a place to stay. This scene looked inviting, but my hope that Jean Claude would save us again was short lived.

"Réserve?" he asked, indicating the building. No, we did not have a reservation here.

"Oh, non." The French have a special knack for blending a look of regret and disapproval. "*C'est complet.*" *It is full.* He said something I couldn't understand, but the meaning was clear. The two men sitting with Jean Claude had snagged the last two available beds.

I could feel Eric doing the math of how long I'd lingered on the porch in Montbonnet, and how much sooner we might have arrived. This second disappointment of the day made my eyes sting with tears.

This whole Camino thing wasn't working out as I planned.

Jean Claude waved down the road. There were other places in town. We must go on. We passed a cafe with patio tables set in the sunshine, and I looked at it longingly. My feet ached. My bag weighed more by the second. I was still hangry. But Eric wasn't going to stop again until we found a place to stay.

Down a side street, I noticed another gîte sign. Following it, we passed through a gate and up a flight of stairs to another courtyard, this one beside a building that was all modern angles and bright white paint. I thought it looked like a Seattle community center, not a place for pilgrims following a medieval path, but if they had space, I would overlook the poor aesthetics.

A young man sat at a picnic table, reading a book. "English?" Eric asked him.

"Yes. A little." We learned that he was German. He had a reservation here, but they wouldn't open until 4:00, another hour away. He didn't know if they had room for more pilgrims. "You should call them," he offered, waving to a phone number printed on the glass door.

Sure, except this was our *offline* sabbatical. Our cell phones were turned off, and even if they weren't, they weren't connected to European phone plans. We weren't supposed to need phones to walk a trail that's a thousand years old.

Since when do pilgrims need reservations? I stewed. Even as I thought it, I realized that almost everything I read—almost everything that was written in English, for that matter—had focused on the Camino *in Spain*. I'd assumed that things were the same in France. Clearly that was not the case.

Eric and I waited, anxious and testy, for the gîte to open. Or at least, *I* was anxious and testy. Eric kept his thoughts to himself.

At 3:30 a woman pulled up in a car, but she ignored us. She puttered around a garden, made a phone call, and smoked a cigarette. I suggested that Eric ask her if they had space for us, but he refused to interrupt. Since I was too afraid to try it myself, in French, I continued to sulk and nurse my tired feet.

A few more pilgrims came into the courtyard, including a Belgian woman I recognized from the pilgrim mass. When someone finally opened the gîte door at 4:00, Eric politely let her go before us. I seethed, convinced that once again we would be turned away. At least this time it wouldn't be my fault.

The inside of the building was as cool and modern as the outside. When we got to the counter, it was obvious that my worrying had been pointless. The man who ran the place even spoke a little English. Yes, they had beds available. They would also provide dinner and breakfast, an offer called *demi-pension*. He took our cash—along the Camino, all of our transactions happened in cash, which we replenished about once a week at the ATMs that were easy to find in most towns—and assigned us to a room with a minimum of words, casually waving toward a stamp pad sitting on a far table where we could stamp our own credentials.

This was a privately owned, for-profit gîte, and it was about as different from Isidore's careful attention in Le Puy as I could imagine.

Our room had three sets of bunk beds, which quickly filled with a varied crew of pilgrims: a slender, serious French teenager who wore a white scarf; an older Frenchwoman with a pinched face and a lot of maps; and a solid, serious Austrian who left his underwear draped on the heater. They all went about their business with a minimum of words or eye contact, and we followed their lead.

I fumbled through my second night of unpacking and awkwardly navigated a shower in the communal bathroom. That left only one more chore: laundry.

Like the good hiker I aspired to be, I was traveling light, so I needed to hand-wash at least a few essentials every day or two. The trouble was, I'd never in my life washed clothes in a sink, and Eric was nowhere in sight to help me.

Covering my lack of knowledge with sheer determination, I scrunched wads of my hiking shirt and underwear under the running water of the bathroom sink, rubbed some of my bar soap across them, and succeeded mostly in splashing water all over the floor. When I'd rinsed out the bulk of the suds, I squeezed some of the water out and hung everything on the clothes bar in our room, where it dripped onto the tile floor.

With chores accomplished and dinner still two hours away, I found Eric and half-heartedly discussed touring the town; the church was supposed to be lovely. But I was tired, sore, and still hungry. I didn't care about seeing anything except a chair and a beer at that cafe on the corner. There would be other medieval chapels.

Ten minutes later we were sitting under an awning, watching package trucks career at impossibly high speeds around sharp corners and down cobbled streets never intended for motor vehicles. Jean Claude and another man came by and, after a questioning nod and smile of acceptance, joined us. They seemed curious about two young Americans walking the Chemin du Puy. I could see they wanted to question us, to help us. But without a common language we mostly just sat with our beers and our maps, companionable but awkward.

Eric and I excused ourselves eventually and went back to the gîte for dinner, which was as anticlimactic as the rest of the day. The food was good, as French food almost always is. We had a three-course meal of lentil soup and a salad, then sausage and potatoes, then a cheese plate and dessert. The meal was served family style to a table of ten pilgrims, including the solemn Brothers Grim. They nodded in recognition, but they spoke no English. Neither did the imperious older woman from our room, who sat at the head of the table.

"Perhaps we could speak English for a little while," the Belgian woman said to the rest of the group, gesturing at us in sympathy.

"Non," the dour woman declared. And then she said something that the German told us meant "I do not speak English. We are in France, and so we must speak only French."

Eric and I were left to ourselves at the end of the table. Mute and exhausted, my mind kept coming back to the same question: Was this a mistake?

La Margeride

43170 SAUGUES

CLIMBING

I slept better that night but was awake long before anyone else stirred, filled with a mix of nerves and jet lag. As the dawn light started to creep into the room, I knew I wanted to be out of the gîte as soon as possible and away from these stern-faced people I couldn't talk to. There was a snag, though. The clothes I'd washed the night before were still wet.

"Oh, non," the Belgian woman, whose name was Virginie, said. She had that regret-and-disapproval look down, too. "You must dry clothes outside. There are always sinks and lines behind the building."

My breakfast carried the taste of my embarrassment as I worried about what else I didn't know. I'd thought I was so prepared. *How did everyone but me seem to understand how this Camino thing worked?* I stuffed my clothes into mesh laundry bags and pinned those to the outside of my pack, so that the things would dry while I walked, and then we set out.

I could already see a difference in the land around us. The soil was no longer black volcanic rock but had softened to a deep brown. The hills, though, were a constant.

GR65 leads west, toward the remains of Saint Jacques. The rivers in France, at least in that area, run south toward the Mediterranean. The result is that we constantly climbed and descended steep, rocky river valleys. Our first few kilometers were all uphill. We occasionally saw other people on the trail who passed us with happy "Bonjours" and "Bon chemins" ("Good way").

Just past a cluster of houses guarded by well-fed French *chats*, the trees cleared, leaving only bright green, early spring scrub grass on a rocky outcropping. And on top of the rock, a castle. Or, at least, the ruins of a castle. A crumbling keep balanced on the crest, watching over the river valley. Below the tower stood an intact chapel, built of stone that seemed to extend directly from the hillside and crowned with a roof of seemingly haphazard tiles and a belfry with real bells. The date on the lintel read 1328.

Where I grew up, a fort three hundred years younger than this would be designated a national monument, with school tours and park rangers. Here, though, there weren't even fences or warning signs to keep us away. Eric and I shed our packs and set out to explore. While he climbed to the keep, I ducked under the low doorway to the chapel. It was cramped and dark inside, with a few wooden benches and a rough floor, broken through in places by the granite bedrock below.

A children's song from Sunday school played in my head: *The wise man built his house upon the rock . . .*

Back outside, I climbed to the keep and looked out over the valley below. I could see a train winding along the river, and in the distance I could make out Monistrol d'Allier. It seemed impossibly far away to be only our halfway point for the day, but at least it was downhill. I tried not to look at the rows of mountains behind it. Those would come later. This was now.

In the opening paragraphs of her memoir *Tracks*, Robyn Davidson says, "There are some moments in life that are pivots around which your existence turns—small intuitive flashes, when you know you have done something correct for a change, when you think you are on the right track. . . . [This] was one of them. It was a moment of pure, uncomplicated confidence—and lasted about ten seconds." That was me. I was on top of a mountain, beside a French castle, on a spring morning. I was past my lists, my maps, my plans.

I was entirely present.

I let the moment linger as long as I could, but the valley was waiting. We slung our packs back on and for the next two hours picked our way downhill along treacherous paths full of loose rocks. We passed through the valley town of Monistrol without stopping, though I saw several familiar faces in the bars along the way, enjoying a second café au lait.

I looked longingly at the cafe tables, but it was hard to slow Eric down long enough for me to find the town's public bathroom; a midmorning snack was out of the question. He was focused on our destination, Saugues, still twelve kilometers away.

This difference in our paces was something I hadn't considered before we left. Eric was like an Energizer Bunny; he kept going and going. He stopped when I insisted I needed to rest, but if he wasn't tired, I wondered, why should we rest? I pushed on. I didn't want to give the impression that I was slower or weaker than he was.

This, of course, was problematic for a lot of reasons, but let's start with the obvious one: I was a lot slower and weaker than him, and we both knew it.

At home in Seattle, Eric managed a gym and taught classes in parkour—the sport of jumping, climbing, balancing, and running to overcome obstacles. My husband literally scaled walls for a living. I, on the other hand, worked mostly from my couch. My sport of choice was yoga, slow and controlled and close to the ground.

When I talk about the Camino, people sometimes say, "Oh, I could never do something like that. I'm not into extreme sports." Trust me, neither am I. But walking wasn't extreme, right?

As we tackled the steep slope that rose behind Monistrol, I started to wonder. The guidebook warned that there would be a steady incline for thirty-one kilometers, and the first ten would be especially difficult. Eric bounced up the exposed dirt trail and out of sight like a mountain goat. I plodded like a turtle—a footsore, out-of-shape, angry turtle.

To distract myself from my labored breath, and to concentrate on something other than jealousy of my husband—and Jean Claude and Virginie, who both strode easily past me on that hill—I tried to practice my French.

The Chapelle Saint-Jacques-de-Rochegude

Un, deux, trois, quatre, six, sept, neuf, dix . . .

Wait, I was missing something. I started to count on my fingers, out loud, with each step.

Un, deux, trois, quatre, cinq, six, sept, huit, neuf, dix!

I didn't hear the Brothers Grim approaching, but they obviously heard me. As they passed—because everyone passed me on that hill, eventually—their solemn faces were twitching. "*C'est bon?*" one asked, deadpan.

I might have blushed, but I was already so red no one would notice. I gave them a dramatic shrug and almost got them to laugh as they, too, disappeared up the hill.

I eventually made it to the top of the mini-mountain and found Eric waiting with the bread and apples and cheese we'd wisely purchased the day before in Saint Privat. After we ate, we walked together for the last few kilometers into Saugues.

Once again, we arrived without a plan for where to stay. Once again, the red-and-white stripes led us straight to a gîte de pèlerin.

Two men stood outside, and one of them was speaking English with what sounded like an Australian accent. My relief at hearing my native tongue almost drowned out what he said.

"No beds?" The Australian's voice was loud, and he carefully enunciated his words the way humans everywhere do when we talk to someone who doesn't understand us and we've run out of other ideas for communication.

The Frenchman beside him shook his head. "Non, non. C'est complet."

Eric and I joined the conversation as the Frenchman held out a guidebook and pointed to the name of another gîte. There was a street address but no map. The man waved toward something farther down the road, maybe around a corner, and dramatically shrugged. They might have space. Maybe not.

The Australian, Eugene, looked more crestfallen than I felt. He dressed like a colonial tourist of the British Empire, with khaki shorts and pulled-up knee socks, a canvas fishing cap full of pins, and a plastic-covered packet of maps hanging around his neck. He also sagged under the weight of a pack that looked twice as big as mine.

As Eric tried to draw clearer directions from the French pilgrim, I shifted my weight from one foot to the other. Standing still felt like I was putting all my weight onto tender, fresh bruises.

The three of us decided we would go on together and find this new place. Eric, ever helpful, set off at a jog (a *jog*!). Eugene and I followed as fast as aching muscles allowed, but we didn't get far before Eric came back to report there was nothing resembling a gîte down that road.

We were still standing there, trying to decide what to do next, when someone behind us called out. "Pardon? Excuse me?" The Frenchman from the "complet" gîte was chasing after us, waving his phone and speaking in Frenglish. He'd called a gîte somewhere and confirmed they had space, and he'd reserved for *deux* Americans and an Australian. Well, huh. The Camino does provide.

I turned and forced my tired feet to keep up with our guide as he led us toward our reservations. When Eugene asked where the gîte was, I told him I had no idea.

The Frenchman turned in surprise. "You understand him?" He gestured to Eugene.

Well, *oui*.

"I did not know Americans and Australians understand one another." He was going out of his way to help us, and I didn't know how to politely point out that Americans and Australians speak the same language, so I said nothing.

Our new Camino angel took us to a modern-looking building surrounded by children. Like most towns and villages along the Camino, Saugues provided a gîte *communal*, municipally run and usually a few euros cheaper than a private one. But Saugues was unique in that they combined their gîte with their public school. While kids shrieked and played outside, an efficient, humorless city employee collected our euros, stamped our credentials, and informed us that dinner would be at 7:00. He directed Eric and me to our room, which was bare but private, with two twin beds and a private bathroom.

I looked at the bed longingly, ready to put my feet up for a while, but we still needed food for the next day. So Eric and I took care of showers and laundry (hung properly this time on a clothesline in the small courtyard behind the building) and then went out again.

The only market in town was inexplicably fermé, but we found an open bakery. Eric went to the counter and, uncertain of the protocol, pointed to a baguette. The shopkeeper rattled off a question neither of us understood. We looked at him, hoping for some physical gesture that would give us a clue. The shopkeeper asked the same question, more sharply.

Je ne parle pas français. And then the other French word I'd learned that day. *Désolé.* I'm sorry.

The baker did not attempt to hide his contempt. He shoved the bread across the counter and scratched something onto a paper. Two euros. He continued to scowl as he took our coin and turned to the next customer. The encounter left us both cringing, reminded that not everyone would be gracious when faced with our lack of French.

We found fruit and cheese in another shop and bought them without incident. There were still two hours until dinner, but the strain of taking care of our basic needs in another language left me with little mental space to admire the architecture. We walked back toward the gîte, prepared for another quiet night, but as we passed a side street I glanced down and saw Eugene sitting alone outside a tiny bar.

The lure of beer and easy conversation redirected our steps, and we joined him. Despite the challenges of an old knee injury, Eugene was enthusiastic about absolutely everything Camino-related, and the conversation flowed smoothly. We told him about Seattle, and he told us about his home on the southern coast of Australia. He planned to walk to Santiago and started in Le Puy because he had family ties in France and a passion for history.

Our cheery table attracted attention. The Brothers Grim stopped by, and I got them to smile again when I showed off my counting skills. Virginie and a Frenchwoman we'd seen the night before in Saint Privat pulled up a couple of chairs, and Eric poked around the edges of the language with them.

Just as they were stuck on a difficult phrase, a thin, weathered-looking man passed by, and he stopped to help. Gabriel was fluent in French, English, and Spanish. We bought him a beer, and he told us he was walking GR65 backward, from Santiago to Le Puy, and then perhaps he would go farther. He'd walked all over the world, he said, as far away as Nepal. I noticed his clothes were ragged and his boots worn. He spent almost no money, camping by the side of the road or sleeping in the free rustic pilgrim huts that still occasionally dotted the Way.

The time passed quickly, and before I knew it we were hurrying back to the school/gîte for dinner. For reasons that weren't clear, a few dozen teenagers also appeared to be spending the night, and their happy voices surrounded the two tables reserved for pilgrims. The Brothers Grim gravitated to a group of French pilgrims, and we joined Eugene and Virginie at the second table, where we could chat in English. Our conversation drifted to the common Camino question: Where will we walk tomorrow?

Virginie was horrified that we had no firm plan. "You must make reservations in France," she told us. "Especially on weekends, when others also travel."

As much as I wanted my Camino experience to be unstructured and spontaneous, her warnings sounded dire, especially after the past two days of what felt like close calls.

Our new friends were all going to Le Sauvage, a historic gîte de pèlerin that had been a hospital for pilgrims centuries ago. The Frenchwoman from the bar offered to call and arrange beds for us, and we accepted. But after some chatter in French, she hung up and shook her head.

"C'est complet." Of course it was.

Guidebooks in multiple languages appeared from pockets and bags, and everyone went to work. Where else could the hapless Americans and the Australian go? We were in a remote part of countryside, and it was generally agreed that we had only two options: we could stop in a town just fourteen kilometers away, or we could continue past Le Sauvage to the next town, which meant walking more than thirty kilometers.

I did the quick math. Eight miles or nineteen? My body, rested and numbed with wine, still shuddered. I looked at Eugene and thought about his knee.

Eric and I did the married-people-mind-reading thing across the table, and he asked the woman to call the closer town, Chanaleilles, and make a reservation for two Americans and an Australian.

Eric and I had left Saint Privat alone, but after a simple gîte breakfast we left Saugues surrounded by friends. The bite in my calves told me we were still gaining altitude, and most of our companions outpaced us by the edge of town.

We walked into a steady wind, which did no favors to our baguette. We'd unwisely left it whole, sticking out of a side pocket of Eric's backpack like a flagpole. I liked the aesthetic, but the bread was dry as a crouton by lunch.

We meandered along slowly with Eugene and still arrived in Chanaleilles at noon, long before most gîtes opened. The village was tiny, though, so it wasn't hard to track down our host—a sullen woman who also managed the local bar. She spoke no English but took our money, stamped our credentials, and wordlessly pointed us to a room with a dozen twin beds.

Eric and I took two beds in a corner, and Eugene spread himself out on the other side of the room. As he unpacked his giant bag, I saw batteries, a pharmacy's worth of medicine, and piles of clothes. No wonder the poor man's knee hurt.

It took about ten minutes to explore the town, which was set deep in a valley and seemed to have more cows than people, and then there was nothing to do with the long hours of the afternoon except explore my doubts. Should we have kept going, pushing ahead another twenty kilometers? It was hard not to feel like a wimp as I watched people continue to trudge past while I cooled my tender feet in a frigid stream.

I tried to remember that we were pacing for a marathon, not a sprint. Many of the people we'd met, like Virginie, were on short holidays, but Eric and I weren't flying home until July, regardless of when we reached Santiago. There was no need to rush. When that didn't help, I reminded myself that this wasn't a race at all. I would probably never again be in this particular corner of France, and if I moved too fast, I could miss something lovely. That helped a little.

Late in the afternoon, three other pilgrims—athletic French walkers who'd started a day after us and had already caught up—breezed in with easy-looking efficiency. One, a woman our age named Gwen, spoke some English, and the six of us passed a pleasant evening, despite the suspicious stares of the locals in the bar.

Eric listened intently to the French conversations. His accent and vocabulary improved by the hour as he peppered our fellow pilgrims with questions. *What is the word for this? How do you say that?* He was fearless about testing phrases and seeing what people understood. Within days he could ask basic questions so smoothly that shopkeepers and gîte hosts would rattle back complicated sentences, assuming he was fluent.

No one ever assumed that about me.

The weather the next morning was damp as the six of us climbed steadily into the wild and remote Aubrac. Cultivated farm fields gave way to rocky pastures, populated only by a few furry horses with tangled manes. The trees were bare, the breeze was sharp, and there were still small piles of snow along the trail. Spring, it seemed, was in retreat.

Our new French friends slowed to our pace for the first hour or two, but in late morning broke briskly away. They were bound for a destination twelve kilometers past Les Estrets, the town where Gwen had kindly phoned a reservation for us. By car they would be less than fifteen minutes away from us, but on foot the distance was insurmountable. As we parted, I knew we likely wouldn't see one another again, given our—well, my—leisurely pace. And we didn't.

Eric and I walked with Eugene for much of the morning, but eventually his bad knee protested, and he stopped in a sheltered field to rest. "Don't keep waiting for me," he assured us. "I'll make it in time for dinner."

Eric and I wound on together through towns that seemed deserted, even on a Sunday. In Saint Albans, where we planned to have lunch, the cafes and shops were fermé. I started to wonder if anyone actually lived in this corner of France.

Then, with ten kilometers still to go, something unexpected happened. The mountain goat developed a limp. Something was wrong with Eric's Achilles tendon. He slowed down. He limped. He took off his sneakers, which rubbed against the tender spot, and walked in his sandals. It helped a little, but he still settled into what another pilgrim, weeks later, would describe as the "tunnel of pain."

That's how I found myself in the unusual position of walking ahead of him when a young woman with a floppy hat and a backpack strode out of a farm driveway. "That's not the way," she called cheerily, in English. She explained she'd taken a wrong turn and found herself awkwardly standing in a barnyard.

She mistook a driveway for the Camino. In hindsight, I should have paid more attention to that.

I was, however, once again infatuated by the sound of English and happy to have someone to distract me through the final few kilometers of a challenging day, so we walked on together up a shaded country road.

Lara was Swiss. She'd walked all of the Camino Francés in Spain a few years earlier but was here in France for just a few days. She'd catch a bus back home in the morning.

GR65 broke off from the paved road, and we followed a rutted dirt road that took us deeper into the woods. Eric lagged behind, the pain in his ankle making him unusually antisocial. Lara and I chatted about home and travel, but after a while, I mentioned that I hadn't seen a trail marker for some time. Typically, the red and white stripes of GR65 pop up every few minutes. They're painted onto fences, the backs of signs, trees, and even on rocks if the ground is flat. They aren't always easy to spot—walking the Chemin de Saint Jacques often felt like an epic game of Where's Waldo—but we were following a wooden fence that I thought should be marked.

Lara brushed aside my concern. "Oh no, this is right. This feels like the Camino."

Well, she's done this before, I thought, as we continued down a steep hill. Ten minutes later, the road ended at an intersection with another dirt road. There were still no stripes to indicate which way to go, and our guidebook didn't mention an intersection. We were officially lost.

We dithered around, aching and tired. If we followed the new road in the right direction, we reasoned, it would lead to Les Estrets. But which way? We looked out over a valley, but there were no towns in sight. With no map, no GPS, and no idea when we'd lost our way, there was no way to know.

Our only real choice was to turn around and trudge, silently this time, back up the hill we'd just descended, until we came to the place where we'd missed the flaglike symbol of red and white stripes that indicated a turn off the farm road and onto a smaller footpath. It was late afternoon, and Lara's reservation was for a town past Les Estrets. She was worried about arriving after dark, so with a wave, she sped up and disappeared down the trail.

Eric never pointed out that it was me who led us astray. He didn't have to. We limped forward for the final three kilometers. Our detour cost us an hour and a half, and it was almost 5:00 when we stumbled down a final rocky embankment and into Les Estrets. I was exhausted, and my feet felt like they were on fire.

Like a horse that senses its barn, though, I sped up when the end was finally near. Eric was at least a block behind me when I arrived at the gîte. The owner, a gregarious man with a big voice, met me at the door.

"Réserve à deux Americans," I managed, figuring that those were the important words, even if my syntax was wrong. When Gwen made our reservation, she'd given the host our nationality, not our names. It's not like there were other Americans out here who were going to show up and take our spot.

"Ah, non!" The man had a florid face and rough English. "You are too late. I give the reservation away."

For a second, I believed him, and panic stung my eyes. By the next second, I realized I didn't care if he meant it. I wasn't leaving.

"No." I sat on the bench by the door and started to unlace my shoes. (Most gîtes required us to leave walking shoes outside, which made sense, considering how many cow fields we crossed.) I repeated: "Réserve à deux Americans."

Eric arrived at that moment to find me looking mutinous and the jokester proprietor looking sheepish. Of course, we did still have *réservés*. We weren't even the last to arrive, although Eugene had made it ahead of us.

Despite his injury, Eric soldiered on, showering and doing his washing before he allowed himself to rest. Me? I collapsed onto my assigned bed in our room for four and lay there for a long time, on the verge of tired tears. *Could I really do this every day for months?*

The gîte was full, and the communal dinner that night was noisy. Eugene, Eric, and I staked out an English-speaking corner, and we were joined by a Dutchman named Jan and a young Frenchman named Xavier. Across the room the group we'd met at the orientation in Le Puy flirted with our host and chatted among themselves like kids at camp. I christened them the Eight Walkers.

The wine flowed, perhaps particularly into Jan's glass. He was a smallish, gnome-like man with rough, guttural English and endearing round glasses. In basic, fractured English, we all connected as our host brought out generous salads and steaming bowls of wild boar that he bragged he'd shot himself. We laughed and carried on through the cheese plates and dessert. I forgot that my feet ached. I felt another glimmer of the Camino I was looking for.

And then, precisely at 9:00, the dishes and wine carafes were whisked away and, feeling a bit bewildered by the abrupt change in emotional energy, I followed my fellow pilgrims off to bed.

Everything I'd heard about late-night life in Europe? Forget it. Pilgrims are asleep by 10:00.

OF FEET
AND FAIRY TALES

Walking through L'Aubrac was like walking through the legends and stories Eric read as a kid. We'd reached the true highlands of the Massif Central, irregular rolling hills of open, treeless country. It was too early in the year for the herds of cows and sheep that would fill the pastures in summer, so the barren landscape was broken only by stone fences built from the rocks that dotted the landscape.

At least, that's what Eric told me it looked like. He took it all in with wide eyes and a permanent grin. The idea that a place like this was real made him forget his tender ankle. Four days into a three-month hike, he was already talking about how to come back, dreaming about becoming a perma-pilgrim like Gabriel.

I, on the other hand, trudged along that day with my head down and my feet screaming. I resented every rock on the path that poked my tender, swollen arches. I hurt too much to appreciate the landscape around me.

On the outside, I looked fine. I didn't have a single *ampoule*, the blisters that have plagued pilgrims for centuries. And my

The winding medieval streets of Saint-Côme-d'Olt

body above the ankles—apart from the outraged complaints from my lungs when I had to climb a hill—was fine. My shoulders had adjusted to my pack, and my knees and shins never complained. But my feet. My poor, tender, inflamed feet. I had no idea what was wrong with them, but I was pretty sure they were ruining my—and worse, Eric's—entire Camino.

We started calling my feet The Princesses, because they felt every pea-sized pebble in the road. I set out every morning feeling fine. After a couple hours of walking, the tenderness would kick in. After another hour, each step sent sharp pain straight through me. It felt like I was constantly walking on giant bruises, and every uneven surface in the path was agony.

The only remedy was to stop regularly, take off my shoes, rub my arches back into peace, and rest. But I was traveling with a mountain goat who practically skipped across his fairy-tale land with his own set of worries, like whether we would get to our destination early enough to do all of what he called "the things" (claiming beds, unpacking bags, taking showers, doing laundry, etc.) before everyone else hogged the shower and the laundry line. That man walked with a mission, so I walked through the pain.

I couldn't Google my problems or distract myself from them with a mind-numbing screen, which made it harder to cover over my misery. Eventually, inevitably, it started to rub into Eric's good mood.

We both were tense when we arrived in Finieyrols, a cluster of houses too small to be a town, set dramatically in the middle of nowhere. Eric left me slumped on a bench outside while he got us checked into the gîte's dortoir. After a few minutes of rest and foot massage, I rallied and plowed through my chores. Then I collapsed again on a boulder outside, soaking the late afternoon sun into my bare feet and letting myself imagine everyone's reactions when I went home and confessed that I'd quit the Camino.

Because, obviously, I wasn't up for this.

That was my mental state when Eric found me and tried to talk about how far we should go the next day. The towns were still sparse, and we either had to stop after fourteen kilometers again or push through our first thirty-kilometer day. Eric was leaning toward the latter, because it would put us in a better position for future stops.

Thirty kilometers wasn't an unreasonable number. But when I tried to imagine walking for three hours longer than I had that day, I cracked.

"I can't do it," I snapped. And maybe I said some other things.

The muscles in his jaw twitched, or maybe I imagined that. I was sure I could see what he didn't say. But Eric doesn't like to argue with me, so he acquiesced. "Fine. We'll stop in the closer town."

Eric's "fine" gets me every time. Guilt flooded over the pain. I hedged. "Well, maybe I can do it."

My indecision annoyed him even more. "I don't know what's wrong," he said, "and I don't know how to help you."

All I could come up with was, "I don't know how to be helped." Eric went off to scrub his clothes while I stayed on the rock and sulked.

People we met on the Camino often expressed playful surprise when they found out we were married. "You're walking together every day for three months? And you're still married?" I always wanted to say, "No, actually we filed divorce papers at the *mairie* (city hall) in the last town," but I never did. Sarcasm is hard to get across to a nonfluent speaker.

We weren't the only married couple on the Camino, of course. But we met plenty of pilgrims who were married but walking the Camino alone. A long trek like this doesn't appeal to everyone, and the general consensus was that it was better to leave a partner at home than to try to walk across a country with someone who didn't want to be there—a thought I suspected Eric was having in Finieyrols while I sat stubbornly on that rock.

Did I really want to quit? I'd known, intellectually, that this would be hard, but it had never occurred to me that I would have to stop. That I would *want* to stop.

That thought jerked me out of my sulk. Did I *want* to stop?

I dragged myself off the rock and down to the main building, where I bought a local beer appropriately called Antidote, tucked myself behind a picnic table, and finally looked around. It was stunning. The late afternoon sun cast warm light over hills that went as far as I could see in every direction. I watched two kids hanging over the fence at the edge of the property, trying to pet a couple of shaggy horses.

Yes, my feet hurt, but that didn't change the crazy beauty all around me. We were in the middle of a remote area that few French citizens see, let alone two American tourists. I'd walked here, and unless those horses were tamer than they looked, I was going to walk out of here, too. We had good weather and new friends. Surely my feet would get better. I would get stronger.

Eric joined me not long after I started to believe my personal pep talk, and I bought him a beer as a peace offering. Without talking, we leaned toward each other and watched the kids play. We both wanted to be here. We would tackle tomorrow together.

At dinner we sat with Eugene and the Eight Walkers. We'd crossed paths with the boisterous group once or twice a day, and they always welcomed us to chat or share a snack. Michelle, the English speaker, explained that they were a walking club from a small town in northern France. They got together for weekly hikes and an annual week-long excursion. The husband of one walker drove a "camping car" with one of their dogs and all their luggage, which explained how they got away with such light-weight day packs on the trail.

Odette, a septuagenarian in the group, took particular delight in Eric, giggling and batting her eyes across the table at him. To my delight, Eric flirted right back. Michelle told me quietly that Odette's husband died earlier that year, and it had been difficult to convince her to come on this trip, to get away from her grief. Now she was beaming.

I thought the night couldn't get better, but then our host brought out the *aligot*, the regional dish of Aubrac. Take a bowl of mashed potatoes and add garlic and a soft, rich, local Cantal cheese. When it's mixed together, it stretches like dough and has to be cut with a knife. It is as rich and delicious as it sounds.

When our host placed the aligot on the table, we all *oohed* and *aahed* appropriately. When she added a bowl of steaming, fragrant cubes of local beef, Eric melted with happiness.

In the glow of the morning light, L'Aubrac stretched toward the horizon in a photogenic landscape, treeless and wild. One of my photos from that day shows Eugene standing on top of a small rise, his enormous red backpack the only bright color on a monochrome field of brown. His back is to me, his hands on his hips, as he surveys what comes next.

For four days we'd shared stories as we walked and communal dinners every evening. I knew about Eugene's adult children, whom he adored. His divorce, which he regretted. His curiosity about everything from military history to space exploration. I knew his knee caused him more pain than my feet caused me.

As Eric and I passed him that morning, I casually said we'd see him at dinner, if not before. But we never saw Eugene again. I later heard that he'd stopped for the day, aching and tired, in the town fifteen kilometers behind us. As we moved forward in subsequent days and weeks, we heard stories about him sometimes, but he never caught up.

I was surprised to lose Eugene, but he must have seen it coming. He'd asked me to exchange email addresses the first day we met, and by the time we got back to Seattle he'd sent a message. All told, he walked for about five hundred kilometers, but his inflamed knee kept getting worse. A French doctor told him that he needed to rest for at least three months, so he flew back to Australia early. Eric and I have an open invitation to visit him there.

As an American, I'm used to landscapes that take days to drive across. But in southern France, a day's walk—what I could easily drive in less than half an hour—often carried us through two or even three distinct ecosystems. Every hour was worth paying attention to, because by the next we might be in a totally different environment.

By midmorning we'd passed out of the rocks and away from the wild horses, only to find ourselves on something better: turf. Eric commented that Tolkien would have called these springy meadows—a cross between grass and moss—"the downs." In mid-April they were bright green under a blue sky. Early flowers bloomed and the air was warm, although lingering patches of snow made it possible to imagine the sudden storms that could descend, even in spring.

L'Aubrac seemed to understand that we were physically battered and still culture-shocked, and she put on her best behavior to welcome us. Well, at least nature welcomed us. Some of the people had other ideas.

We descended around lunchtime into a town that was also, confusingly, called Aubrac. We needed water, a bathroom, and a place to eat our lunch, but Aubrac the town was, of course, fermé.

Our first stop was a visitor's center that advertised a cafe and a patio overlooking the valley. The sign on the door said they were open from Easter to October, but the employees eating lunch on the patio, complete with espresso shots and a glass carafe of water, ignored us. When Eric tried to talk to them, they shot a barrage of French that came down to fermé.

We huddled at the edge of the deck and ate our dry bread and dwindling supply of sausage while the cheerful party continued. When I asked if I could use the bathroom just inside the door, they waved me away to the center of the village and a locked public toilet.

I was getting used to things in France being arbitrarily closed, but this was the first time a bathroom failed me.

Before I left for the Camino, I worried a lot about bathrooms. If I was going to be outside, walking, for eight or ten or twelve hours a day, where would I, well, go? I couldn't find consistent answers anywhere, but when we arrived, I happily discovered that almost every town in France, regardless of size, had a public water closet, or WC. They varied widely in cleanliness and modernity, and I learned to always carry a few squares of my own toilet paper, but still, WCs were always there, saving me from the embarrassment of the alternative.

As I've mentioned, I don't camp, which means I never had to master the art of the female squat. As an adult, I learned an awkward variation, which required holding on to a tree. That's probably too much information, but it's relevant here because

Eric and I had just spent five hours walking across soft, green, *bare* landscape. It was all very exposed. And now we were in a fermé village full of people, including nonhospitable visitors-center workers who were happy to watch tourists wander in circles around locked buildings.

My temper rose with the tension in my bladder, but the visitors-center workers just went back inside and locked the doors. The only other way to get access to modern plumbing was to go to the only restaurant in town and order cafés we didn't need. Which meant, of course, that in half an hour I would need another WC.

Fortunately, after Aubrac, the trees came back. For ten kilometers, we wound steeply downhill through a forest of oaks and chestnuts. The older pilgrims around us groaned and pointed at their knees, but I was much happier walking downhill in the shade than uphill in the sun. When we arrived in Saint-Chely-d'Aubrac, deep in a valley and spread over a stream, we'd walked thirty kilometers, and I hadn't felt as good in days.

Such is a paradox of the Camino: often a "good day" or a "bad day" happens despite the distance, not because of it.

The previous night Michelle had made a reservation for us at a private gîte on the outskirts of town. There were only three other pilgrims there that evening: a pretty young Parisian named Stephanie, who was fluent in English, and two stern-looking older Frenchwomen, who were not.

As we gathered around the dinner table, I noticed that one of the older women had a bandage on her hand and a deep bruise forming on her face under her glasses. She looked shaken. As our host brought out thick vegetable soup and a casserole of potatoes and duck confit, she told her story, which Stephanie translated.

Apparently, as the two women descended the last steep hill into town, the injured one tripped and started to fall forward. Human instinct would have had her put her hands up to catch herself, protecting her face, but the woman was using walking poles, and in her panic she didn't let go of them. She face-planted onto a rock, bruising her eye but somehow not breaking her glasses.

The woman still seemed upset, but she mimed her fall and the impact of hitting the rock so well that Eric burst into laughter.

Now, my husband has a big, rich, loud laugh that fills a room. Usually, it's wonderful, but that night I froze, trying to read the change in the air. *Did he seem rude? Would she be offended?*

Not at all. The injured woman smiled for the first time, and then she laughed. Eric had another fan.

Wearing sandals had relieved the pressure on Eric's Achilles tendon, but as he got ready the next morning, we realized that it had caused another problem: the dreaded ampoule finally struck, and in an awkward place between his toes.

We stopped to buy supplies at a market that was miraculously open, and when Eric sat down outside to adjust a bandage over his blister, he was immediately surrounded by concerned pilgrims. The two women from dinner offered their antibiotic ointment. A Frenchman we'd never seen before waved away our American adhesive bandages and whipped out his own (presumably superior) supply. Others paused with opinions.

When we finally got on the road, we joined the Eight Walkers for a while along a wooded path, teasing them and being teased in return. Odette continued to make eyes at Eric. As we joked, I noticed our language barrier seemed to be shrinking. Maybe I understood a few more words, but I was also getting better at paying attention. I couldn't think about other things while also miming my way through Frenglish. I had to stop worrying about whether my floppy sun hat made me look dumb, or about how my left toes were starting to ache again. These conversations needed my full attention.

We split with the Walkers when they stopped to wait for their camper car and lunch. The trail continued to run perpendicular to rivers and streams, and as the morning wore on we climbed and descended several times through forests full of chestnut trees. Despite the hills, I loved the woods and the soft, padded ground. I loved the shade and the way the trees framed pastoral valleys and lonely stone cottages.

Eric, it turned out, was not having the same experience. Wearing sneakers protected his blister but ate into his ankle. Wearing sandals protected his ankle but rubbed the blister on his toe. He soaked his feet in an icy stream when we stopped for a break, but found little relief when we were moving.

Two days earlier, my feet had beaten me. Today, his were winning. "I have one job to do, and I can't do it," he said in exasperation.

Fortunately, we were past the most remote portion of wilderness, and we had more options. When we saw the spires of Saint-Côme-d'Olt rising in front of us, we tossed the plan to walk another ten kilometers. According to the guidebook, there was a gîte communal here, and the book even indicated that the hosts spoke English. If they had room, we agreed, we would stop. I repeated what was becoming my mantra: We weren't in a hurry, and this wasn't a race.

That spontaneous decision, driven by the only blister either of us had on the whole Camino, led to one of my favorite afternoons in France.

The twelfth-century heart of Saint-Côme-d'Olt is walled and medieval. To enter, we passed through a narrow gate and discovered the kind of twisted, cobblestone streets that could never support modern technology or cars, but even as I thought about the impossibility, a tiny French hatchback zipped by.

The gîte was as old as the town. A door right in the thick city wall led us up steep stone steps, deeply rutted by the thousands of feet that had passed the same way. In a long, narrow common room a man introduced himself as Sylvain, from Montreal, and welcomed us in English.

"You're the Americans! I heard you were coming!"

Wait, what? "We didn't know until ten minutes ago that we would be here," I stammered. "How did you . . . "

He laughed and waved us to rest at the table. "It is Radio Camino," he explained. "There are no secrets along the Way." Someone who had met us, perhaps Gwen, had stayed here the night before. It was natural to tell the Canadian host about two other English speakers on the trail.

Sylvain led us up another flight of stairs to our low-ceilinged room. Four bunk beds stood on a rough wooden floor, but Sylvain said that so early in the season we'd have the space to ourselves. The walls were stone, and casement windows opened out to a view of tiled roofs and the uniquely twisted steeple of the town's church.

Every quirky corner and dark beam here made me happy. Eric could have the wild country. This was my kind of fairy tale.

I left Eric sitting in the sun, doctoring his feet, and went out to explore what the guidebook said was one of France's most beautiful villages. Streets jutted at odd angles and wove in circles, with arches and unexpected staircases turning every alley into a postcard-worthy picture. The sixteenth-century church—practically modern history for France—was unlocked and deserted, and I explored it slowly, taking in the statues of the saints and the way the late afternoon sun glowed in the stained-glass windows.

I reveled in the chance to linger and study an image of Saint Roch, the popular figure who seemed to grace almost every road-side chapel of the region. In a sometimes overwhelming lineup of saints, Roch stands out. In every image, no matter how simple or ornate, he's always lifting the hem of his robe and showing off more than a little thigh. And there's always a dog leaning ador-ingly against his leg. Who was this flirt?

Saint Roch, I later learned, was a French nobleman who lived in the early fourteenth century. Both his parents died when he was twenty, and the pious Roch gave up his inheritance, sold all of his possessions, and set out on a pilgrimage to Rome. This being the Middle Ages, there were plagues and mysterious ill-nesses afflicting the Italian towns along the way. Roch stopped often and cared for the sick and dying, frequently healing them miraculously either by touch or the sign of the cross.

But hanging around contagious people has its price. Eventually Roch contracted the plague himself, and he went to the woods to die. He built a shelter of branches, and a spring rose miracu-lously from the ground to provide him with a steady supply of fresh water. Then a local nobleman's hunting dog brought him bread and licked his plague wounds, which began to heal. Well, that explained the paintings and statues. He's not flashing us; he's showing off a plague wound.

Miraculously cured, Roch returned home to France. His uncle, failing to recognize him, arrested him and accused him of being a spy. Roch did not reveal his identity because he did not want to glorify himself. He died in prison five years later. I'm not sure what the takeaway of that last part is supposed to be, but I was becoming quite loyal to Saint Roch, the patron saint of dogs and knee problems.

After a long, quiet time in the church, I meandered to an outdoor cafe, where I sipped a Leffe beer and half-heartedly caught up on my journal while watching the people go by.

"C'est bon?" the Brothers Grim asked, when they paused by my table to say hello.

Oui. C'est bon indeed.

When dinnertime approached, I went back to the city wall and my home for the night. A small group of pilgrims gathered at a long wooden table to share a simple curry dinner with Sylvain and his wife, Sabine. The couple had met on the Camino ten years ago, Sylvain explained, and walked to Santiago together. He moved from Canada to France to marry Sabine, and now they ran this gîte for the city while saving money to open a pilgrim house of their own.

As the wine flowed, Sylvain described what he'd learned from his time as a pilgrim. "It is a monastic life," he said. "You wake up, you walk. When you arrive, you take care of your feet, you take care of your basic needs, and you eat. Do it day after day, and it becomes a meditation."

He'd hit on one of the things that had been scratching at my mind all week. We walk, we eat, we sleep. Is this *it*?

According to Sylvain, yes. And the way he said it, it was enough.

NOS AMIS

I tried to take Sylvain's advice the next day, to find a peaceful rhythm of walking, but my body wasn't ready to let my mind settle into monasticism.

We left Saint-Côme-d'Olt and navigated the outskirts of Espalion, where the ruins of a castle guarded a bustling town that blended modern (and open!) retail with turreted manor homes lining the river. We bought oranges and sipped midmorning espressos at an outdoor cafe, and I thought about how much I loved France.

Four hours later, as I approached Estaing, I thought about how much I hated France. I was limping, swearing, sweating, and generally making a scene along a sunbaked commercial road, braving blind curves and speeding trucks.

If you talk to two pilgrims who have walked any part of the Way of Saint James, you'll get three different opinions about what the path is like.

"The Camino is all busy roads and hard pavement. There is no nature!"

"The Camino is all mountains and rocks and mud. There is no smooth path!"

"The Camino trails are so soft and easy that you could do it in slippers!"

In spring, the mist on GR65 can be as thick as rain.

Reality, as it usually does, lies somewhere between the extremes. The Camino that Eric and I walked in France and Spain was a mixture of paved roads—usually remote country lanes, where cars were infrequent—and natural paths of gravel or dirt, wide enough for two people to walk abreast. Of course there were exceptions: entering larger towns or cities meant pounding the pavement through busy and not-so-picturesque suburbs. There were some stretches in France where we walked on roads with narrow shoulders, dodging moderate traffic, for a few hundred meters at a time. There were plenty of sections in both countries that were steep, rocky, muddy, and slippery.

The only consistent thing I can say about Camino paths is that every day, and sometimes every hour, brought something different.

My traffic-clogged walk into Estaing was not the fault of the GR65 planners, though. The official path had veered off the road and uphill a kilometer behind me to follow a protected path through the woods. But I was tired and footsore, and I refused to follow the sadistic red and white stripes up another hill when, according to the map, following the road would be a more direct route to the city.

Eric, being sensible, took the marked path, so I was alone in my ill-considered shortcut. Once again, I obsessed on a single thought. My feet hurt.

By this point I'd seen pilgrims with terrible blisters. I'd seen people younger than me hobbling sideways down hills because of knee injuries. I'd heard about walkers who had to go home early. I had none of those problems.

But man, my feet *really* hurt. Was I just a wimp?

The internal doubt weighed me down as much as my pack, and the hot pavement pushed back against my swollen feet. When I came around a corner to find Eric—who had walked the hillier, longer, *harder* path—already waiting for me, I lost it.

The next ten minutes weren't pretty, but eventually I followed him, grudgingly, into Estaing, past the beautifully restored riverfront and down crooked streets where gray stone buildings seemed to be held up by sagging doors and broken windows.

Eric stopped in front of one of the weathered doors and rang the bell. This was the donativo gîte run by the Catholic Order of

Saint Jacques. A middle-aged woman wearing normal, middle-aged clothes welcomed us. Only later did I realize she was a nun.

I was still in a haze of pain as the sister checked us in and showed us the simple dorm where men and couples slept. Women traveling alone or with other women slept in a separate room for privacy.

As we settled in, the Brothers Grim arrived. Though we never talked to them about their travel plans—or anything, given the language barrier—we'd seen them every day and often stayed in the same gîtes. They always greeted us, and we made as much small talk as we could manage. ("C'est bon?" "Oui, c'est bon.") Yet I still rarely saw them talk to each other.

I distracted myself by pondering their mystery as I limped through the daily chores. There was a lovely yard where I hung my laundry next to a chicken coop, and I sat there with my journal for an hour as the sun slowly revived me.

I eventually found Eric in the library, a creaky-floored room full of books in French about the lives of saints and missionaries. The place was cool and soothing, as was the cheerfulness of the two nuns who stopped in to check on us. They moved silently through the echoing residence, a relic of the time the diocese attracted more than two nuns and a single priest, and apologized for not speaking better English, as if we weren't the interlopers in their world.

After our communal dinner, we all helped to clean up, and there was a bit of a production while the priest stamped our credentials and recorded our information. Then the pilgrims were invited to join the convent's permanent residents for their evening prayers.

It may seem odd that two recovering Baptists, walking the Camino without spiritual motivations, would consider going to a Catholic service in a language we barely understood. And there were definitely times it felt odd.

But to understand the historical significance of the walk to Santiago, I couldn't ignore the faith that created it. Without James the apostle of Jesus, and the church that the Romans built from their story, there would be no Camino. The church cared for pilgrims for centuries before a secular government put red and white stripes on trees to guide us.

These nuns and priests weren't here to convert us. No one in a faith-based gîte ever even asked what we believed. They simply welcomed us as pilgrims in need of shelter. It was the grace of people like these, night after night, who got me through the tough days. So when the nuns of Estaing invited me to join their evening prayers, I said yes.

We gathered in a windowless room, paneled in wood infused with centuries of incense. One of the Brothers Grim was there, but the other was not. I followed the French liturgy as well as possible, and at the end the priest prayed by name for the pilgrims who had passed here before us. Tomorrow, I knew, he would pray for Eric and Elizabeth.

I slept well among the memories of the thousands of pilgrims who had passed through this shelter before me.

The next morning, Eric and I crossed the stone bridge back out of Estaing and started yet another steep climb. We were about a kilometer up the hill when it hit me. "Did you put money in the donation box?"

Eric froze. Damn. Neither had I.

The nuns in Estaing never asked for anything; our beds and our meals were freely given. But there was a donativo box on the wall by the front door, with an invitation for pilgrims to contribute what they could to help provide for those who followed. We'd planned to put money in this morning, but in the rush of packing and getting our shoes tied and packs strapped, we'd forgotten.

They'd been so gracious, so kind . . .

Eric took off his pack and set it by my feet. "I'll be back." He jogged back down the hill, across the bridge, and through the streets. He rang the bell, and when the surprised nun opened the door, he gave her our donation—more than we would have spent on a demi-pension in a private gîte.

And then he jogged back *up* the hill to where I waited.

I love that man.

After that, it was a relatively easy walk under an overcast sky to Espeyrac. We arrived without reservations, but that hadn't been a problem for the past few days. We easily found the gîte communal, which appeared empty, but a note on the door said otherwise. *C'est complet.*

Eric went to find the mairie, where someone explained that two groups, including the Eight Walkers, had reservations. There were no other gîtes, but the town had an inn. It cost more than two bunks in a common room, but it wasn't budget-busting.

Before we flew to France we'd agreed that we would stay in hostels as much as possible. But there would be times, we assured each other with a wink and a nudge, when we might want a private room. So what did we do when, after more than a week of communal living, we found ourselves in room with a double bed and a lock on the door?

We did the daily chores and immediately left to find our friends, of course.

The Eight Walkers had arrived in town, cheery and full of energy. Their walking holiday would end in Conques the next day, and they were ready to celebrate. They pressed appetizers and wine on us, and together we laughed and shared stories. Once again, I was surprised how much more of their French I understood after just eight days.

I tried to imagine our Camino without them. Who would translate and make our reservations for us? Who would ogle Eric? Who would be our friends?

Before we left for the Camino, I read everything I could, including plenty of Camino memoirs. I was desperate for practical information and advice, but I noticed that every personal story focused mostly on the people the authors met along the way.

Wait, I wanted to say to the writers. You're walking through this magnificent country, and all you can talk about is the Austrian guy you met at dinner? Where are your priorities?

And then I went to France, started walking, and met the people. And they became the center of my story, too.

It doesn't matter how old you are or where you're from, whether you're traveling alone or with a group, or whether you consider yourself an introvert or an extrovert. If you walk the Way of Saint James, the people around you will make or break your experience. The Camino is as much about the hours of conversation in the evenings, with people you'd never meet otherwise, as it is about the physical challenge of the mornings. This was a social experience in ways I never expected, and the people I met are bound to my memories.

With just one-tenth of my journey complete, losing the Eight Walkers meant I already felt a sense of something ending.

The next day we set out through a thick mist that was almost rain. We strolled first with the Eight Walkers, and then with the Brothers Grim. Eric peppered them all with questions and practiced his French. They all loved him.

I lagged behind as we crossed a field of brilliant springtime green, so I was alone when two deer leapt gracefully across the dew-wet grass, chased by a black dog that seemed more determined than vicious. The dog didn't bark, and the whole scene was weirdly serene. They disappeared over a rise while I stood frozen, trying to remember the French word for "deer" to alert the others.

The moment was magic, and all mine.

The day's walking distance was short, and we made the steep, almost stairlike descent into Conques before noon.

I'd been looking forward to this stop, which is always mentioned as a high point of the Chemin du Puy. Conques clings to its medieval history as tightly as it clings to the steep hillside. Every effort is made to retain the original architecture along terraced, cobbled streets. There are no motorized vehicles, and the power lines are buried underground.

At the center is the Abbey of Sainte Foy, with a massive cathedral built for the thousands of pilgrims who flowed through the remote valley in the ninth and tenth centuries to pay their respects to the relics of the virgin Saint Foy.

As far as the stories of the early Camino go, the history of Conques is particularly twisted. Saint Foy was a third-century French aristocrat who was brutally tortured and killed for her refusal to deny her Christian faith and marry a pagan. That's a pretty common saint story. But what's interesting is that Foy was not from Conques. She was born and died in Agen, more than two hundred kilometers away.

Early Christian pilgrims traveled to Agen, where Saint Foy's remains were protected and displayed in a monastery. The town flourished with the influx of their donations and commerce. The tiny abbey of Conques wanted a piece of that, so they sent one of their monks, undercover, to work at the Agen monastery. For ten years the man gained trust, until finally he was put in charge of protecting the sacred relic—which he immediately stole and carried back to Conques.

The monks of Conques never denied what they'd done, because that would have thrown doubt on the credibility of their new relic. Instead, they simply announced that Saint Foy had moved to a new valley. Pilgrims, without any historical record of a fuss, changed their course and continued to seek the blessing of the stolen saint.

Today, the modern abbey of Saint Foy provides a gîte de pèlerin right beside the cathedral, in a building that once housed the monks themselves. We arrived several hours before it opened, so Eric and I left our bags in its sheltered courtyard and set out to explore.

Conques, we discovered, is not just a stop on the Way of Saint James, but also a popular destination for nonpilgrim tourists. They filled the narrow streets and stood out in their clean clothes and designer shoes, but there were still plenty of faces we knew. We said a proper goodbye to the Eight Walkers and waved to both the man who'd bandaged Eric's feet in Saint Chelys and the group of teenagers who'd taken the rest of the beds in Espeyrac the night before. Everyone, it seems, stops for a night or two in Conques.

Of course, the Brothers Grim were there. When they approached us, for the first time they had more to say than "Everything good?" Slowly and in French, the older Grim told Eric that they would leave the Way in two days, in Figeac. In case we didn't see each other again, they wanted to exchange email addresses. Here again was the weight of goodbye. Losing these generous strangers-turned-friends brought tears to our eyes.

Eric went off to find a quiet corner of the abbey's courtyard and gather his thoughts while I wandered the town. On the surface Conques was charming, but I thought it also felt "Camino commercial," with shops selling everything from cheap "pilgrim" walking sticks to high-end scallop shell jewelry. Nothing I saw was worth adding extra weight to the pack I carried every day.

As I walked the postcard-perfect streets, I thought about Saint-Côme-d'Olt, where the church had been smaller and shabbier, but there were posters by the door about food drives and children's activities. There was a market nearby where families did their daily shopping. There was a school. *People lived there.* The more I explored Conques, the more I suspected that no one called this place home.

I found out later I was right. According to a woman we met later, who'd once worked for the abbey, the summer population of Conques was all shopkeepers and artisans who lived elsewhere and came for the tourists. In the winter, when the gîte closed and the tourists went home, just seventeen people stayed in the village—the monks and the people who worked for them.

Eric and I met up again at 3:00, when the gîte opened, and joined a few dozen pilgrims in the abbey courtyard. Volunteers gave us cookies and showed us where to stow our hiking shoes and how to cover our backpacks with giant plastic bags coated with insecticide that would supposedly kill bedbugs. The whole thing was cheerfully inefficient, but eventually someone took our money, stamped our credentials, and led us up a circular stone staircase to the biggest dorm room I'd seen so far, with eight bunk beds. (Two months later, in Spain, a room with only eight beds would seem practically private.)

The two stern women we'd met in Saint Chelys were already there, and I noticed the bruised woman was crying, quietly, in her bunk. Her feet were wrapped in bandages, and she looked utterly miserable. I offered her a small smile that I hoped was empathetic. *I've done some crying in a bunk, too. I understand.*

Wanting to avoid the crowds and commercialism outside, Eric and I escaped to a small reading room upstairs, where we sipped bottles of monastery-brewed beer and caught up on our journaling. The rain beat on the single-pane window and stained the brick of the cathedral just across the courtyard.

After a couple hours of peace, I was ready for Conques again. I skipped down the stairs, on my way to hear the monks sing their evening vespers, but stopped when I heard a familiar, guttural voice.

Jan, the older Dutchman we'd met over the dinner of wild boar in Les Estrets, stood by the registration table, hunched under his enormous backpack. We had seen Jan several times since then on the trail and usually slowed to chat for a few minutes. But he walked unfathomably slowly, even by my standards, and carried a tent, so he often camped at night. It had been days since we'd seen him. Now, on the edge of saying goodbye to so many other friends, I was disproportionately glad to see him.

The abbey volunteer didn't seem to feel the same way. She shrank back when Jan spoke, as he always did in French, at top volume, one syllable at a time, and with a heavy Dutch accent.

"AH VAY VOO UN LEE SEE VOO PLAY?"

Even when he was sober, Jan gave the impression of being a little drunk.

"Jan!" I called. He looked up and brightened. "Elizabeth!"

The volunteer looked up and brightened. "You know him?" she asked me, and then, "Is he real?"

Why yes, I could verify that Jan was real, and I supposed I knew him as much as I knew anyone in this country, where I slept two feet from people I couldn't talk to. I joined them at the table, and between my terrible French and the volunteer's limited English, we got Jan checked in, stamped, and someone led him upstairs to settle into a room while I continued to vespers, where ancient chants echoed off the cavern of the cathedral.

Dinner that night was a noisy affair, with more than fifty pilgrims crammed around tables. Eric and I joined a table of pilgrims from Germany, Hungary, Austria, Ireland, and the Netherlands, including Jan, who all got by with English.

After we ate, the volunteers called for quiet. They pulled out an easel, a flip chart, and a couple of guitars, and then they taught us the Camino song.

Yes, there is a Camino song. It's in French, of course, with some throwbacks to Latin to liven things up. All I learned that night was the chorus—*Ultreia!*—but later I looked up the rest. Roughly translated, it is:

Every morning we take the Camino,
Every morning we go farther,
Day after day the route calls us,

It's the voice of Compostela!
Onward! Onward! And upward!
God assist us!
Way of earth and way of faith,
Ancient road of Europe,
The Milky Way of Charlemagne,
It's the Way of all the Santiago pilgrims!
And over there at the end of the continent,
Santiago waits for us,
His smile always fixed
On the sun that dies at Finisterre.

The cynic in me held back. Did I really want to sing motivational choruses in the equivalent of a church basement? The pilgrim in me looked around at fifty faces, from a dozen countries, connecting through a song that was a thousand years old.

An hour later our group joined dozens of others for compline services in the vast, echoing cathedral. I struggled to follow most of the French service, but at the end we sang *Ultreia!—onward!—* again, and my pilgrim side won. I sang.

This didn't seem silly anymore. This town I'd written off as too commercial had surprised me.

My goodwill lasted until the next morning, when my room-mates started to get up and rustle through their bedbug-proofed plastic bags at 6:00 a.m. What were they doing? Breakfast didn't even start until 7:00, and most of us didn't start walking until 8:00. It's not like anyone primped for a day on the muddy trails.

At 6:30 the quiet woman with the black eye got up, walked across the room, and turned on the overhead lights with no acknowledgment of the people who were still trying to sleep. I lay there, blinking in the harsh fluorescent glare, wondering why I'd felt so sorry for her the night before. From that point on, the injury-prone woman and her stern companion acquired a new nickname: the Black-Eyed B's.

Conques sat deep in a valley, and I'd spent the previous afternoon with one eye on the tree-covered wall that I'd have to climb to get back out. I didn't see its natural beauty. I saw an obstacle.

Like most things I fret about, it turned out not to be as bad as I expected. It helped that I was learning, finally, not to try to keep up with Eric. The path was muddy and slippery, and I plodded upward at my own pace. I stopped often to catch my breath. I plodded again. As long as I made steady progress and didn't cry, I decided, I would eventually get to the top. Eric was long out of sight, but instead of feeling guilty for slowing him down, I relaxed in the knowledge that he'd wait for me at the top.

Or not. I was still plodding when he came skipping lightly back down the hill toward me. He'd made it to the top, got bored, left his bag there, and came back for me. He took my pack, slung it over his own shoulders, and went bounding up the hill again, playfully daring me to keep up.

Without the extra twenty pounds of weight, my pace picked up, and I passed a dozen pilgrims, most of them slack-jawed as they watched the young American.

I was pretty impressed, too.

Eric may have already gotten choked up at the idea of losing the Brothers Grim, but the Camino wasn't ready to take them from us yet.

As we dropped altitude and moved south, spring advanced at hyperspeed. Just ten days earlier, the trees around us were bare, and there were still occasional drifts of snow. Now there were flowers blooming everywhere, and I was sweating in my T-shirt.

When we stopped for a lunch break in a children's playground covered knee-deep in weeds, we tried to decide where to spend the night. None of the towns on the map looked right. They were too far, or too close, or there wasn't a gîte that seemed right.

We were still waffling when the Grims walked by, and Eric flagged them down to ask if they could phone a reservation for us somewhere. When they saw we didn't have a plan, the Grims suggested that we stay with them in Livinhac-le-Haut, at a private gîte listed in their French guidebook, but not ours.

We knew it was their last night; they would board a train in Figeac the next day. Of course we said yes.

Once that was settled and reservations made, we split up again and walked at our own paces through modern towns full of pastel houses and over still more hills. France was still, as far as I could tell, a never-ending roller coaster.

In Livinhac, Eric and I found the gîte, the Coquille Bleu, on a quiet residential street. The talkative owner, Claire, ushered us into a cool stone sitting area on the ground floor. It had been a cow barn in 1610, she told us in English, so she didn't care if we wore our shoes. She produced a tray of *sirop,* the popular French beverage of water flavored with syrup, and ordered us to drink three glasses each while she unleashed a barrage of instructions about where to sleep, where to wash our clothes, and where to hang them. Later, she waited by the laundry lines and rehung everything when she decided we were doing it wrong. And though she didn't offer dinner, she told us where to go and what to order. Her bossiness could have been infuriating, but she was so friendly that she was easy to forgive.

Eric and I were lounging in the sunny yard, hiding from Claire, when the Grims came to find us. They'd explored the town and found a bar that would make us dinner. It wasn't what Claire recommended, but would we join them? Of course we said yes.

We also invited the two other gîte guests, a Canadian man and a Frenchwoman, and at 7:00 we all made our way across the deserted town square and into the deserted bar. The meal itself was disappointing. The bar owner clearly wasn't a cook, but when pèlerins had come in with their euros, he'd seen an opportunity and had scrounged whatever he could from the local market.

The mediocre food didn't matter, though. We were with the Brothers Grim, our companions since the beginning. For nine days we'd shared meals and smiles, slept in the same rooms, laughed and struggled together. Heck, we'd heard each other snore and seen each other's underwear.

Yet even as our (well, Eric's) French improved, we'd intentionally avoided personal questions. We'd reveled in the mystery. But they were leaving, so it was now or never. "Excuse me," I asked the Frenchwoman. "Will you please ask them their names?"

The Grims were Jean Rene and Clebert. They were brothers-in-law, married to sisters, so both Eric ("they look nothing alike") and I ("they act like they're related") were right.

To us, they are always the Brothers Grim.

THE SAGGING MIDDLE

We woke the next morning to a sound we hadn't heard yet in France: heavy rain. Sure, we'd walked through drizzle and slogged through mud from overnight showers, but this was different. This was the kind of rain that was so thick you couldn't see the end of the block.

Reluctantly, we got up and geared up. Most European pilgrims we met assumed "the more rain gear, the better." They had waterproof boots, rain pants, and ponchos with deep hoods. At the first drop they disappeared under a pile of Gore-Tex.

Eric and I had a different approach, probably because in Seattle, rain is our daily companion nine months of the year. We had rain jackets, but to keep our packs light and our bodies mobile, we both opted for "quick-dry" instead of waterproof. When it rained, we just rolled up our pants and lived with being wet. We lined the inside of our packs with plastic trash bags, hid water-sensitive papers and gear deep in the middle, and then wrapped the rain fly over the whole mess and hoped for the best.

We all ate a subdued breakfast, glancing often out the window, while Claire clattered around us and told us how to put jam on bread. With the rain as a distracting backdrop, our parting from the Grims was anticlimactic. They pulled on their jackets and disappeared into the rain fifteen minutes before us without saying goodbye, and we never saw them again.

Splashing through the rain was almost fun at first, even though the water soaked my pants and turned my shoes into swamps. We dodged mud puddles and sang nursery rhyme songs from childhood, changing the lyrics to make them dirty.

We came upon Jan, plodding at "Jan pace" under a giant poncho and hat. We slowed to chat about where he'd camped the night before, and how heavy his waterlogged tent was. We made sure he had enough food for a long day. But the rain made it hard to talk, so we kept moving.

GR65 that day mostly avoided towns and followed dirt trails that wound through and behind farms. On a good day it was probably lovely. On that day the unpaved paths turned to flowing streams. I tried to skirt the overgrown edges, cursing my "breathable" shoes and snagging my clothes and skin on thorn bushes. It was slow, painful, and ultimately pointless. I was drenched and mud-covered no matter what I did, so I eventually just gave up and slogged through water up to my ankles.

After two hours my body asked for its midmorning break. But there was no shelter, and nowhere to rest that wasn't just as wet and muddy as we were. We walked on. The rain never let up, and the mud got deeper. We stopped singing. Lunchtime came and went.

Finally, after five long hours on our feet, we came to a cafe—well, a garage filled with picnic tables in the yard of an entrepreneurial family. The sign out front promised hot soup. Nothing ever sounded so good.

There were a dozen pilgrims like us already inside, seeking shelter. We all shivered in the unheated space, but at least we had dry seats. We draped raincoats and gear around the edges of the room, dug out dry socks, and commiserated about the lousy weather. We consumed gallons of soup, coffee, quiche, and anything warm the family offered us.

After an hour, feeling fortified for the final ten kilometers, Eric and I squished our feet back into soaked shoes, slid into clammy raincoats, and set off.

The rain never let up. It was still coming down, light but steady, when we limped into Figeac at 4:00 in the afternoon and discovered that compared to everywhere we'd stayed since Le Puy, this was a major metropolis. Ten thousand inhabitants filled a warren of streets, and we had no map, no reservation, and no idea where the gîtes were. And there was certainly no one lingering outside in this mess who we could ask.

But when you need it most, the Camino provides. We abandoned the red and white markings and crossed an unmarked bridge into the heart of town, and a block away we saw a red sign: GÎTE DE PÈLERIN.

The young owners of Le Coquelicot were from Morocco. They welcomed us despite our mud and offered us a double room with a private bathroom. We couldn't give them our money fast enough.

We took long, blessedly hot showers, rinsed as much mud from our clothes as we could, and curled up in the stone common room, probably another centuries-old cow barn, with other tired, rain-shocked pilgrims to journal and wait for dinner.

We didn't know any of the other pilgrims there that night, but the rain bound us together. At 7:00 we gathered to eat spicy Mediterranean chicken, couscous, and vegetables. The warm flavors and bright colors made it feel like spring again.

As we lingered over one last glass of wine, our host came over. He spoke no English, but through pantomime and simple French, he commiserated over how difficult the language barrier could be. He'd emigrated here as an adult without knowing a word of French, he said, and it took him two lonely years to become fluent.

I went to sleep that night feeling like an adventurer who was conquering great obstacles.

At home I make my living helping writers develop their ideas into books. One of the places where many storytellers struggle is what editors like me call the "sagging middle." Writers start with a great idea and plenty of drama. And then, at the end of the book, there's a resolution: the murderer is caught, the couple discovers true love, the main character sets out on a new life. But between those Big Events, things can get flat. The writing is often still good, but chapters slide by and nothing significant changes. People in the "sagging middle" follow established routines, marking time until it's time to introduce some new tangle.

As we walked out of Figeac the day after the epic rain, we entered the sagging middle of France. Our friends were gone, and after almost two weeks of walking fifteen to thirty kilometers a day, we were tired. The novelty of springing out of bed before dawn, donning the same clothes, and putting one foot in front of the other for hours had worn off. The days started blending together into what Angela and Duffy Ballard, in their book *A Blistered Kind of Love*, called "the spectacular monotony."

More rolling hills, medieval roadside chapels, and picturesque fields of French cows? Sure, whatever.

It didn't help that The Princesses were still in full revolt. Every day would start okay, but after two or three hours my feet would swell and throb. I'd already blown through the bottle of ibuprofen we brought from home, and I was spending a small fortune at French pharmacies to restock. We tried taking a half-day off after Figeac, walking a scant five kilometers, but it didn't help. Different socks, looser laces, and end-of-day ice baths brought temporary relief that never lasted.

I needed a real rest day, the kind where I didn't have to put on a backpack at all. Eric was willing to take a break if it would help me, but it was up to me to make it happen, and I couldn't find the right place to linger. The communal gîtes, like the one in Cajarc, were inexpensive and efficient, but allowed people to stay only one night. The private gîtes where we stayed in Cassagnole and Varraire were full of thoughtful details and kind hosts, but I deemed both too remote to linger for a full day.

I knew how to walk in France but not how to stop.

I waffled and complained for days, testing Eric's patience. We got testy with each other more often. But without a better plan, we kept moving forward, day after day.

There weren't many other pilgrims on the road; we often had gîte dorms to ourselves and rarely saw others on the trail. We continued to walk at our own paces, which is the nice way of saying that Eric sped off out of sight and then stopped every couple of hours to wait for me to catch up.

We got braver about ordering food in restaurants when demipension was not available and occasionally attempted to buy groceries and cook for ourselves. (Lessons learned after trial and plenty of errors: a half kilogram of chicken is not comparable to a half pound, and is way too much for two people. Also, it's not appropriate to pick up your own produce in most markets; a person at the counter wants to put that apple in a bag for you.)

The weather was kind, and we enjoyed a week of bright sun and spring temperatures. We were outside from dawn to dusk, every day. My skin grew tan, and despite all the French food and wine, my pants became so loose I needed a belt to keep them up.

The landscape, too, was changing. The hills softened from "vertical" to "rolling." Dew-covered green fields, dotted with postcard-perfect shepherds' huts shaped like beehives, more often gave way to commercial and light industrial areas. Pastures gave way to factory farms, and we passed windowless barns that smelled so bad outside that I couldn't think about what happened within. The first time I saw a dusty, smelly lot filled with miserable, fat, open-beaked geese, panting in the sun and unable to stand, I swore off foie gras.

We stopped in every open church so that Eric could sign the guest books and I could study the memorials to "l'Enfants" of the Great War. Every village had one, inscribed with the names of the hometown sons who'd died in trenches and hospitals. As an American, it was hard to imagine the impact of an entire lost generation. But when I looked at the empty houses and crumbling towns, I saw the farmers and schoolteachers, bankers and doctors, who would never have a family or grow old there.

Even in the sagging middle, there were surprises. None were as memorable as the cows that chased us.

Eric and I were walking along a single-lane farm road early one morning. The light and the temperature were just about perfect, and we were moving along smoothly when Eric pointed out that a cow was on the wrong side of the pasture fence just ahead of us. A dozen or so black-and-white heifers were inside the fence, but one brave explorer had somehow gotten out to graze on the taller grass by the roadside.

Clearly, I said, he'd heard the cliché.

Before Eric could respond, the rest of the cows noticed our approach and started to trot toward us, sending up a chorus of discontent. The escapee ignored the excitement and continued to enjoy the feast spread before him.

There are a lot of *vaches* in this part of France, but these black-and-white milk cows seemed smaller than average. I assumed they were the bovine equivalent of teenagers and that they were now tattling on the defector. Their concern gave me the giggles, and I stopped to take pictures of the scene.

Eric did not share my amusement. He moved to the far side of the road, away from the pasture, and told me to do the same. "Keep walking and don't make eye contact."

Well, okay. We reached the edge of the pasture where the cows inside the fence were waiting for us. When we passed without stopping, they turned and followed us down the fence line, still complaining.

Our noisy parade reached the escapee cow, and his herd instinct kicked in. He lifted his head and started strolling with his companions, albeit on our side of the fence. This made Eric even jumpier, but I thought the cows were adorable.

When we got to the far corner of the pasture, the road split. GR65's red and white stripes pointed to the left. To the right, I could see a farmhouse, presumably belonging to the cows' owners. I considered going to their door to tell them they had a cow loose. But did I know how to say, "Your cow is outside the fence" in French?

While I was mentally conjugating verbs, the cows in the pasture got to the corner. In the place where their fences should meet, a single piece of rope hung across an opening that served as the gate. Cows, I remembered reading somewhere, are so domesticated that a single line of string can keep them contained.

Well, most cows. This rope gate was strung for taller animals, and our new teenage friends could walk right under it, which probably explained how the loose cow got out in the first place. Now, three more followed his lead, their eyes on us.

We had four cows outside the pasture, ambling our direction and blocking my path to the farmhouse.

"This is not good," Eric said more than once.

I abandoned my plan to report the escapees, but I couldn't get over my giggles.

"Keep walking," Eric urged. "Cows are big." And then, "Don't look back. But know where they are. A cow could head butt you and trample you."

Really? Trampling heifers?

Two of the cows were distracted by the roadside grass and stopped. The other two, including the initial intrepid explorer, followed us down the road as we walked briskly away.

We walked faster, which was a bad idea. Our new mini-herd started to trot. Eric sped up again, and told me at least three times not to look back. Just as often, I suggested that we turn around and lead the cows back to their farm, but Eric refused, because we'd have to double back past them, increasing the risk of head butting and trampling.

We kept walking. The cows kept following us. I kept laughing. This all continued for about half a kilometer. We passed a few houses, but the gates were all closed and the heavy metal shutters drawn.

Finally, we saw an open driveway and a sign for a *chambre d'hote*—essentially a French bed and breakfast. It seemed to be open.

"I'm going to ask for help," I announced, both to Eric and our cows.

Eric nodded. "I'll stay out here and distract them."

Not sure what he thought he would distract them from but pretty sure it involved the word "stampede," I turned up the driveway. Our bovine friends let out a chorus of discontent. They were confused by our separation, not sure who to follow.

An older, frowning woman opened the door when I knocked. "Do you speak English?" I asked, too rattled to ask the question in French.

"Oui. A little," she said.

I explained the situation with the cows.

"They are not my cows," she said.

I told her I understood. "But they are not our cows, either. They belong to your neighbor. We have no phone, and we do not know who to call. Can you help us?"

She reluctantly agreed to call someone and closed the door in my face. Assuming that meant I was dismissed, I retreated to the road to find out if Eric had been head butted and trampled in my absence. Instead, I found the cows ignoring him and happily munching grass in what they must have considered their new pasture. When we tiptoed away, they didn't even look up.

I spent the next couple of hours relentlessly teasing my brave, strong husband. How had it taken fourteen years of marriage for me to discover that he was afraid of cows?

When I finally wound down, we talked it out and concluded that although Eric had never spent time around farm animals, he had spent those summers in the Canadian wilderness near another bulky, hoofed animal: moose.

A moose *will* charge a person, head butt them, and trample them. It was a valid point, but one that I chose to forget many times over the next few weeks, as I watched Eric stride off ahead of me and knew I couldn't keep up.

I may be slow, I'd think, but at least I wasn't afraid of a cow.

Day after day, we continued to follow the Chemin du Puy as it wound toward Cahors, a town that has guarded a strategic bend of the Lot River since Celtic times. Cahors is famous for its wine, especially a rich Malbec so dark it's called black wine, and for its ahead-of-its-time medieval policy of allowing lenders to charge interest, an affront against church rules that earned it a comparison to Sodom in Dante's *Inferno*.

Despite all its history, the modern city of Cahors was remote, and reaching it meant we had to cover a punishing thirty kilometers in a day. Most of the walk was relatively flat, along an old Roman road that bisected a thick, muddy forest. But in the early afternoon we started to climb the series of rocky hills that surrounded the city.

It was here that we found Jan sitting on a rock by the side of the path. We hadn't seen our strange Dutch friend since the rainy walk to Figeac, but even as we said hello, I could see something was wrong. Jan seemed to droop, and his voice was flat even for him.

"This is a long way, and there aren't any fountains," he said. "I am out of water. I am sitting here because my brother called. His wife died." He said it all in a rush, and while I was still sorting out the implications, Eric unstrapped his pack, handed over his water bottle, and sat down next to our friend.

See why I married him?

We knew from previous conversations that Jan had intended to walk the Chemin du Puy with his brother, but a few weeks before they left, the other Dutchman (I always imagined him as Jan's opposite, six feet tall and rail thin) stayed home because his wife was sick. I hadn't realized how sick she was. Maybe Jan hadn't known.

"What will you do?" I asked.

"My brother says to keep walking." His eyes were distant. "I would not get home in time for the funeral. So I will continue."

We sat with Jan for a while longer, gave him as much of our water as he would take, and tried to guess how much farther it was to Cahors. His tent was once again soaked from a midnight rain, and he was low on other supplies. We encouraged him to get to town and splurge on a gîte, a warm meal, and a shower. We told him the name of the place where we had reservations, Le Papillon Vert.

Eventually, we got up together and set out. Jan waved us ahead, knowing that his pace didn't match ours. We reminded him again to come and find us at the Green Butterfly.

That last stretch to Cahors wasn't short, and it wasn't easy. We wove through remote hills for hours, without a city in sight. It was late afternoon by the time Eric and I finally crested the last hill and descended back into civilization. We'd given up on Jan by then, sure that our plodding friend would still be in the woods when the sun went down.

Dazed by the sudden appearance of people and cars, we crossed a traffic-filled bridge and stopped at a welcome center to get directions. The women there plied us with cookies and sirop while they stamped our credentials and gave us directions to our gîte.

Le Papillon Vert stretched five stories tall and just a single room wide, in the middle of a street no wider than an alley, just two blocks from the cathedral. Our hostess was a tiny woman with a halo of frizzy blonde hair and a breathy, whispery voice. If Luna Lovegood, from the Harry Potter books, had grown up, this was who she would have become.

Crossing the Pont Valentre of Cahors

Luna-the-Elder welcomed us in English and offered us poetry to read as she stamped, and then meticulously hand-colored, our credentials. As she led us up four flights of narrow stairs, she mentioned that the building was nine hundred years old, so we should watch our heads.

Eventually we found ourselves all the way in the attic, in a low dormer room under the eaves with just enough room for a twin bed and a cot. I leaned out the window and soaked in enough of the view to fuel my energy for the trip back down two flights to the bathroom.

After a long day I was in no shape to explore the town, so I lingered in our attic hideout until twilight descended and the restaurants started opening. Le Papillon Vert was too small to serve dinner, so Eric and I were on our own.

We'd just reached the end of our block when we saw Jan, flanked by two of the volunteers from the welcome center. They had that same dazed, politely appalled look that I remembered from the volunteer in Conques.

"Elizabeth! Eric! I have arrived!" Jan bellowed in greeting. "They want to take me somewhere else, but I said no, I must go to the *PAPPY ON VERT.*" We found out later that he'd stopped "for salad and beer" at the edge of town. I suspected the beers outnumbered the salad, but again, with Jan it was sometimes hard to tell.

We were delighted to see him. The volunteers seemed delighted to leave him in our care. It was only when we got Jan back to our home for the night that I realized what a terrible idea this was. The Green Butterfly, and its ethereal hostess, were narrow, thin, quiet, and delicate. Jan was solidly connected to the earth, especially after several days of sleeping in a tent without showering. He swayed under his heavy bag and filled the small space with his booming voice. He was a bull in a china shop, and there was nothing to do but sit back and watch. Eric couldn't stop grinning.

An awkward hour later, Luna had colored Jan's stamp and settled him in the last available dorm bed, and Jan had cleaned himself up. We ventured out again, Jan in tow, to find dinner at a noisy, inexpensive Italian restaurant. The next two hours were full of local wine and pasta and laughter.

The Camino really is all about the people.

Our walk the next day was going to be shorter, only twenty kilometers, so Eric and I lingered in Cahors for a few hours, exploring the cathedral of Saint Etienne. At 9:00 in the morning on a Tuesday, the twelfth-century church was practically deserted, and we circled it slowly, taking in the details of gargoyles along the eaves and intricate but time-worn carvings in the quiet cloister.

We lingered again on the Pont Valentre, with its three distinctive towers, on our way out of town. Built at the beginning of the fourteenth century, the bridge was a defensive structure against river invasions.

Construction took seventy years and was plagued with delays. There's a legend that the frustrated master builder made a deal with the devil: if the devil would help in every way the builder needed, the builder would give him his soul when the bridge was complete. As the end of construction neared, the man reconsidered his eternal prospect. So he told the devil to bring water to make the mortar to place the last stone and handed him a sieve to carry it in. Not even the devil could transport water in a sieve, so the final stone was never laid and the master builder kept his soul.

When the bridge was restored in 1879, the architect added a small sculpture of the devil at the summit of the central tower, where the stone was still missing. We waved to him as we passed under his watchful glare.

After the first tough climb out of the valley, we expected an easy walk to Lascabanes. By 3:00 that afternoon the sun was bright and hot, and I was footsore and tired. We took a break in a chapel in a town called L'Hospitalet, where the air was cool and the light shone through stained-glass windows under high Gothic arches. It felt peaceful, and we emerged refreshed.

And then we realized L'Hospitalet wasn't on the Chemin du Puy.

France's many Grande Randonnée walking trails sometimes overlap and cross, and they're all, confusingly, marked with identical red and white stripes. At some point that morning we'd accidentally started to follow GR6. We pulled out our maps, studied our options, and realized that our beds were still ten kilometers away.

The next two hours weren't pretty. Eric was frustrated by our mistake and eager to make up for the lost time. I was exhausted and couldn't walk fast enough. As we entered town at the end of our second thirty-kilometer day, I had vague impressions of a beautiful European village set in a green valley, with tall church steeples and whitewashed cottages.

Our gîte de pèlerin was in the lovely former rectory of the parish church. I vaguely registered a group of pilgrims outside, clean and refreshed. They'd probably been there for hours and were gossiping about why it took the Americans so long to walk twenty kilometers.

I was too miserable to talk to anyone. I left Eric to do whatever chores he thought were necessary and limped off to find my bunk and have a cry. My feet hurt. My body hurt. I couldn't imagine another seven hundred miles of this. It was my lowest point of the Camino.

But it was also when things started to turn around.

SOMETIMES YOU WIN, SOMETIMES YOU LOSE

Lascabanes would have been a good place to rest, but the gîte was already full the next night. No matter how tired and broken my body felt, I had to get up the next morning and walk again. So I did.

First law of inertia: an object in motion tends to remain in motion . . .

We left in the company of a group of five young, friendly, English-speaking pilgrims we'd met at dinner the night before. They'd come from around the world, each planning to walk the Camino alone, but they'd met by chance in Le Puy and had stayed together every night since. The Camino has that effect on people.

It was Saturday again, which meant that gîtes would fill quickly. As soon as we found a hilltop where our new friends could get cell phone reception, we clustered together and waited to find out if there were available beds in Lauzerte.

The first three places they called were already full, but we got lucky with the last gîte on the list. Yes, they had space for all seven of us that night. It was three kilometers outside town, and the person on the phone said that we should call again when we got

Inside the Cathedral of Saint Peter in Condom

to the market at the edge of Lauzerte and they would come get us. It seemed complicated, especially without a phone, but what choice did we have?

Once that was settled, we all spread out to walk our own paces. Eric and I reached Montcuq midmorning and stopped for a second coffee and my second dose of ibuprofen. This was the halfway point of the Chemin du Puy and our time in France, so we added a pain au chocolat to celebrate.

In eighteen days we'd walked 380 kilometers, or more than 230 miles. I tried to come up with some profound thought about that, but instead I ended up trying to calculate how much more ibuprofen I would need for the next 770 more miles.

While I was doing the math, the French pilgrims at the next table were having a different kind of conversation. Montcuq, it turns out, sounds a lot like the French phrase for "my ass." Even the most serious retirees couldn't say it without a bit of a smile.

Great. I still couldn't make a gîte reservation in French, but now I could swear.

We continued to the walled town of Lauzerte, which sat like a good medieval fortress should, on top of the steepest hill in sight, with a clear view of open land all around it. The market our hosts had referenced turned out to be a modern grocery store at the foot of the hill, so for once I was spared the climb.

On the other hand, our new friends, the ones with the phone, were nowhere in sight. We lingered in the grass at the edge of the parking lot until a pilgrim we sort of recognized passed. He called the gîte for us, and after a quick and incomprehensible French conversation, he told us that they were on their way. Then he continued up the hill toward town, where he, of course, had a réserve.

We waited some more.

Finally, an old car rolled up. The man inside could have been Nicolas Cage's French brother. He spoke no English, but he knew our names, so we got in. He drove away from the town, turning several times until we were on a dirt road that led to a secluded house. In other stories, in other places, that might have made me nervous. But this was the Camino, and the sprawling stone house at the end of the lane had its own tower. I felt nothing but peace.

French Nic's wife, Frederique, met us in their glassed-in porch, which looked over rolling fields of golden safflowers toward Lauzerte rising on its hill. Frederique didn't speak English either, but she showed us to a private room with thick walls and a double bed. There was a kitchen where we could cook, or Frederique would provide dinner if we preferred. There was a hammock in the backyard.

I had found our resting place at last.

By the time the others arrived, Eric and I were lounging in the yard while our clothes spun clean in Frederique's tiny washer. We passed a happy, boisterous evening listening to their stories, but when they invited us to join them in Moissac the next day, I demurred. Frederique had already agreed to let us stay in our private room for another night.

On Sunday morning, French Nic drove us into town to pick up supplies, and then Eric and I spent the afternoon napping, reading, and making plans for the next few days. We sat quietly and watched the light change in the fields of flowers. The tension of the past few days faded from my body, and even Eric acknowledged that a rest day had been a good idea.

The next morning, Frederique drove us back to the trail and we started walking again. There was a drizzly mist that never turned into rain, but it left the path muddy and the grass wet. We didn't pass through any towns that morning, and there was nowhere dry enough to sit, so we spread our lunch on the hood of an abandoned car buried deep in the weeds and laughed at our romantic picnic.

The rest day had refilled my physical and emotional tanks, but it didn't magically heal my feet. By the time we reached the dreary suburbs of Moissac, I was limping and footsore again.

Our gîte was high in the medieval part of town, in a former convent just around the corner from the Saint-Pierre Abbey. Once we were settled, I wandered over to the church and spent a quiet hour studying the Romanesque murals and carvings, while nuns in full habits prepared for their evening vespers. A brochure by the entrance told me that the cloister of this abbey was famous for its intricate and well-preserved carvings, but there was no door to get there from the sanctuary. I had to cross the square and pass through a tacky gift shop. When a humorless employee told me I would also have to buy a ticket, I left in a huff. We'd seen some fabulous cloisters already, I told Eric, in places that served God, not tourists. Churches should never charge pilgrims for admittance. (This became a harder line to hold in Spain, where most of the larger cathedrals, and even some churches in smaller towns, charged an entrance fee. But I didn't know that yet.)

The next day the Chemin du Puy gave us a break from the mud and the hills, and all day we followed a smooth, flat path along a canal, shaded by ancient sycamores. Before railroads and highways, this waterway was the primary way to move people and goods from the Atlantic Ocean to the Mediterranean Sea. Now it was mostly recreational, with only houseboats and pleasure craft cruising through the locks.

We'd just cleared the limits of Moissac when I saw a familiar blonde figure walking ahead of us. I'd first met her in the bathroom of the abbey gîte in Conques, of all places, after the pilgrim mass. During the service the priest had invited several pilgrims to read the evening's Scripture aloud in their own languages. The young woman had stood and read in English, so when I saw her later, I complimented her reading and said something about how it was good to hear English.

She seemed embarrassed. "I don't read English well. Someone gave me a paper and told me I had to do it." She studied me. "You're American? Why didn't they get you to read?"

I suspected it was because I was so bad at French that I didn't even know they were looking for English readers. Or because this girl from Denmark was very pretty. We'd seen each other a couple of times since, and I always thought of her as The Dane, mostly because I couldn't remember her name and felt bad asking again.

Eric and I caught up to her when she took a break along the canal, and we gossiped about where we'd stayed and who we'd walked with. Before she strode off again at a pace that left even Eric in the dust, she mentioned that she, too, was bound for the town of Auvillar that night.

One of Eric's favorite mantras on the Camino was "sometimes you win, sometimes you lose." It was especially appropriate for describing the imaginary roulette wheel we spun every day when we decided where to stay. In Auvillar, we won.

We climbed up the final hill, following a road that curved under battlements on the way to a fortified gate, as the afternoon sun warmed the town's red stone. Bright flowers bloomed around the distinctive circular granary in the town square, which was flanked by art galleries and bars. Outside, old Frenchmen played *petanque,* a bocce-like game with heavy balls and a lot of drinking.

Auvillar's Office of Tourism managed the gîte communal, which from the outside looked like a private home on a residential street. Behind a gate was a modern building with a row of guest rooms, each with real sheets on the beds and curtains on the windows. Across the courtyard was a two-story stone building, renovated from an old rectory, with a full kitchen, sitting area, and a walled yard with thick grass. The Dane was already there, resting in the sun, and my nemeses, the Black-Eyed B's, arrived shortly after we did.

The B's busied themselves with laundry, Eric set out to watch petanque, and I spent the evening puttering in the kitchen, making a simple meal of pasta and mushrooms and talking to The Dane. Her name turned out to be Amanda, but Eric and I never used it. Even to her face, we always called her "Dane." We got away with it because she was so young, I think, and because that night, the three of us developed a strong, sibling-like bond.

The Dane was in her early twenties, with the corresponding mix of confidence and uncertainty. She'd biked the Camino with her family when she was a kid, so when she found herself between jobs and without a plan for the next season of life, she decided to come and try it alone, on foot. She was fit and competent and fluent in three languages, but none of them were French, and I gathered that the last three weeks had been lonely for her. She needed friends even more than we did.

The weather and our good luck held the next day. The paths were soft and dry, and there were things to see around every corner: the ruins of a cathedral destroyed in the sixteenth-century Wars of Religion, an abandoned castle rising from a densely planted farm field, and a small roadside snack stand selling perfect pain au chocolat. With the added perspective of our new Danish friend, everything was interesting again.

The afternoon air was warm when we arrived at the gîte communal in Castet-Arrouy. But in Castet, we all lost.

The town, if it could be called that, was two blocks long and consisted of a crumbling church, a cafe, and a used car lot. The gîte was an echoing community hall, with twelve cots shoved under portraits of local priests from the 1950s and 1960s. One bathroom was under construction, and the other was crammed into a dusty closet under the stairs.

The manager, a gruff and impatient woman, showed up at 4:00 to take our money and stamp our credentials. There was a kitchen, but when we asked about an *épicerie*, or general market, she announced, "I am the épicerie," and waved at a shelf of ancient and overpriced pasta packages and canned tuna. Eric and I decided to take our chances on the dingy cafe, since even the simplest French dinners we'd had were well prepared.

Not in Castet-Arrouy. A surly woman who could have been the gîte manager's cousin served an eclectic mix of what appeared to be leftovers. It was a night worthy of a scathing one-star Yelp review, except that we shared the whole experience with The Dane and Marieke, a Dutch woman The Dane knew who was also staying in Castet.

Looking at Marieke made it easy to see my own Dutch heritage; in the right light and after a bottle of wine, we could have been sisters. But Marieke, an occupational therapist who specialized in helping people sleep, had an easy, laid-back attitude that I could never replicate, and she helped us find the humor in our "losing" day. After all, it was just one night. The Camino would carry us out of this grumpy town in the morning.

But the next day my losing streak continued. My poor Princess feet, which had been almost agreeable for the past few days, collapsed again and took my attitude with them.

Are you tired of reading about my feet? Because I assure you, by this point I was utterly sick of them myself. But every day they demanded my attention.

There was no one particular thing that made that day's walk worse than the rest. We were going thirty kilometers, but we'd done that before, and there was little elevation change. The real problem was that the dirt roads we followed were rocky and hard to navigate, and I was walking alone.

The Dane and Eric outpaced me early, and Marieke stopped to "have a nap" after our lunch break. We hadn't seen Jan since Cahors. There was nothing to distract me from myself. That kind of solitude can be meditative. It could have given me the opportunity to think deep thoughts and explore corners of my psyche that rarely saw the light of day. But no. As the day wore on, and my feet hurt more, I worried that I would miss a turn and get lost. I fell into a downward spiral of thinking about how everyone was faster than me and how no one cared enough to wait to see if I was okay. I seethed with resentment buoyed by a sense of failure. I obsessed about my aching feet.

By the time I finally caught up to Eric, who was sitting under a shade tree and waiting for me, just as he'd done for weeks, I was angry and he had no idea why.

"I'm awful at this. You'd be happier if I wasn't here," I told him tearfully.

He didn't deny it, though he wisely didn't agree, either. "I don't know how to help you," he said again. "These are your feet, your shoes. You have to figure out what you need. I don't know if you should replace the shoes, or see a doctor, or . . . "

I think he kept talking, but I stopped listening.

Replace the shoes? These state-of-the-art, ill-considered footwear? I could do that?

It seems obvious now, but at the time I missed it. I'd spent months researching my packing list, but when it came to shoes—arguably the most important piece of equipment a person has on a thousand-mile hike—I'd choked.

That's partly because there is nothing in the Camino community that is debated as much as footwear. The opinions basically came down to this:

A: This is a long-distance backpacking trip, so (duh) you need to have sturdy, waterproof hiking boots to trek over mountains and through mud.

B: You're not trekking in the wilderness. The Camino is a well-groomed trail, and heavy boots will cause blisters. You need lightweight, breathable sneakers.

The latter seemed to be the more common attitude among Americans, and I was swayed by the counterintuitive idea. Eric and I had both been wearing minimal, "zero drop" sneakers and sandals in the city for years. Thinking of the Camino as something I could do in the same shoes I wore to stroll across town made it far less intimidating.

The sporting goods salesperson backed me up. When I mentioned the Camino, he handed me a pair of lightweight trail runners. "This is what people who walk the Pacific Crest Trail wear now," he assured me. The shoes were thinner and less supportive than most traditional running shoes, but they were bigger then Eric's ultraminimal shoe choice (which he wore for the full thousand miles with no ill effects). So without trying anything else on, I bought them. I didn't even bother with inserts, despite my high and drama-prone arches.

So when my feet utterly collapsed under the stress of twenty-five unpaved kilometers a day and the unfamiliar weight of a twenty-pound backpack, the first thing I should have considered was my footwear. Yet somehow, I just got up every morning and put on the same shoes, and then expected some kind of change that never came. In all of my self-pity and genuinely awful pain, and even though I was in a first-world country with plenty of stores, I never considered replacing the damn shoes.

There were no stores that sold shoes in La Romieu, where we stayed that night in an airy former hospital, with cots spread out in wards that echoed every snore and cough. But I had a plan, and with that came hope. Long after everyone else was in bed, Marieke and I sat in the kitchen, sharing stories and drinking the half bottle of wine that someone left after their dinner.

Eric and I set out the next morning for Condom, a city that the French—the same French who thought Montcuq was funny—said without a trace of a smile. Me? I snickered like a fifth grader.

It was lightly raining again, and Eric and I entertained ourselves by coming up with mottos and tourist slogans. The best one? "Condom: Come Inside."

Unfortunately, "come inside" was not going to happen in Condom that day. It was May 1, which I learned is a much bigger holiday in France than it is in the United States. In Seattle, a few labor marches might snarl traffic, but business pretty much continues as normal. In France, not only does everything shut down, but the people all disappear. In a town of seven thousand, we didn't see a single local in Condom. Even the bars and cafes were closed.

A few tourists braved the drizzle to explore the town square and take pictures with a life-sized statue of the real-life D'Artagnan, who was born in a castle near Condom and made famous in *The Three Musketeers* by Alexandre Dumas. Eric and I watched them as we ate a meager picnic of leftovers and tried to formulate a plan. We'd walked fast and arrived in town early, hoping to shop, but that clearly wasn't going to happen. We could go on another five kilometers to the town where we were staying, but our gîte wouldn't be open for hours. The only thing open in Condom was the cathedral, so we ducked inside.

By this point the novelty of "ooh, a really big building with amazing architecture and beautiful stained glass, and it's a gazillion years old!" had started to wear off. We'd been in a dozen cathedrals of this size, many older. But the church in Condom was the one that stole my heart.

Built at the turn of the sixteenth century, the Cathedral of Saint Peter is all white marble and delicate carvings and impossibly high Gothic arches. The flat gray light outside filtered through hundreds of panels of stained glass that ringed the top of the building, seeming too delicate to hold up the roof. Each pillar supported a realistic-looking saint, apostle, king, or angel. A few tourists and visitors wandered the aisles, and a painter stood at an easel, trying to capture the space.

We lingered, soaking up the details instead of soaking in the rain, until it was time to walk on to the medieval fortress of Larressingle, where the bishops of Condom retreated in times of war. By the time we reached the walled stronghold, it was pouring and we were drenched. It was also still May 1, and while the single gate over the dry moat was open, nothing inside was. I caught glimpses of stone and turrets and thatched roofs, but it was too wet to linger, and after a quick stop in the chapel to get a stamp in our credentials, we went on to find our gîte, where The Dane was already waiting.

Martina, the gîte owner, was a chatty woman who had walked the Camino herself in the 1970s, long before there were designated GR routes or pilgrim accommodations. She'd had only a map of France and a general idea of where the original Camino went, so she'd wandered from place to place, stopping at farms and working for her room and board. I thought it sounded risky and uncomfortable. Eric thought it sounded ideal.

Martina was a blur of words and energy all afternoon and evening. She made an incredible four-course dinner, of which the crowning glory was a dessert cup of preserved prunes, crème fraîche, sugar, and a generous shot of Armagnac, the local alcoholic specialty. Eric still talks about that dessert.

The next morning, as we were lingering over an equally elaborate breakfast, Martina pointed out the window. "This is your first view of the Pyrenees," she told us. And there they were, faint and distant, still ten days away by foot. But ten days was a lot less than the twenty-five we'd already walked, and seeing snow-capped peaks was a lot different than abstractly thinking that eventually we would have to walk over one of Europe's most famous mountain ranges.

We walked that day to Eauze, another town that it's hard to say in English without snickering. The rain had stopped, and the landscape remained flat and soft. We took our time and arrived in the early afternoon to find a bustling town square.

Though the town was small, it was lively enough that I thought there might be a store with shoes. We went to the Office of Tourism and asked where I could buy new walking shoes, and the woman behind the counter whipped out a map and circled something just a few blocks away. Well, that was easy.

When Eric and I followed her directions, though, we found ourselves standing in front of a garden store. It didn't look promising, but I was desperate enough to go inside anyway. I passed the seeds, the trowels, and the watering cans, and sure enough, in the far back I found a rack of gardening clogs and a few pairs of men's leather work boots.

Sometimes you lose. The shoe search would continue.

We wandered on to Gîte Bethanie, a donativo privately run by a family of devout Catholics who turned the second story of their home into a fully equipped refuge. "We want to treat everyone who passes through our home as if they're Jesus," Marcel told us, and my jaded heart melted a little.

That night their only guests were the two of us and The Dane. She walked by herself during the day, but this was our fifth night in a row together. She got annoyed when older French pilgrims talked to her about "the Americans who are your age." There was a big difference between her and the pushing-forty married couple. Yet she stuck with us.

Marcel, who spoke English, brought up a modest dinner that he shared with us while his wife, Pauline, stayed downstairs with their two small children. They alternated dinners, he told us, so tomorrow Pauline would visit with the pilgrims while he ate with the children. Their generosity, humble and genuine, meant as much to me as Martina's extravagant hospitality the night before. Both loved the Camino for their own reasons.

The next day our little group of three spent an uninspired night in Nogaro, a town that even the guidebook called "not scenic," and then set out with a loose plan to meet again in Aire-sur-l'Adour. But that day I just couldn't do it. I was short-tempered with pain, and by midafternoon Eric and I both knew it was time to cut our losses. The Dane would be disappointed when we didn't show up where we said we'd be, but even for her I couldn't go farther.

We stopped in the town three kilometers short of Aire-sur-l'Adour with an agreement to take the next day off if necessary and go wherever we needed to find me some new shoes.

Barcelonne-du-Gers didn't appear to have much going for it, and we approached the first gîte we saw, prepared for a lonely night.

But sometimes you win.

Just inside the gate we found Stephanie, the physical therapist from Paris who had translated the night the Black-Eyed B's earned the first part of their name. We'd seen her, on and off, since then, but she'd taken a side trip and we hadn't expected to cross paths again.

Then we saw a cheery older French couple we'd met in Cahors, at the Papillon Vert.

Then Guy, a mustachioed playboy we'd met a few times before, arrived. Guy was full of bright colors and flirty attitudes. "He's from Marseilles," other French pilgrims told us more than once, as if that explained everything.

Then, to my delight, our Dane walked in. She, too, had felt too tired to make our rendezvous. The party was complete.

We all spent the afternoon on the shaded patio, buying each other rounds of one-euro beers, and then over dinner we bought each other bottles of wine. Stephanie translated what we couldn't understand and told us about her own adventures.

"I have had many conversations with women of a certain age," she said with a grin, "who all tell stories about the American with the warm brown eyes who went back down the hill in Conques to carry his wife's pack."

I looked at a pair of embarrassed warm brown eyes and remembered again that sometimes you win.

PART II

A TEST OF THE MIND

The cobbled streets and Chemin markers of Saint-Jean-Pied-de-Port

THE GIFT OF THE PRESENT

Sometime that night, Stephanie convinced us that we should meet again the next night in Miramont-Sensacq, a short twenty-one kilometers away. She made reservations, and I reasoned that there was plenty of time to check out the shoe shopping and still make it to the gîte in time for dinner.

Eric and I arrived in the bustling town center of Aire-sur-l'Adour before 9:00 the next morning to find the tourist office already open and the woman who worked there happy to help. Yes, she said, there was a *sportif* store that would have what I needed, but it was not in town. She pulled out a map and circled a spot by a freeway three kilometers away, in the opposite direction from where the Camino path would take us.

A six-kilometer round trip would take an extra hour and a half of walking, along modern and unfamiliar roads. I hesitated.

"Distance changes utterly when you take the world on foot," says Bill Bryson in *A Walk in the Woods*. "A mile becomes a long way, two miles literally considerable, ten miles whopping, fifty miles at the very limits of conception. The world, you realize, is enormous in a way that only you and a small community of fellow hikers know. Planetary scale is your little secret."

Testing a handmade bamboo flute during a moment of rest in a pilgrim oasis

Then the tourist guide mentioned that she could call a taxi for us, and my planetary scale realigned to the modern world. A few minutes later, Eric and I climbed into the backseat of a car that yanked us from the Camino, away from medieval villages and the speed of the human step. Ten minutes later, we pulled into the giant parking lot of a strip mall, and I could only stare. This was not the France I knew. This looked just like a mall in middle America.

That wasn't bad in this situation, though. I knew how to navigate a mall. The sport store felt familiar, and the staff was quick and efficient, despite the language barriers. While the cab waited outside, they set me up with the best hiking sneakers they had, high-quality inserts that cost almost as much as the shoes but would protect my arches, and a pair of walking poles for good measure. I handed over a credit card and tried not to think about how in twenty minutes I'd spent more than we usually did in five days.

Eric and I were back in the medieval part of town an hour after we started. The new gear, of course, didn't fix everything. I found the poles awkward and swung them erratically. The new shoes and inserts tempered the daily pain, but never totally beat it. Actively doing something to control what was happening, though, helped me get past the mind-set of pain that had plagued me. I'd spent every morning anticipating the hurt, counting the minutes until the aches set in, and then counting the kilometers until I could be done for the day. I'd been tolerating the walk in order to experience the rest. But now, as the French landscape spread before me, I started to pay attention to the walk itself. The impossible idea of a thousand-mile trek was almost cut in half already. While I sulked about what my body couldn't do, I'd walked 360 miles across most of southern France.

Not bad for a person who, a few weeks before, considered three miles a significant hike.

Because of our side trip to the twenty-first century, we were the last pilgrims to arrive at the crowded gîte communal in Miramont-Sensacq. We barely had time to claim the last two open bunks in the dortoir before The Dane found us.

"It's about time you got here," she said in welcome and complaint. "I've been so bored."

I glanced around at the other pilgrims, the countryside, and the preschool children playing in the yard next door, and wondered how anyone could be bored here, even with the language barrier. But then again, I wasn't walking the Camino alone.

The Dane and Eric sat on a sunny patio, trading stories and sipping beers provided by a gregarious volunteer. I listened to them for a while, but my mind was full of my new perspective, and I needed a break from people. I wandered off to the town square to sit under a gazebo and catch up on my journaling.

That night, the volunteers from the local Amis de Saint Jacques made us a feast, asking only for donations to fund the food the next day. The pilgrims who had passed through the day before us must have been generous, because the volunteers kept pushing more servings of chicken and carafes of wine toward us. When we were finally stuffed, they serenaded us with folk songs, ending in a rousing round of "Ultreia."

Over breakfast the next morning the pilgrims around us discussed a shortcut option. We could follow GR65 through the fields, they said, or we could cut three kilometers off the day's distance by following the local road to Pimbo and picking up GR65 there.

For the last three weeks, if anyone said "shortcut," I jumped at it. But now something drew me to the countryside. Maybe it was a concern about missing a turn on a road. Maybe it was my new shoes and renewed sense of optimism. Probably it was the knowledge that our opening act was nearing its end. We were suddenly just a week from the French border.

Whatever it was, when the crowd of pilgrims left the gîte and turned right, Eric and I turned left.

Eric slowed his pace to walk with me, wanting to talk about the monasteries that dotted the Way. Most had long since closed and crumbled, but a few were still active. The simplicity of a life like that—a communal purpose and clear structure—has always appealed to him, when stripped of any religious motivation. What would a monastic life look like, he wondered, in a modern, secular capacity? Was it, as Sylvain had said back in Saint-Côme-d'Olt, becoming a pilgrim, setting aside modern distractions, and following the daily routine of putting one foot in front of the other?

Big questions like this were not out of character for Eric, who likes to play with ideas. He'll switch sides and suggest impractical castles in the clouds (or, as he'd say, design perfect systems in white boxes) just to see what they look like. When we're at home, I confess, it's sometimes hard for me to engage on that level. I'm pragmatic, content with observations about life as it is, not as it could be. But we were wandering along the edges of farm fields in France, and I'd just decided I wanted to spend more time thinking about the world around me and less about my feet.

So as the cows stood at safe distances and watched us pass, we untangled our assumptions and ideas. The monastic life, we eventually decided, was not the same as a pilgrim's life. Monasticism was a lifelong decision to live selflessly. When they join a structured, defined community, monks (male or female) accept permanent limits on their autonomy in order to serve and become part of something bigger than themselves. In return, they get the spiritual satisfaction of serving God (or country or family or cause), and a level of protection. Monasticism shelters its members from the constant noise and temptations of technology and consumerism—the very things that burned me out and sent me on a pilgrimage.

But I was certainly not a monk, and this was where the difference lay. Being a pilgrim is an inherently self-focused experience. If monastic life gives up the desires and uniqueness of "Me" in order to join "We," the pilgrim's life sacrifices the comforts of "We" (family, home, community) in order to focus exclusively on "Me."

And that wasn't a bad thing. Sometimes we need temporary, self-centered endeavors. A pilgrimage that is long enough to demand a sacrifice but not permanent offers a unique opportunity for self-reflection and clarity—or in medieval terms, penance and gratitude—that a person can then bring home.

A person can't be a permanent pilgrim, because pilgrimage is a journey with a specific destination. Eric and I hadn't abandoned our old lives; we'd just left them behind for a while. This temporary retreat from the modern, familiar world would give me a deeper perspective on . . . well, something. I had six hundred more miles to figure that out.

While we talked about why we walked, we skirted open fields waiting to be planted. There were no buildings or people in sight, so I wasn't expecting the small chapel to appear on a hill in front of us, or for it to be so important.

The Église de Sensacq was small and weathered, with tiles missing from the roof and patches of stone visible in the walls. It didn't look like much from the outside. The guidebook had a passing reference to it as a local place of worship eight hundred years ago. It had been rebuilt after the Wars of Religion and wasn't considered an important stop for early or modern pilgrims.

Yet of course it was unlocked, and of course we went in.

There were no gilded altars or icons of saints and martyrs. There was no stained glass. There was a simple stone basin at the door and a large baptismal in a corner. By the altar there was a Baroque-style plaster statue of the Madonna and child. Both were, kind of creepily, missing hands.

We shed our packs and quietly poked into the corners of the single-room chapel, navigating the uneven stone floors and touching the much-used fireplace in the sacristy. We studied how the light coming through plain windows set into thick stone walls bounced off the exposed beams of the arched ceiling. There were flowers, both fresh and fake, scattered around the altar. Someone visited this place. Someone cared for it.

I would have missed it if we'd taken the shortcut.

As the day progressed, I realized Eric didn't seem to be in as much of a rush as usual. He'd had a personal revelation or two as well, which led him to downshift and focus on the journey, not the destination. When we stopped for coffee in Pimbo, we lingered long enough to eat an entire box of cookies while we chatted with the pilgrims arriving on the road.

After that, the Chemin du Puy wound through a modern park and around a small lake, where Eric cut a piece of fresh bamboo to use as a walking stick. Green bamboo, however, doesn't hold up well to pavement, and it shredded quickly.

It was close to lunchtime when we came across a fenced yard with a small sign on the chain link gate: PILGRIMS WELCOME.

Under the shade of the carefully tended trees was a rustic picnic table and soft, recently mown grass.

We'd seen oases like this before, places where someone, presumably the landowner, had created a place for pilgrims to rest. Sometimes there were pitchers of fresh water or a thermos of coffee. Sometimes there was a guest book. Once, there were hammocks strung beside a stream. Here, there was plenty of soft grass. We let ourselves into the yard and ate our lunch. Then, instead of rushing ahead, I stretched out in the sun while Eric tried to carve a flute out of the bamboo. The Dane came by and joined him, and the two of them gave an impromptu and out-of-tune concert to other pilgrims walking past.

I smiled drowsily as I watched them. Were we having fun? Up to that day, hiking the Camino had been mind-blowingly beautiful, culturally enlightening, and personally challenging. Many of our evenings were full of laughter. But this was the first time that the walking part had been this enjoyable.

I liked this Camino.

We eventually made it to the private gîte in Larreule, where we spent one last night with Stephanie before she left the Camino to meet friends in Bordeaux for a weekend party. I would miss her. She had been part of our journey since the first week. She walked through knee problems, loneliness, and Guy's terrible flirting, and she continued to tolerate our terrible French. At the same time, I wondered what it would be like to live so close to the Camino that you could just leave it.

Over dinners, conversations sometimes turned to "What would it take for you to leave the Way?" A death in the family? How close in the family? An emergency at work? An injury? How about an important party?

For me, it would have taken something catastrophic. Eric and I had traveled across the globe for this, and we didn't have the option to just come back in a few weeks, or even months. I'd planned this trip for longer than I planned my wedding. I was here to the end. But that certainty could push me down the slippery slope to the bigger, messier, don't-go-there question, where of course all pilgrims eventually go after the second bottle of wine is poured.

What makes a real pilgrim?

Is a pilgrim "real" if they walk for only a week?

If they hire a company to transport their bags?

If they take a bus or a taxi?

If they take a shortcut?

If they make reservations, or sleep only in private hotels?

Is the pilgrimage real if you stop in Saint-Jean-Pied-de-Port, or do you have to go all the way to Santiago?

Those questions followed us from table to table for a thousand miles. I tried not to answer them, because as soon as I started to define what made someone else's experience "not real," I opened up my own journey for scrutiny. I wasn't Catholic, and I wasn't walking for religious reasons. Was I a "real" pilgrim? And what about those who started walking from their front doors in Geneva or Amsterdam? Were they more "real" than someone who took a train and started closer?

"Real" was a dangerous word when it came to pilgrimage.

Stephanie's departure to be with her friends inspired me to sit down with a calendar and consider our own social commitments. Eric and I had been walking for thirty days now, and in that time we'd never mapped out more than a day or two in advance. When people asked when we would reach Saint Jacques—and the question came up often in France, where Santiago was incomprehensibly far away—I would shrug. "Whenever we get there," I would say. "It takes a long time to get to the end of the world."

But in fact, we had a couple of commitments to keep before we walked into the ocean at Finisterre. When we were still home in Seattle, planning and talking incessantly about our upcoming trip, friends would often say, "I wish I could do something like that." My standard flip response was always, "You can. Come walk with us for a few days."

To my utter surprise, two friends, Emily and Ian, took me up on it. They each had other reasons to be in Europe that summer and thought a few days of hiking sounded like fun. So we set tentative dates for when we would meet, and I flew to France and forgot about them.

Now I realized that our appointment to meet Ian in Logroño, Spain, was seventeen days away. I made some rough estimates of how far we typically walked in a day. Logroño was, at most, thirteen days away. We were early.

Those numbers were bouncing around in my mind as Eric and I began the long, slow climb to another medieval town on a hill, Arthez-de-Béarn.

We were walking with two older Germans, Wolfgang and Margarete. We'd seen them almost daily for about a week, occasionally staying in the same gîtes or passing each other on the road. Radio Camino loved to gossip about them. Were they a couple? Siblings? Friends? When everyone slept in twin beds in co-ed rooms, it was surprisingly hard to tell.

Adding to the mystery, they kept mostly to themselves. Wolfgang was fluent in English, but Margarete was not, so they didn't spend much time with our English-speaking crowd. That afternoon, though, as we plodded up paved farm roads under a relentless sun, Margarete dropped behind, and Wolfgang chatted happily with us about work and travel.

"You should be sure to get anything you need from the market tonight," he casually mentioned. "Tomorrow is the holiday."

"Another one?" I remembered how deserted and dreary Condom was on May 1. "What is it this time?"

"It is the 8th of May." I might have admitted I didn't know what that meant, or I just looked clueless. He continued: "The day that Germany surrendered to the Allies in 1945."

I paused for a beat while the irony sank in. Here was a German telling a couple of Americans that we all were about to experience a holiday in France to celebrate my ancestors defeating his ancestors in a war. There was no discomfort in his voice, no animosity.

I was intrigued to see how the day would unfold.

Arthez-de-Béarn stretched for five kilometers along a winding road that followed the ridge of a hill. There was a plaza in the middle of town overlooking the valley to the south, the Pyrenees now looming large. Many of our friends, including The Dane, planned to pass through this town altogether and spend the night farther along. Eric and I weren't specifically planning to stop here either, but in the moment, I thought it was a good place to stay for a day and just look around. I wanted one last rest day in France, and Radio Camino warned that things would get more crowded as we approached the border.

I was also, reluctantly, starting to realize that we needed a little space from The Dane. She'd been with us, usually in the same room, every night for ten days, and while we loved her, I craved some one-on-one time with my husband. I mentioned all of this to Eric, and we decided to see what was available.

Wolfgang and Margarete had reservations at a private gîte that was full, so we went on alone to find the gîte communal. We found the unlocked building in the center of town, large and modern, with a full kitchen and an inviting backyard. There was no one there so early in the day, but when we checked at the mairie, a woman named Marie-Frances told Eric that we could stay. She would come over at 4:00 to take our money and stamp our credentials.

We'd been through that routine before, so we took it as an invitation to settle in. We looked at the different dortoir rooms and spread our sleeping bags on a couple of beds, showered, and sorted our things. No other pilgrims arrived, which seemed strange. Would we have the place to ourselves?

I was in the middle of wringing out my freshly washed hiking pants when I heard Marie-Frances bustle in. Eric went out to meet her. I heard her say a rapid string of things in French. Eric asked her a question. She said something else. I couldn't understand the conversation, let alone add to it, so I kept doing laundry in the next room.

After a few minutes, he came to find me. "So . . . ," he said in that don't-get-mad tone. "She says all of the beds upstairs are reserved. We have to sleep on the couches in the lounge."

Wait, what? We'd talked to her two hours ago, and she hadn't said anything then about the place being full. The "lounge" was more like a lobby, with bright lights and humming vending machines, open to whoever happened to walk through the front door. I wasn't sleeping there.

I followed Eric back to the lounge, which, to my point about the inappropriateness of it, was currently Marie-Frances's office.

She looked like any other middle-aged bureaucrat, with a pinched nose and a permanent frown. I pointed upstairs, and in my pathetic, useless French told her we had beds.

She rattled a string of French that included "c'est complet" and "réserve." "If you were complet you needed to tell us that two hours ago," I snapped in English, too rattled to care if she understood. "I'm not sleeping on a cot in the lobby. Non." I can't remember, but I may have stomped my foot.

Eric was quiet. He doesn't like it when I argue over poor service or unreasonable behavior. If Marie-Frances said he had to sleep on the bare floor, next to an empty bed, he would probably accept it. I, on the other hand, assume that everything is negotiable. Negotiating without a common language, though, was difficult.

Without any other words in my arsenal, I stormed out of the room, my "non" hanging in the air as I went back to the laundry area and started to collect our things. Could I find different lodging at such a late hour, the night before a holiday?

Breathing deeply and fighting indignant tears, I suspected that I was going to sleep on a bench in the lobby next to the snack machine. I would carry the bluff a little longer, though.

In the other room there was the distinct sound of French exasperation. Marie-Frances appeared in the laundry area door, holding a key and glaring daggers. Without a word she motioned me to follow her down the hallway toward the kitchen. She unlocked a door that I had assumed was a closet. It turned out to be a small bedroom with two twin beds, tucked awkwardly in the center of the building. It smelled musty, but it was a room.

"Okay?" she asked in English with a roll of her eyes.

I beamed. "Oui, okay. Merci beaucoup."

Eric did not appreciate my coup right away, but he would. We went out to shop for supplies, and while we were gone our fellow gîte guests finally arrived. It was a single, noisy group of about twenty people on a religious pilgrimage. The pilgrims, as I understood it, were disadvantaged people from an urban center somewhere. The leader was bearded and young, probably not over thirty, and wore a hoodie. Everyone called him Father. He was assisted by two women in thin pastel uniforms that bore a passing resemblance to pink nun's habits. They also had a film crew, a dog, and a support vehicle carrying their supplies. They unloaded crates of food and gear everywhere, completely taking over the kitchen and every inch of floor space in the common areas. When I walked past the lounge, I saw four cots crowded wall-to-wall, and I wondered where Marie-Frances would have had us sleeping.

Eric and I retreated to a nearby bar for a Leffe beer or two, then got take-away slices of pizza and ate them on the open plaza over-looking the valley. When we finally returned to the gîte for the night, we slipped into our room and locked the door, and I sent a mental blessing to Marie-Frances.

The next morning I lingered in bed as the pilgrim posse spent several hours getting packed. When they left, they took all the toilet paper in the building.

Marie-Frances had agreed to let us stay in the same room for a second night, so we had the luxury of not having to wad up our sleeping bags and shove everything into our packs. We ate break-fast in the trashed kitchen and wondered what a small town like this would do to commemorate a holiday.

Whatever it was, I assumed it would be in the plaza, so I wan-dered over midmorning and waited, half-heartedly reading a book. Eventually, two old men arrived and began to fiddle with an even older-looking sound system. Not long after, the locals, most dressed up for the occasion, started to gather around the flagpole.

I hovered across the street, on the fringe of the crowd, as a short procession arrived, led by teenagers in uniforms—volunteers training to be firefighters, perhaps—and then old men in suits decorated with military medals. A few officials read speeches, then two young girls stepped up to the squeaky microphones and read a list of names I took to be the locals killed in the war. Two of the fire brigade kids lowered the flag to half mast, then the ceremony ended. Everyone kissed and chatted and wandered off to lunch.

There wasn't much obvious emotion in the ceremony, yet history felt close to me here—not the medieval history that left castles and artifacts, but the close history I could see reflected in the eyes of old men. From now on, I'll always remember why the 8th of May is important.

THE END OF
ACT ONE

We spent the remainder of our second rest day much as we spent the first, napping and reading and making plans. Someone came and replaced the missing toilet paper, and we shared the gîte that night with two couples we'd never met. Everyone seemed happy to keep to themselves.

Eric and I set out at dawn the next morning, feeling rested but sad that our spontaneous day off had probably separated us from our friends. The week before, our favorite grumpy trailmates, the Black-Eyed B's, had stopped for the night one town before we did, and that set them on a course that never overlapped with ours again. We assumed that it would be the same for us.

But a few kilometers out of town we came across Guy, the flirt from Marseilles, standing beside the path as if he had been waiting for us to come along. He was with Martin, a Brit who was conveniently fluent in both French and English. (Guy's English was worse than our French.) They were making plans for where to stay in Navarrenx, and they graciously agreed to reserve two beds for us as well.

The four of us walked together for an hour or so, but on the first significant hill, Eric and I outpaced them, and we all

Approaching the Pyrenees under a bright, hot sun

agreed to meet in town that afternoon. It had taken a month and 650 kilometers, but I was finally not the slowest person on a hill.

That was good, because we were approaching the Pyrenees, and the day's walk took us up and down a series of hills, full of lazy-eyed cows and long-haired sheep. Eric continued his new habit of walking with me, or at least waiting for me to catch up more often. He was lingering on top of one particularly steep incline while I shuffled my way toward the top when I noticed him holding a small white bag.

"Is that . . . ," I gasped.

"Pain au chocolat," he confirmed. "But you have to keep walking to get it." Oh, the things I will do for a fresh French chocolate croissant.

A few hours later, just as we were thinking it was time for lunch, we found another familiar pilgrim, Jean-Francois. We'd first met him at the gîte in Miramont-Sensaq and had shared meals with him several times since. Now here he was, sitting in the grass by the roadside, lingering over his lunch.

Jean-Francois was a retired French executive who, as a young manager, had sought out an English tutor to help him become fluent so that he could work with his American clients and suppliers. Not for the first time, I wished I'd made the same commitment to French.

We rested and talked for an hour, while fending off an overly friendly farm dog that was determined to share our picnic meal. Before I walked the Camino, I'd heard horror stories about "wild dogs" that would attack pilgrims, but the only dogs I ran into were like this one, demanding belly rubs and food scraps, but not blood.

Jean-Francois eventually set off, saying he'd see us in Navarrenx. Eric and I were still gathering our things when we received another surprise: Marieke. Our Dutch friend had taken a break from the Camino after La Romieu to visit friends in the area, and we'd lost track of each other.

As we walked together, we caught up on Radio Camino gossip. At some point the pastures gave way to a lightly wooded forest, and it was there that we found Jan, our other favorite

Dutch pilgrim. Eric's entire countenance brightened at the sight of him.

We hadn't seen Jan since our night together in Cahors. He told us that he'd tried to avoid the steep climb out of town the next morning and then lost his way. Cahors was another place where two of France's Grande Randonneés intersect, and Jan had followed the wrong red and white stripes for half a day. Despite that, it seemed the time had treated him well. He'd acquired a bigger water bottle and traded his heavy jeans for lighter hiking pants, and even his pack seemed smaller. "I don't camp anymore," he told us. "Amanda tells me I don't meet people when I sleep in tents." I grinned, thinking of a conversation between our favorite Dane and Dutchman.

With Jan, Marieke, and a German couple who quickly became new friends, we were a merry group as we walked into Navarrenx, where it seemed as if we knew everyone we saw. Wolfgang and Margarete were there, and the Papillons (so named because they told us every time we saw them that they had met us at the Papillon Vert), and the three Pinks (who wore matching pink T-shirts every day), and the Happys (they were always smiling). Guy and Martin caught up with us and, to top it off, there was The Dane herself. She'd sped past us in Arthez-de-Béarn but at Navarrenx decided to take her own rest day.

Guy had made us all reservations at the gîte communal, but when we checked in we were told that it was overbooked. Jean-Francois, Marieke, and The Dane all had beds in the main building, a tall stone manor that had once housed the kings of Navarre. Guy, Martin, Eric, Jan, and I were waved off to an "overflow" building a few blocks away that made that drafty town hall in Castet-Arrouy look good. One wall of the three-story dortoir was literally crumbling into the empty lot beside it, and the smell of mold in our bare room was stronger than the smell of my four sweaty male roommates. Even after a thirty-kilometer day, I suspected I was cleaner than the shower.

It could have bothered me. I was, after all, the same person who'd thrown a fit two days before when told I had to sleep in a clean lounge. But today, I didn't care. This day felt special. I left the gîte with barely an eye-roll and set out to regather the troops. A party was brewing.

I'm told that Navarrenx is full of unique history and that the ramparts and ammunition garrisons from the Wars of Religions are worth exploring. But my memories of that night are all about the people. Our group found a restaurant with a large outdoor patio, and we stayed for hours. We had a primarily English-speaking table of me, Eric, Jan, and Marieke, while a few feet away Guy, Jean-Francois, and Martin kept a parallel conversation going in French. Others dropped in and then went off to their own pursuits. We waved to everyone who went by and feasted on a multicourse menu and plenty of Bordeaux.

We might have gotten a little loud at some point, because an older woman—a local or a tourist, I couldn't tell, but she wasn't a pilgrim—at the table behind us turned and snapped that we should speak French if we were in France. It was a rare encounter with the snobbish French stereotype, and after a month of grace and kindness the assault left me speechless.

Marieke, an unflappable diplomat, engaged. With a smooth voice and a warm smile, she explained—in French—that we came from different countries, and when we were together we were most comfortable in English. If someone *in our conversation* spoke only French, of course we would accommodate that. Our French friends at the next table toasted Marieke, and the woman behind us didn't speak to us again.

The French border loomed large in our minds that night. Most of our group was walking only as far as Saint-Jean-Pied-de-Port, so we were nearing the end of our time together. There was an unspoken agreement to make these last days count. We'd created a pilgrim family—that collection of people who share the journey together for days or weeks at a time—and we wanted to keep it going.

Radio Camino spread the word that the next day we all should go to a place described only as The Farm, just before Aroue. It would be a short walk, less than twenty kilometers, so Eric and I took our time, stopping for morning croissants and a chat with one person, then speeding up to walk for a while with someone else. The sun was bright and hot, and we lounged with Guy for an hour beside a stream and waded in its icy waters while minnows nibbled our feet. When we finally pulled our shoes back on to tackle the last five kilometers, we met Jean-Francois as he emerged from under a giant shade tree, where he told us he'd had a nap. It was that kind of day.

Our destination was a collection of buildings on a green hill far removed from anything else. The original farmers had offered a room or two to passing pilgrims as a side income. Their adult daughter saw an opportunity and built a full gîte with a wing of breezy guest rooms that all opened onto a long, covered patio. A dozen of us gathered there in the super-saturated colors of late spring, laughing and sharing stories. We ranged in age from twenty-two to at least seventy, came from at least five different countries, and spoke half a dozen languages.

Eric and The Dane sat at the edge of the patio with a pair of borrowed binoculars, watching the road below for signs of Jan's distinctive walk. As always, he was the last to arrive. Our dinner was generous even by French standards, with endless platters of food and eight kinds of cheese on the cheese plate. Jan, awkward and happy and probably a little drunk, was at the center of everything.

Eric and I shared a room that night with The Dane, Marieke, and Caroline, a young Parisian The Dane had met in our absence. I called it Eric's International Bevy of Women and laughed when he self-consciously left to give everyone time to get into bed. By that point most of my awkward feelings about sleeping (and sometimes dressing) in rooms full of strangers had long worn off.

The next morning we all set out together, confident and comfortable pilgrims by now. The Dane soon disappeared over a rise, but we, along with Marieke and Caroline, paced ourselves with Jan. After an hour or so, his cell phone rang, the shrill sound breaking the morning quiet. He stopped to answer, speaking loudly in Dutch. He waved us on and we went, reminding him of the name of the gîte where we all would stay that night in Ostabat. He would catch up, we assumed.

He never did.

When Caroline suggested it, we all agreed to take a shortcut that trimmed a few kilometers from the route. At the time, what mattered to me was keeping these friends near me. In hindsight, the shortcut was probably a mistake. The path we took skipped around Hiriburia, where three of the French routes historically met.

But the historic stone monument wasn't the only thing we missed. Late that afternoon, in Ostabat, we finally caught up to The Dane. She'd stayed on the marked path, and while she was taking a break, she saw Jan. He stopped long enough to tell her that he'd had another phone call from home. His brother—not the one who had lost his wife, but another—had died unexpectedly. Jan planned to get a taxi to Saint Jean as soon as he could, and would take the first train home. This time, his family needed him.

None of us had any contact information for Jan, or even knew his last name. In the way of the pilgrimage, he just drifted away.

The loss cast its shadow, but this would be our last night together, and we were determined to make one last grand party in Ostabat. Caroline led us to a private gîte on the far side of town that she'd heard was a can't-miss experience. The International Bevy of Women, plus Eric, stayed together again in a large, airy room with doors that opened to sloping lawns outside.

There were only two showers for our group of five, so Eric told us that he would wait and went outside to chat with some familiar pilgrims who were lounging outside. He wanted to practice French while he still could. I rested in the room and caught up on journaling. After a while, Eric came back, looking sheepish. "I was just naked with the German women," he said.

I knew, casually, who he referred to. They were a few decades older than us, with a bit of a hippie vibe. It seems that they were all sitting in the grass, chatting and enjoying the sun, when one of the Germans noticed a tick on her leg. Then the other German woman found a tick. This made them visibly uncomfortable, and they told Eric he must go inside and check himself for ticks right away.

He said he would, but the showers were still occupied. So instead he washed his laundry in a utility sink. When he went outside to hang his wet clothes, the Germans were there.

"Did you check?" they asked.

Eric explained that the showers were full. "No, you must check. You must check now." They seemed very concerned. "We will all check. Take off your shirt."

Now, Eric is not really a take-off-your-shirt-in-public kind of guy. But he's also super-sensitive about not acting like the prude American stereotype. So he took off his shirt. They took off their shirts as well. They weren't wearing anything under their shirts.

This is how Eric, who was discovering he was rather prudish after all, found himself with two topless German women who wanted him to closely study their skin. To his credit, he did so with a straight face. That pathological helpful streak saved the day. But the women weren't done.

"Take off your pants."

Was this a joke? Nope, he realized, they must mean it, because they were taking off *their* pants. Fortunately, Eric noticed without wanting to notice that they were wearing underwear. So he took off his pants. They all checked one another's legs and confirmed that they had no ticks.

When they looked at his underwear, he decided he would have to draw a line. But they said only, "You should have your girlfriend check you." (One of the great things about walking across France, surrounded mostly by retirees, is that they constantly underestimated our ages by at least a decade. We clearly weren't sixty-something, so we must be young twenty-something lovers. There was no in between.)

I was still laughing two hours later when we sat beside the German women at dinner. The food wasn't all that memorable, but our hosts made up for it with the after-dinner show. The patriarch of the house, with a black beret and a sizable belly, serenaded us with Basque folk songs, and then he invited the guests to sing the songs of their own countries. His patter was clearly rehearsed, but there was something endearing about singing "The Itsy-Bitsy Spider" in English, while across the table The Dane sang it in Danish, and somewhere across the room a French voice chimed in a third language.

We finished the night, of course, with a rousing "Ultreia."

And onward we went the next morning, for the final twenty kilometers of the Chemin du Puy. We were now well into Pays Basque, Basque country, home of the unique indigenous people who have straddled the border between France and Spain since long before either country existed. Fiercely independent and prone to occasional separatist uprisings, the Basques cling to their own language and customs. Even my untrained eye picked up that the municipal signs were full of q's and odd spellings. My more practiced palate appreciated that the Basques are also artisan producers of some of the best cheese and cider in the world.

The twelfth-century author of *Codex Calixtinus* had some strong feelings about the Basques:

> *In this land . . . there are evil toll-gatherers who will certainly be damned through and through. In point of fact, they actually advance toward the pilgrims with two or three sticks, exhorting through force an unjust tribute. And if some traveler refuses to hand over the money at their request, they beat him with the sticks and snatch away the toll money while cursing him and searching even through his breeches. These are ferocious people; and the land in which they dwell is savage, wooded, and barbarous. The ferociousness of their faces and likewise of their barbarous speech scares the wits out of those who see them.*

The Basques have been subjected to this kind of xenophobia ever since. More than one person in France warned us to be careful with our possessions when we were in Pays Basque, because the locals would rob us blind. In my experience, however, the stone-faced locals waved sticks only at the sheep they guided from one field to another.

The real enemy that day was the sun. As soon as the morning fog burned off, the temperature soared. We were with Jean-Francois midday when we arrived in a town. We'd spent the last two kilometers looking forward to the chance to buy cool drinks and food to supplement our meager remaining supplies. But as we entered the town square, I noticed that the tables outside the local cafe were empty. When we reached the door, it was locked.

Fermé.

Thirty-five days earlier, a closed cafe in Montbonnet had been shocking. Now, I accepted that this was how rural France worked. Jean-Francois, on the other hand, was outraged. Eric and I retreated to a courtyard table to watch, bemused, as he pounded on the door until someone opened it. He demanded they open. The person refused. The cafe was closed on Tuesdays.

"Closed on Tuesdays!" Jean-Francois huffed, when he returned to us. "Why would anyone be closed on Tuesdays?"

I shrugged. In France, *pourquoi pas?* Why not?

We reached the Porte de Saint Jacques, the historic gate through which generations of pilgrims have passed into Saint-Jean-Pied-de-Port, at 2:00 that afternoon. It was early by our standards, since most gîtes on the Chemin du Puy didn't even open until 3:00. But Saint Jean was also the beginning of the Camino Francés, where, we learned, 2:00 put us well behind the first wave of arrivals.

And that was just the beginning of the changes.

Our French friends and hosts had warned us, repeatedly, that everything would change in this little border town. In their eyes the Spanish sections of the Camino were crowded, uncultured, and dangerous, barely related to the French Chemin. I'd taken them seriously, but I wasn't prepared for the cultural onslaught that began just past the gate.

Saint-Jean-Pied-de-Port, which translates to Saint Jean at the Foot of the Pass, has been Europe's gateway to the Pyrenees for more than a thousand years, and today it's the second-most popular starting point for pilgrims who walk to Santiago. Only Sarria, where one begins to cover the minimum one hundred kilometers for a Compostela, draws more eager, untested pilgrims.

Eric and I paused for an obligatory photo at the gate and then passed into the older, walled part of Saint Jean. The cobbled street is closed to motorized traffic, forming a long, steep pedestrian arcade. The first thing I noticed was that everything on the street was Camino-themed. There were gîte de pèlerins and chambres d'hote but also hiking supply stores and gift shops selling Camino

T-shirts, overpriced chocolate, and racks of identical white scallop shells printed with the red cross of Saint James. There were touristy bakeries and health food stores that looked nothing like the boulangeries and épiceries I was used to.

A few blocks away, past the walls, the roads widened and an open-air *petit train* offered a "hop on, hop off" tour of the town, narrated by a tour guide with a microphone. Cars whirled around roundabouts. Crowds poured out of tour buses, filled the sidewalks, and gathered at dozens of bars and cafes—all of them open on a Tuesday. It was like leaving a country and walking into the Disneyland version of it. I felt bad about ever disparaging the softer commercialism of Conques.

Dazed, we followed the Rue de la Citadelle to the Pilgrim Office, where we hoped someone would help us arrange lodging. With so many options listed in the guidebook, we had assumed there would be plenty of rooms and hadn't made reservations. But now, looking at the crowds, we weren't so sure. Besides, we also needed new credentials; our six-paneled booklets issued by the American Pilgrims on the Camino were full of thirty-five colorful days in France.

Finding the office was easy enough, but there was a line out the door, with people speaking enough languages to make Babel's builders proud. Huge, heavy backpacks swung awkwardly, wielded by those who hadn't yet figured out how much extra clearance they needed. Their excitement and nervousness shimmered in the humid air.

I couldn't get over how many of them there were. In France the most pilgrims we'd ever seen in one place was maybe fifty. Radio Camino later reported that the Saint Jean Pilgrim Office issued more than four hundred credentials on that Tuesday in May, and that didn't include the arrivals who brought a credential issued in their home country.

When it was our turn with the Pilgrim Office volunteer, we easily acquired new credentials, but we hit a snag when we tried to ask about reserving a gîte. Although I loved our nights with the International Bevies of roommates, I wanted to spend my last night in France in a private room. I needed a good night's sleep before I tackled the Pyrenees. But the volunteer, who spoke only French, kept trying to send us to the gîte communal.

"Non," I said. "No dortoir."

She shook her head and rattled a flood of words that not even Eric understood. "Something about going outside and then back in?" he guessed. The conversation wasn't working, and there was a line waiting behind us, so we shrugged and got up to leave. We'd find a place on our own.

We went back outside and blinked in the sunlight, getting our bearings. But before we could set out, the volunteer was outside next to us. She gestured to the unmarked door of the house next door.

"She says we should stay here," Eric translated. I shook my head. This wasn't in our guidebooks.

The woman knocked on the door anyway and waved us over when a tall, stiff woman opened it. The pilgrim volunteer said something to her and gestured to us. The woman frowned. It had been weeks since I'd felt that regret-and-disapproval look, but it seemed I would end my sojourn in France just as I'd begun, doing something wrong. What was it this time?

She nodded once, and the volunteer told Eric something, then turned and went back through the crush of people into the Pilgrim Office. The tall woman stepped back and waved us inside. Not sure how to say no, or even what we were saying no to, we followed.

It was dark and cool inside the narrow hallway. We were obviously in a private home, but there were some familiar signs as well. There was a bench along the wall, and under it two sets of dirty boots that could only belong to pilgrims. A set of walking poles leaned in the corner.

The woman pointed toward the opposite wall, where I noticed a handwritten price list for rooms. The writing looked curiously like my grandmother's.

Ah, now I got it. This was a chambre d'hote. There was a price for a double room, and it was lower than what I'd thought we'd have to pay.

"Oui?" she asked.

Eric and I exchanged the married-people glance. Would we offend her if we said no? The place made me nervous, but the whole town made me nervous. Maybe a quiet night in an unmarked building would give us a break from the crowds. I mini-shrugged.

Eric turned to her. "Oui."

Her expression didn't change. She pointed to the bench and instructed us to take off our shoes. With each step we were deeper into this. She led us into the gloom and then up a creaking wooden staircase to the third floor, where off a narrow attic landing she pointed to a small, windowless room with a double bed and a small skylight.

It wasn't ideal, but we stayed. It was only one night. We showered and unpacked, then we set out to discover what was lovely about this last French town.

To be honest, it took a while to find it.

I know that most pilgrims, especially Americans, consider Saint-Jean-Pied-de-Port one of their favorite places of the whole Camino. I've seen hundreds of pictures of the canal-like river that winds through the town and the picturesque stone buildings that hang over it. New arrivals climb to the citadel on the hill, visit the cathedral, and feel themselves becoming pilgrims. They feel about Saint Jean the way I feel about Le Puy—the beautiful, foreign, welcoming gateway to the adventure of a lifetime.

But Saint Jean, for me, was an ending, not a beginning. It was where I had to let go of France.

We wove through crowded streets until we found an épicerie where we could buy fruit and nuts and a baguette to sustain us over the next day. There would be no markets in the mountains. After that, we found The Dane, who was staying in a hostel with Caroline and a group of young, attractive Frenchmen. They'd planned quite the dinner party, and I was glad our Dane finally had some people her own age. But dinner was still several hours away, so we did what good Chemin du Puy pilgrims did: we commandeered an outdoor table at the first bar we saw, ordered a round of Leffe, and sat back to watch the people.

One by one, familiar faces emerged from the crowd to join us. Wolfgang and Margarete. Guy. Jean-Francois. We shared rounds of drinks, and toasts, and memories. We'd done something amazing together.

Finally, Eric and I wished the others good night. They were off to do their own things: Amanda and Caroline to drink the night away, Wolfgang and Margarete to attend a concert, and Guy to do whatever men from Marseilles do.

Eric and I weren't ready to go back to our dreary attic room yet, so we wandered the town's quieter corners. We found an alley, then a staircase, and eventually the original city's defensive walls. The archer's turrets now looked down on rows of European hatchback cars, and across to satellite dishes on hotel rooftops, but it was quiet up there.

I watched the mountains become dark shadows as the sun set. Act Two lay beyond them.

THE DAY I
WALKED OVER
THE PYRENEES

I slept poorly in our tiny attic room. My mind wouldn't settle. For as long as I'd known I would someday walk the Camino, I'd been dreading the day I would have to walk over the Pyrenees. Approaching them now, with thirty-five days of experience, didn't make me feel more confident. It just made me know how hard it would be.

The Napoleon route from Saint-Jean-Pied-de-Port, France, to Roncesvalles, Spain, is by most standards the single most difficult stretch of trail on the Camino. It's a twenty-six-kilometer hike, including fourteen hundred meters of elevation gain to the Napoleon Pass and then a sharp descent on the other side. I realize that forty-five hundred feet isn't extreme by most American standards. Appalachian Trail hikers spend six months climbing mountains higher than that, and then descending, and then doing it again. And they do it while carrying tents and water and freeze-dried food. But there were reasons I wasn't an AT hiker.

There were signs all over Saint Jean reminding us that there is an alternative Camino route to Roncesvalles that follows an

The miracle sheep of the Pyrenees

early trade route along the Nive River. The Valcarlos route winds *between* the mountains, rather than going up and *over* them. Not only does that shave five hundred meters of elevation off the total, but there are towns and services all along the way. In winter and bad weather, it's the only alternative.

But most of the original pilgrims to Santiago didn't take the river route. They climbed to the Port-de-Cize (as it was called then, since Napoleon did not yet exist) because the open countryside above the tree line was safer from the robberies and assaults that were supposedly common in the heavily wooded valleys. *Codex Calixtinus* romanticizes it this way: "to him who climbs it, it seems as if he was able to touch the sky with his hand."

The weather reports for the next day were good, and my eyes, like everyone's, looked up to the Cize Pass. Even I was curious what it would be like to touch the sky.

On a normal day on the Chemin du Puy, we started walking somewhere between 8:00 and 9:00 a.m. But this was not a normal day. The guidebook said to plan for at least seven hours of walking, plus breaks, and I suspected I would want a lot of breaks. Eric and I agreed we needed to set out by 7:00, at the latest.

Our hostess reluctantly agreed to have our breakfast ready at 6:30. In gratitude, I tried to swallow a slice of bread and jam, knowing I needed the energy. Mostly, though, I sipped my coffee and waited.

All too soon, we strapped on our packs and passed under the Porte d'Espagne, the Gate of Spain, just as the church clock above us chimed 7:00. It was the earliest we'd ever started, but there was already a line of people with backpacks ahead of us.

The first thing I noticed was that I didn't recognize any of them. These were all new pilgrims, beginning the Camino Francés with the hardest day of walking they'd face. The second thing I noticed was how quiet everyone was. After the noise and enthusiasm in town the previous night, I expected this to be a boisterous bunch. Maybe I wasn't the only one feeling nerves.

As soon as we crossed the Nive River, the road started to climb. I set a slow, constant pace, focused on keeping my heart and breathing steady. Eric wished me luck and disappeared up the hill. We'd talked earlier about how we shouldn't even try to walk together today; our paces on inclines were just too different. He promised to stop every hour or so and wait for me to catch up.

The sky was overcast but dry, and the sun shone weakly behind the flat layer of gray. I looked back every few minutes to see the white walls of Saint Jean behind me until they disappeared as I went around a corner. And then I climbed some more.

The steady ascent was relentless. Each step was like a staircase. My leg muscles were burning when I reached Hunto, the cluster of houses four hundred meters above and five kilometers past Saint Jean.

That had only been five kilometers?

I tried to imagine doing what I'd done so far four more times, and as my mind slipped away from the present and into the future, I lost my battle to stay calm. There was an undercurrent of panic in my steps and my breathing was labored when the Camino path, now marked with Spain's yellow arrows alongside the familiar GR65 stripes, split from the paved road and shot up an even steeper set of rocky switchbacks.

The wind picked up as I left the cover of trees and started up the open incline. It was a breeze on my face at first, enough to cool the sweat. But as I got higher it picked up some more, and then some more. Of course it was blowing against me, making each step harder. I felt myself drift under its pressure toward the outer edge of the trail, which fell steeply, though not dangerously, down the mountain.

Logically, I knew I wasn't going to blow off the side of the mountain. The wind wasn't that strong. Rationally, I knew that I just had to keep putting one foot in front of the other. This mountain was steep, but I'd climbed steeper (albeit shorter) hills in France. This was something I could, eventually, do.

My mind *knew* all of that, but all I could *feel* was panic. I've never had a full-on panic attack, or at least not one that's been confirmed by a medical expert, but I came pretty close that morning on the side of the Pyrenees. I couldn't catch my breath or slow my heart rate. Then the tears started, and with them the mortification of knowing that all these strangers were watching me melt down. (Of course, most of those strangers weren't watching me at all. They were fighting their own battles with the windy, steep, terrible mountain.)

I was barely six kilometers in, and it was over. I'd have to retreat to Saint Jean and admit defeat. Eric would have to come back for me. The inner chorus predicting my failure was almost as loud as the wind. Through all of it, though, I kept planting my walking poles and pulling myself forward, foot by foot. *An object in motion tends to remain in motion . . .*

And then, as I rounded yet another hairpin turn and passed another pile of rocks, it happened.

Sheep.

Before we left for the Camino, people often asked what I was most looking forward to. I think they expected me to say something like "the cathedrals" or "a life-changing revelation" or (if they didn't know me at all) "spending a day hiking over the Pyrenees." My standard answer, though, was "sheep."

It was a bit of a blow-off. I was trying not to create specific expectations for myself or anyone else about would happen on my Camino. But there was one thing I had to confess that I really, really wanted to experience. My Camino dream was to walk along a narrow country lane, lined with walls or hedges, while a flock of sheep herded by a solemn shepherd flowed around me like I was a rock in a river. That, from the perspective of my city and technology-driven life, was the quintessential "Camino moment."

I had no way of making my fantasy become real, but I knew it was possible. I'd seen plenty of videos of sheep encounters on the Camino. So far, though, I hadn't been so lucky. Eric and I had shared the road with farmers herding cows a few times. (We always stayed on the far side of the road and never made eye contact.) And I'd had a close encounter with sheep near Ostabat, when a small flock crossed a road a few hundred yards ahead of us. By the time we got there—and I practically ran to get there—the sheep were already settled in their new field, the gates were secured, and the shepherd had moved on. My sheep dreams remained unfulfilled.

Until now.

Meandering down the mountain toward me was a flock of the *ugliest* sheep I had ever seen. Seriously. They'd been shorn recently, so they were all bristly, mud-colored fuzz and knobby shoulders and ears. Several had bright blue marks on their sides, as if they'd been tagged with graffiti.

There was no pastoral road, and no fences to keep the flock together. I wasn't sure I even could legitimately call this a flock. There was no shepherd or caretaker in sight, and the animals seemed to move at their own pace and direction. They were coming generally downhill, toward me, but they kept their heads down, nibbling what little grass existed on the open hillside. They were less like a flock and more like a collection of grazing sheep under the effect of gravity.

But gravity was working in my favor, so I stopped, delighted, as they swarmed past me and into a field on the other side of the road. The sheep paid little attention to the steady line of humans crossing their path and, to my surprise, most of the humans paid little attention to the sheep. Pilgrims, too, kept their heads down and their feet moving forward.

Not me. I stayed until the last gangly lamb passed. And in the process, my pounding heart slowed, and my breathing evened out. When I started walking again, the road was just as steep. The wind blew just as hard. The only thing that had changed was my perspective. All my attention was on the piece of magic that had just happened.

Later, when I caught up with Eric, he told me about a conversation he'd had with a devout Catholic from Eastern Europe at about this same time. It was her first day on the Camino, and she could barely control her excitement. This was a holy place, she told Eric. When he mentioned that he'd been walking for a few weeks already, she asked if he'd had a "Camino miracle" yet.

Eric pointed at the miles of rolling mountains that were a hundred shades of summer green, dotted with flowers and farms and dappled by sunlight. "Look around. This is the miracle," he told her. He thought she seemed disappointed by his answer, and they soon parted to walk their own Caminos. But he'd hit on something.

"The sheep!" I told him. "The sheep were my very own Camino miracle."

Orisson is perhaps the single most famous gîte de pèlerin of the Camino Francés. It's the last stop in France along the Napoleon route, about eight kilometers and six hundred meters of elevation from Saint Jean. I knew many Americans stayed here, breaking the arduous mountain climb into two days, so I was expecting a sprawling, historic structure. Instead, I found a small, modern building set right against the narrow road. A busy cafe counter served coffee to dozens of passing pilgrims, who overflowed the outdoor picnic tables and crowded the patio across the street, where the view was stunning.

I found Eric in the crowd, saving me a seat and chatting with whoever passed by. English was suddenly the common language, and I noticed how many of the accents sounded like home. We were no longer *the* Americans on the Camino. The new pilgrims were also younger, on average, than pilgrims from Le Puy. College-aged adults sporting North Face gear and sneakers replaced the retirement-celebrating crowd wearing Quechua and leather hiking boots.

I shed my pack and sipped coffee as we observed the steady stream of hikers coming toward us. But the more people who passed by, the more I worried. Where would they all sleep tonight? Where would *we* sleep tonight?

That thought pushed me off the bench and back to the steady climb. Eric practically skipped away, promising to stop for me in another hour or so. If I was having the hardest day ever, he was having the best day ever. He loved the mountains. I suspected that in an hour, he would be at the summit. It was hard to be miserable when he was so happy.

I followed the long line of walkers and the occasional intrepid bicyclist up the single-lane paved road for another few kilometers. The wind was still relentless, but the incline wasn't as steep. I still hated climbing, but I could see that I was making it, step by step.

At about a thousand meters up and ten kilometers in, I passed the tree line and approached the Pic d'Orisson, where a statue of the Virgin Mary, supposedly brought from Lourdes centuries ago, stands on a point of rock a few dozen meters off the trail. It's probably the most iconic and photographed place of the entire crossing, but I had some momentum going and didn't want to stop.

Besides, I was hungry again, and Eric was carrying our food.

To distract myself, I watched the stout horses that roamed freely across the mountainsides. We'd left the fenced pastures and farmyard animals far behind; these were free-ranging animals, their only sign of domesticity the bells on their necks. Most of the horses grazed on the steep slopes above and below us, but two stood side by side and perpendicular across the pilgrims' single-lane road. They leaned into the wind, immobile, and looked out over the valley.

They were beautiful. Regal. And seriously in the way. The horses were as wide as the road. Pilgrim after pilgrim approached, took a few photos, and then had to scramble off the trail, jumping across a thorn-filled ditch and then scooting along the prickly embankment to get past. The horses never deigned to notice. I kept climbing.

The views were stunning in every direction, with miles of uninhabited mountains and valleys in the peak of their spring colors. My feet complained. My lungs complained. I kept climbing.

Finally, two hours after my Orisson break, I caught up again with Eric, who was waiting for me beside one of the last things I expected to see up here in the wilderness: a food truck.

Actually, it was a brilliant business strategy. Some enterprising soul had realized that pilgrims, deprived of sustenance for hours and still not in sight of the summit, would appreciate a snack and a stamp in their credentials. A sign on the truck promised that there was just one more kilometer to climb, then five flat kilometers, then four downhill. I focused on that one (kilometer up) and not the ten (kilometers total).

I kept climbing.

Actually, fueled by the unexpected Coke and a handful of nuts, the last scramble up to the top wasn't so bad. And just as the road mostly flattened out, almost as a reward for the hard physical and mental work I'd done all morning, I found Marieke resting on a wall along the path. She was as happy to see a familiar face as I was, and just about as tired, so we walked on together, distracting ourselves with unflattering assessments of our new trailmates. After so many hours trying to control my thoughts, it was lovely to let go.

According to the books, there's a cattle guard that marks the official border between France and Spain. I never noticed it, and realized we'd crossed only when we came across a monument that read Navarre, which I had a vague notion was the Spanish border province. It was all rather anticlimactic. But it was also, literally, all downhill from there.

For many people who hike the Napoleon Pass, those last four kilometers of steep descent are the hardest of the day. Knees buckle and injuries happen. Marieke slowed down, but sensing the end, I picked up a final burst of speed and energy, barreling forward into a thick forest and letting gravity carry me downhill.

After a few minutes, I noticed the quiet. I was actually *alone*, with no other people in sight, for the first time all day. The pilgrims had spread out, and I had a pocket of peace to carry me. Even the wind had stopped. I had summited the Pyrenees, and it was over.

I arrived in Roncesvalles before I expected to. One minute I was plunging downhill through the woods, and the next I was crossing a stone bridge and looking across a parking lot at an enormous stone building. Eric sat on a rock wall outside, waiting for me. I didn't ask how long he'd been there.

The monastery of Roncesvalles has welcomed pilgrims since the twelfth century, when Augustinian monks moved their hospital from its original location at the top of the Cize Pass because the violent weather made year-round service there impossible. They chose the "valley of thorns" for their new home because this was where the emperor Charlemagne's nephew, Roland, was killed in a battle against the Basques. To sleep near the place of his death was somehow an honor.

Today, the abbey's *albergue*—because, in Spain, gîtes de pèlerins are now called albergues—is run by volunteers from around the world, who are given quite a logistical challenge. The abbey's new, modern dormitory could house almost two hundred people a night, which sounds like a huge number, but when I arrived at 3:00, the Dutch volunteers assigned Eric and me to the last two beds in the building, and the people were still coming off the mountain. Marieke, who arrived half an hour after me, found herself on a flimsy bunk bed in a crowded, windowless overflow area in the basement. The tired pilgrims who arrived after her were sent to temporary dormitories made from storage containers. Our early start that morning had been a smart idea.

There were tired, awkward, happy pilgrims everywhere, waiting in lines for showers and getting in each other's way in the hallways. I knew from experience it would take time for them all to find their routines, so I decided the best thing to do was stay out of the way. Eric and I got settled as quickly as possible, then left in search of a celebratory beer.

We found a bar, but as I looked around Roncesvalles I realized that's about all there was. For all its historical significance and legendary status along the Way of Saint James, it was not a true town as much as it was an isolated collection of services for the Camino. There was the abbey albergue, of course. Attached to the abbey was the chapel of Roncesvalles, with a museum of religious artifacts I didn't have the energy to consider. Beyond that, I saw two modest hotels, two or three restaurants, and a gift shop or two. That was it. No one seemed to permanently live in Roncesvalles.

This was the second time that I felt like a targeted tourist, not a guest in a place that thrived without me. It seemed like a bad sign of what was to come.

Eric and I found The Dane and Caroline at an outdoor table, surrounded by their group of French admirers. We greeted one another, even the French guys we'd barely met before, like old friends. Beers were passed and stories shared. The group kept the conversation mostly in English for our sake.

I noticed that a man sitting alone at the table behind us was obviously eavesdropping. Probably in his fifties, he wore a button-down shirt stretched tight over a sizable paunch. When I heard him talking to the server with an American accent, I smiled and said hello. It was still so novel to meet an American.

So yes, what happened next is all my fault.

Without more of an invitation, the man—we'll call him John—pulled his chair up to our table and started to talk. And talk. And talk. Have you heard the stereotype of the ugly American abroad? You know, the uncomfortably loud, arrogant, ethnocentric, insensitive clod with the white knee socks and the loud opinions? That was John.

He told the group he was from northern California, and how perfect it was there compared to everywhere else in the world. This had been his first day on the Camino, yet he told us about the best gear to carry and the right food to eat. He told us about all of the other long-distance hikes he'd done in different parts of the world. "Those were real hikes," he said, waving a hand dismissively around him. "This Camino thing is a walk in the park."

I laughed and challenged him a bit, telling him about the five hundred miles that everyone else at this table had already walked, through mud and over roller-coaster hills. "Hell of a park," I said.

"Six weeks in France?" John not only didn't take the hint, but he picked up a shovel and dug himself deeper. "I wouldn't want to do that. I've been to Paris." He puffed up a bit at this, and I wondered if he understood that several of the people at the table *lived* in Paris. "I don't get what the big deal is. Just a lot of people too interested in what clothes they're wearing. The language is terrible. The whole place isn't that great."

There was a long, awkward pause. Not all of our friends spoke English fluently, but they understood enough. I saw a few quick glances in our direction. Would we defend him?

Hell, no. Eric turned and said something to Caroline in French. I had no idea what, but it didn't matter. Our allegiance was clear. Without another beat, the conversation switched exclusively to French. I could follow enough to laugh at the right places and throw in a word here and there.

Effectively shut out, after a few awkward minutes John got up and moved away. When we tried to apologize for his behavior, our friends waved us off. Every culture has someone like him.

We stayed on the patio until it was time for dinner inside the attached restaurant. With so many hungry pilgrims in town, the dining room sold tickets in advance for two seatings a night. Eric, The Dane, and I had signed up for the early seating so that we could go to the pilgrim's mass and blessing after. Inside, we found Marieke, a Swiss man named Hans Peter, and a Frenchwoman we'd seen occasionally over the past week but never talked to.

As we ate, we drank the modest carafe of wine that was on our table and asked the waiter for more. "It will be five euros," he said.

What? We'd never been charged for a refill of wine before.

"Fine," Hans Peter said. "I will buy it."

The waiter brought another carafe, and we filled our glasses. Five minutes later, the waiter came back and told us that we had to leave. They had to clear the room to prepare for the next dinner seating. We'd never been sent away from a dinner table, either.

It wasn't the waiter's fault, of course. They did have to prepare for the next wave of fifty people. But it added to my growing sense that I was no more than a number here.

The bigger issue at that moment, however, was the half carafe of wine still on the table. Hans Peter waved it away. "It's fine." But I eyed it. I had not been raised to let good food—or drink—go to waste. Marieke and I looked at each other and then the carafe, and then filled our glasses again. We drank too fast and too much, then stumbled out of the restaurant with a case of the giggles that followed us to the church. The pilgrim blessing, the first I'd heard in Spanish, was a blur. I'm sure it was lovely.

The volunteers in the albergue had warned us repeatedly that they would "shut down" at 10:00 p.m. We were back inside long before that, knowing that they would lock the doors, but I didn't expect them to also abruptly shut off the overhead lights in the building, and while I was in the bathroom, no less. I tiptoed carefully back through the darkness to my bed at the end of the long aisle, listening to forty people rustle and shift and snore.

I'd walked over the Pyrenees.

It was beautiful. Amazing. And something I was never, ever going to do again.

CULTURE SHOCK

The Dutch volunteers at the Roncesvalles albergue had warned us about the 10:00 p.m. curfew, but they'd saved the wakeup call as a surprise. When we checked in, we were told we had to leave the albergue the next morning by 8:00, no exceptions. That wasn't a problem. The abbey didn't offer breakfast beyond a bank of vending machines, so there was no reason to linger. We would wake at 7:00, go through the routine, meet Marieke and The Dane, and leave by 7:30 at the latest.

But the abbey volunteers had other plans. At 6:00 a.m., while I was still deeply asleep, the bright banks of overhead lights flashed on. Remembering Conques and the Black-Eyed B's, I sent silent curses toward whichever novice pilgrim just woke up dozens of people, and then tried to go back to sleep.

Five minutes later, the door at the other end of the dorm burst open, and the guitars started. Three overly cheerful Dutchmen started singing "Wake Up, Little Susie" at the absolute top of their lungs.

What the hell?

Mornings, like hills, are things I need to approach slowly. I need snooze buttons and soft light. I need to drink coffee. I do not need singing. Yet from my sleeping bag cocoon, I could tell the guitars were getting closer.

Just an ordinary day in Pamplona

Sleep was impossible, but I refused to get up. There was no *reason* for me to get up. They couldn't *make* me get up. I burrowed deeper under the cover of my lightweight bag and waited for the sadistic concert to end.

I heard everyone around me getting up. *Lemmings.*

I heard Eric laughing. Of course he would find this funny.

The guitars reached our beds and stopped. I stayed in my sleeping bag, tiny travel pillow pressed against my head. The noise got closer. At least one of the players, with a booming voice, stood just beside me. I saw camera flashes through the thin bag as others gathered to watch the showdown. But I refused to move.

"Little Susie doesn't want to get up," the guitar player told the crowd, and everyone laughed. Little Susie refrained from telling him what she wanted to do to him and his guitar.

Finally, when he understood that I wouldn't play along, the guitar player gave up and moved on. His work was clearly done, anyway; there was no chance that I, or anyone else in the building, was still asleep. Still, I waited a few more minutes out of principle before emerging from my sleeping bag, spitting every foul word I could think of. If this was what Spain was like, I told Eric, I was going back to France. I hadn't walked five hundred miles and crossed a mountain range just to be herded in and out of dinner like cattle or treated like a child who couldn't make her own decisions about when to sleep or wake up.

We packed our things, drank terrible vending-machine coffee, found our friends, and were out the door before 7:00. We followed a wooded path that continued to descend from the mountains. It passed through charming, whitewashed Basque towns and soft forests, but I had a hard time seeing any of it. My attitude was shot, and my anger spilled over to the crowds of innocent pilgrims who swarmed the trail.

More than two hundred people flowed out of the Roncesvalles albergue all at once, creating a bit of a human traffic jam. Groups walked three or four abreast on the path, blocking others. The sounds of nature were drowned out by dozens of conversations.

When we got to the first town, we discovered that the cafe was not only open this early in the morning, but overflowing.

Backpacks lined the walls outside. People crowded around dozens of outdoor tables and stood three deep at the counters. Fermé was a word from the past, it seemed.

Instead of appreciating the new convenience, though, I grumbled about having to wait for my *café con leche*. After so many weeks of walking mostly alone and living quietly among people I couldn't talk to, the sudden flow of words and bodies was overwhelming. I felt like we'd left the countryside and entered a circus, and it left me with the same unsettled, unsatisfied feeling I had the first day after I left Le Puy. *Was this a mistake?*

At the same time, there was a lot to appreciate. The trails were well marked, the views across the valleys were beautiful, and the shade trees kept the heat away. Eric and I stayed close to Marieke and The Dane all day, the four of us building a tight clique to ward off the changes. As we started the final descent into Zubiri, a young man with fancy sneakers and fluent English picked us out of the crowd walking past. He and his friends had opened a new albergue, he said. It was small, just twenty-two beds total, and there was a room with four beds. If we wanted it, he would call ahead and reserve it for us.

Yes, we wanted the room. Although none of us had said it out loud yet, we all knew that this was probably the last night the four of us would be together. Marieke needed to speed up her pace to get back to her job in Amsterdam, and Eric and I had to slow down to wait for our friend Ian to meet us in Logroño. The Dane, meanwhile, seemed restless for something, and I couldn't figure out what. But at least we'd have one last night of Eric's International Bevy of Women.

Zubiri was small and working class, with wide swaths of weed-rutted blacktop surrounding a few cafes and shops. We found our albergue on the far edge of town, in a modern townhouse stuffed with bunk beds. The room was basic, but big enough to string an improvised laundry line for our clothes when fat raindrops started to fall outside.

The four of us spent most of the evening in that room, just being together, and I left Zubiri the next morning feeling better than when I'd arrived. For one thing, no one serenaded me at

6:00 in the morning. In fact, when we emerged from our room a little after 7:00, everyone else in the albergue was already gone. Spain's early risers would take some adjustment.

The real reason for my optimism, though, was that we were going to Pamplona. If I'd dreaded the Pyrenees for as long as I knew about them, I'd been excited about Pamplona for just as long. I had images of eating tapas in the cafes where Hemingway once sat, and wandering the crooked streets where, two months later, the bulls would run for the festival of San Fermin. What little I knew about Spain was almost all tied to this city, and I was eager to take a break from the Camino to see it.

As we left town, Marieke and The Dane each split off to walk alone, but Eric and I plodded through the steady drizzle together. Just past Larrasoaña, we noticed a crumbling church by the road. The doors were open, so we went to check it out and sign the guest book.

When we got to the doorway, we discovered that this wasn't an active church at all, but a restoration project in progress. The chapel's interior was gutted, and there were huge holes in the brick floor and the plaster walls. But there were also lit candles near where the altar used to be, and I could make out the edges of a simple fresco on the wall above it.

A man emerged from the choir loft and introduced himself as Neil, from South Africa. This abbey was his project. With great enthusiasm he showed us around the chapel, parts of which he said dated back to a chapel built by the Knights Templar for pilgrims in 1150. The order had been established earlier that century and recognized by the pope in 1139, with the primary mission to protect Christian pilgrims on the road to Jerusalem, especially during the tumultuous years of the Crusades. It was a natural extension to also guard and provide support for pilgrims to the tomb of Saint James.

The Templars hadn't been active since the fourteenth century, though, and the Spanish Church had been steadily declining for centuries. Neil's chapel building sat empty and abandoned for decades before he and his wife, Catherine, purchased it from the Archdiocese of Pamplona.

I stopped him. "You bought a nine-hundred-year-old abbey? A person can do that?"

They can, he assured me, but it takes a lot of work. The local Spanish diocese didn't have the financial resources to sustain all of its aging buildings, and for them it was better to sell it to Neil than to leave it to rot.

"Gypsies," Neil told us, waving at the belfry. "They come and steal everything—the wires in the walls, the bells from the belfries. I have to sleep here every night for now, to let them see that the place is inhabited again."

Templars and gypsies, belfries and frescoes . . . I started to see past the crowded modern Camino and into the intriguing corners of a pilgrimage in Spain. Eric, too, looked interested for the first time since we crossed the border.

Neil described his plan to renovate the abbey using volunteer labor as much as possible, and then open it as a pilgrim oasis, maybe even an albergue.

While we were talking, The Dane wandered in, and I watched her perk up at the word "volunteer." For as long as we'd known her, she'd talked about taking her time on her walk and possibly stopping for a while if an opportunity came up. She wasn't limited by a job to return to, like Marieke, or a visa that would eventually expire, like us.

The Dane and Neil started talking and wandered across the room. When she returned, she looked both nervous and happy. "I'm going to stay here to help," she told us.

And just like that, her Camino was on hold. There were hurried hugs and exchanged email addresses, but it hardly felt like a proper goodbye.

As soon as we passed through the gate and into the medieval part of Pamplona, I forgot about the steady drizzle and the culture shock, and I fell in love. Bright buildings of every color, four stories high and lined with tiny Juliet balconies, loomed over crooked streets. Well-dressed people went about their daily lives. The Camino pilgrims, who had seemed like an overwhelming mob just the day before, blended and disappeared into the crowd.

Eric and I wound through streets set at odd angles and into the plaza of City Hall. Tucked across from the elaborate buildings was a practical, modern Office of Tourism—a welcome sight for two tired, muddy pilgrims without reservations on a Friday night. After a short wait, a woman helped us reserve a surprisingly affordable hotel room just half a block from the famous Plaza del Castillo. It was on the second floor of one of those perfectly Pamplona buildings, with a balcony overlooking a narrow street where I could imagine crowds in white being chased by bulls. I leaned over the railing, taking it all in and wondering how we got so lucky.

I would learn the answer to that, but not for a few more hours.

Showered and reenergized, Eric and I set out to explore. The first stop was the Plaza, with its cafes shaded by wide awnings. The Café Iruña claimed to be one of Hemingway's favorite haunts, and in his honor (and for the tourists) it retained all of its 1920s Art Deco magnificence. We sipped wine and people-watched for a while before wandering on.

The cathedral and the famous bullfighting ring were both closed (I learned a new Spanish word: *cerrado*), but we ran into Marieke and shared a plate of tapas before she went off to a concert and we went to find dinner.

True to our pilgrim routine, Eric and I were back in our hotel and ready to sleep not long after 10:00, which is when we realized why our room was so cheap. All of the ground-floor businesses on our street, which had been closed all afternoon, now threw open their doors and became open-air bars. Cocktail tables lined the cobblestones, and Pamplona's biggest weekend party happened ten feet below our window. The crowd drank, shouted, broke glasses, smoked, argued, and sang until dawn. Sleep, even for bone-tired pilgrims, was difficult.

When Eric and I ventured out the next morning, it looked like a riot had passed through, with broken glass and unidentifiable liquids filling the street. Two maintenance workers were already on the job, wielding power hoses and giant brooms. I could have been annoyed, I suppose. But I'd read Hemingway, and I expected nothing less from Pamplona.

The whole day was full of a similar exuberance. Eric and I went looking for breakfast and instead found a band in traditional Basque dress—kilts and fur capes and large cowbell-looking percussion instruments strapped to their backsides—parading down a side street. A few hours later we wandered back to our hotel room, thinking we would nap, but something outside our hotel window caught my attention. When I climbed onto the balcony, I found myself almost eye level with a fifteen-foot puppet wearing a vest, shirt, and long skirt, which hid the human who balanced the whole contraption on his shoulders, making it bob and dance.

When a giant puppet walks past your hotel room, you really have no choice but to follow. Or at least, I had no choice. Eric chose to nap.

Two blocks away, in the plaza in front of the Church of San Nicolás, I caught up to my giant puppet as he joined several others. They were dressed as soldiers and matrons, pretty young women and priests, and while a band of men in black berets played traditional tunes, the puppets danced for a growing crowd. Meanwhile, a serious boy wearing a soldier costume and "riding" a papier-mâché horse wandered around and hit small children on the head with a stuffed toy mace. Everyone laughed when he did it.

None of it made any sense. I was enchanted. I asked someone what festival or holiday we were celebrating, and he shrugged. "It's not a special day. This is just Pamplona."

"Just" Pamplona celebrated all night again on the street below our window. When Eric and I left our hotel the next morning at dawn, backpacks strapped and walking poles in hand, the sounds and smells of the party still hung in the air. Near the city gates, a few well-dressed stragglers still wandered, their high heels and button-down shirts looking worse for the night, their expressions dazed.

As we left the city behind, I took a deep breath and committed myself to this new Camino. I would stop thinking of Spain as "not France," I told Eric, and give it a chance to be something unique and wonderful.

Eric wasn't ready for that commitment yet. He was having even more trouble adjusting to this new Camino than I was. With all of the problems I'd had with my aching feet, I had mixed memories of France, but Eric had loved every single minute, even the rainy ones. Now he missed the bread-and-jam breakfasts, and the challenge of the language, and the small, familiar groups of overly prepared people, and the shared meals with passed plates and endless helpings. Albergues didn't do demi-pension, and eating on our own in the local bar just wasn't the same.

We'd already left the wooded hills of the Pyrenees and entered a new countryside. As I started the long ascent to Alto de Perdón, the famous Hill of Forgiveness, I made a conscious decision to stop focusing on what I didn't like. I looked away from the people stretched on the trail in front of me like a line of ants and instead looked to my left and right at the fields of grasses rippling in the breeze, splashed with color from spring poppies. I studied the ruins of crumbling castles and the toppling towers of hay bales.

The trail up the hill was steep, and it looked like it would be a muddy, slippery mess on a wet day. But today a cool, steady breeze blew the low clouds past. A row of wind turbines on the ridgeline above me turned steadily, but with surprisingly little noise, as I plugged away up the switchbacks. I'd climbed the Pyrenees, I reminded myself. This was nothing.

Eric, as always, waited for me at the summit, where a silhouette sculpture of a line of pilgrims looked west toward the tomb of Saint James. Inscribed on one figure were the words "donde se cruza el camino del viento con el de las estrellas" ("where the path of the wind crosses with that of the stars").

That morning, the wind's path was the one we really noticed. The views from the top of the hill were incredible, stretching in every direction, but the breeze on the exposed ridgeline had changed from cool to downright biting, and the few pilgrims who lingered huddled behind a boulder to escape it. Most of us moved on quickly, taking a few photos and then picking our way down the steep descent into the next valley.

Before I knew it, we were in Uterga, a village of sunbaked tan bricks and red-tile roofs, with a locked church, a single private albergue, and not much else. Although it was not even noon, Eric and I stripped off our packs and declared ourselves done for the day. It was an unusual but intentional move. Most of the people around us would walk another ten kilometers that afternoon to

Puente la Reina, the next "big" Camino town. But we were still ahead of schedule, and I thought getting away from the more popular stops might help Eric and me break away from the crowds and ease into this new Camino.

Our albergue doubled as the town's cafe and bar, and dozens of pilgrims stopped for lunch and a rest as they passed through. I was happy to see most of them move on, but here we finally had to say goodbye to Marieke, who needed to be back in Amsterdam by the end of the week. She stopped for a coffee and a hug, then strode off toward Puente la Reina. Her easy grace and outrageous stories had carried me through difficult days, and my eyes stung when I watched her walk away.

Before I could get too morose about what felt like the last big goodbye, an unexpected arrival caught my attention: Guy, our Marseilles flirt. We hadn't seen him since Saint-Jean-Pied-de-Port, and we'd heard through Radio Camino that he'd taken an extra day or two of rest before he tackled the mountains. The break seemed to have served him well, because he was now walking with two new friends, pretty young women who looked like they were still in college. As they left together, he said something that made both women giggle and blush. It looked like Guy would do all right in Spain.

Eric and I spent a quiet night in the tiny town, and when we left Uterga early the next morning, we were totally alone. The handful of people who'd stayed at our albergue had mostly left before us, and everyone else was at least eleven kilometers behind, on the other side of Alto de Perdón.

With plenty of time on our hands, we decided to make a side trip. In Muruzabal we left the official Camino trail and walked across two kilometers of wide, flat fields that were already brown and dusty in mid-May. The sun was bright even at 8:00 in the morning, casting sharp shadows and making the air shimmer around the mysterious Romanesque Church of Saint Mary of Eunate.

Built in the twelfth century, the octagonal Eunate is surrounded by a delicate, freestanding cloister. Most scholars agree that the design indicates a Templar connection, and archaeologists found evidence of scallop shells adorning some of the bodies buried beneath the structure, so we know it has a place in the Santiago pilgrimage. Beyond that, there are no records. There are competing theories that it was a personal chapel for a powerful noble, a hospital, a burial site, or even a landlocked lighthouse of sorts. (It has a distinctive lantern tower, which in the open country would have been visible for miles.)

Until recently, the volunteer guardians of Eunate offered it as a primitive albergue, letting a small number of pilgrims sleep on mats under the domed roof of the chapel after sharing a candlelit dinner. But the increasing numbers of Camino pilgrims overwhelmed them, and they'd closed the overnight program and now opened the chapel to daytime visitors from Tuesday through Sunday.

We were there on a Monday, though, and Eunate was cerrado. But the beauty of a cerrado chapel was that it was quiet. We were the only people in sight as we put down our packs and lingered, circling slowly, soaking in the peace and the details of the architecture. I studied the weather-worn faces—of saints or gargoyles, it was impossible to tell anymore—carved on the sides of the building. I hummed childhood hymns I hadn't thought about in years. It all felt a little mystical and mysterious, at least until a tour bus pulled up. Then it was time to go.

We got to Puente la Reina late in the morning and lingered over a meal of fresh-squeezed orange juice and *tortilla española*. I was already in love with these wedges of potato omelet, sometimes with onions or cheese, which were available in almost every bar for just a few euros.

After splurging in Pamplona and on private albergues, it was time to tighten our belts and try a big, inexpensive albergue again. We were in line to check into the church-run Padres Reparadores, which housed a hundred pilgrims a night in ten simple rooms, before it opened. The building filled swiftly with pilgrims of every age, and within an hour the air was full of a dozen different languages and several dozen different smells.

But it was something *outside* the building that captured all of my attention that afternoon. As Eric and I walked into town earlier, I'd noticed the tall brick smokestack of a long-closed factory. More specifically, I'd noticed something on top of it. A nest? It seemed too big, wider than the tower itself. But then something moved inside the nest.

It was my first stork sighting, but many more would follow. I got a little obsessed with the huge, awkward birds that were seemingly everywhere. I later learned that there are three thousand stork pairs living in Spain and raising their young in giant nests of sticks and mud, which they build on anything that's tall and easy to defend. Church steeples are especially popular, and it was rare to see a Spanish belfry on the Camino that didn't have a stork nest or three. Later, in other towns, I would be close enough to hear storks throw their heads back and make their distinctive clacking sounds.

I spent the afternoon in the plaza across the street, watching transfixed as the birds flew in long, slow circles, coming in for what were always awkward landings. I could relate. I'd have a hard time controlling a three-foot body and a seven-foot wingspan too.

Eric finally lured me back inside with the promise of food. We took advantage of the albergue's communal kitchen and cooked our standard dinner of pasta, mushrooms, and chicken in jarred pesto, accompanied, of course, by a two-euro bottle of the local Rioja.

I was at the stove when a young blonde woman, probably in her early twenties, bounced into the kitchen and up to me. "Hi, where are you from?" she asked, but didn't give me time to answer. She was from Arkansas. She was walking the Camino alone after working in Madrid for a year. She was meeting everyone, and this was all *amazing*. Cooking dinner was *amazing*. She noticed two Korean teenagers, who as far as I could tell spoke neither Spanish nor English, and spontaneously hugged them. "They don't know what I'm saying, but they understand this."

I thought they looked more terrified than understanding. But Arkansas—the name stuck—had already forgotten them, and turned her attention back to me. "Look at my legs," she said, waving a young, tanned, and toned calf my way. "I haven't shaved in over a week. If I don't find a razor soon, how will I ever find a boyfriend?" Fortunately, I wasn't expected to answer.

I still wasn't ready for these people. I was in love with Spain— its cities and storks and dramatic skies and castles—but I still didn't love my fellow pilgrims.

ENFERMA

Leaving Puente la Reina the next morning, we crossed the iconic six-arched stone bridge that has provided a safe passage for pilgrims since the earliest days of the pilgrimage. Eric pointed out that in France, the Way of Saint James took us from church to church. In Spain we seemed to be walking from bridge to bridge.

As if to prove his point, that morning the Camino path wound several kilometers out of its way, passing under a busy highway and through some less-than-picturesque towns, to take us along a Roman road and to another centuries-old bridge, this one over the Rio Salado, or Salt River.

The *Codex Calixtinus* talks about this place: "In a place called Lorca, towards the east, runs a river called Rio Salado. Beware from drinking its waters or from watering your horse in its stream, for this river is deadly." He goes on to claim that when he was there, two Navarrese waited on the shore with knives, tricking innocent pilgrims like him into watering their horses in the unhealthy waters and then skinning the carcasses on the spot.

That poor writer had a hard time in Spain. And while no one tried to kill my horse, of course, I could sympathize a little with the feeling of being unwelcome. The local Spanish residents who provided cafés con leche and *bocadillos* and clean bunk beds

The bridge over the Rio Salado

and *vino tinto* day after day were all professional and polite. But our hosts didn't join us for dinner or share their experiences. Camino pilgrims like me flowed by like drops of water in a river so dense that it was all they could do to keep up. I missed feeling an engagement.

I pushed myself to talk with people as we walked on to the town of Estella, where we spent a fine but unmemorable night in a donativo albergue provided by the local Church of San Miguel. The hairy-legged girl from Arkansas was always around, but so was a cheerful teacher from Manitoba, and a college student from San Francisco, and an older Australian man who made me miss Eugene, our very first Camino companion. They all had great stories, but no one really connected longer than an hour or two. Maybe it was because there were so many distractions here.

Not even the wine fountain of Irache could excite me, although that didn't prevent us from stopping. We passed it just before 9:00 a.m., which seemed early for a shot of *tinto*, even in Spain. But the monastery of Santa María la Real de Irache had shared wine from its vineyards with pilgrims since the twelfth century. It was our sacred duty, I explained to Eric, to support the history and culture of the Santiago pilgrimage.

Considering the history, I expected "the wine fountain" to be a grotto in some ancient stone building with a freely flowing . . . well, fountain of wine. Instead, we found a modern tap in the wall of a concrete warehouse, monitored by a webcam. The wine fountain is maintained as a marketing tool by a collection of local wineries, which long ago bought out the monastery's vineyards. A gate keeps out overnight revelers, and the webcam probably acts as social pressure to not get greedy and fill a water bottle.

Despite the modern precautions, the Irache fountain felt welcoming. A sign by the gate read: "Pilgrim, if you wish to arrive at Santiago full of strength and vitality, have a drink of this great wine and make a toast to happiness." We all drank to that and then walked on through vineyards that stretched for kilometers, the plants still too small to bear fruit this early in the season. There was no shade, but our weather luck continued to hold, and a low bank of clouds protected us from the heat of the day.

After two restless nights in crowded albergues, Eric and I were ready to splurge on something smaller and nicer in Los Arcos. There were still bunk beds and shared rooms in the private albergue we found, but the mattresses were thick and the bathroom—one floor down a lovely tile staircase—was clean and modern. Our *hospitaleros* were cool and distant, but our host had the richest, deepest, most Spanish voice I'd ever heard.

The church in the center of town was open to visitors for a few hours that afternoon, so we ventured to check it out. We hadn't been inside many churches in Spain; most were closed and locked, and guest books and empty chapels seemed to be things of the past.

On the outside, the Cathedral of Santa Maria looked like a normal Spanish church, with smooth stone walls and a couple of storks nesting on top. But as soon as we walked through the doors, it was obvious that this was like nothing we'd seen yet.

I knew, in theory, that Spanish architecture would have a different aesthetic than the stark Romanesque and Gothic styles of France. Everything here was Baroque, covered with King Ferdinand and Queen Isabella's gold from the New World. Even older buildings had been remodeled and covered with chubby, naked cherubs that stared mournfully from cluttered altars. But nowhere and nothing, before or after, was quite like the Church of Santa Maria, where every single inch of every single surface was a visual representation of eight centuries of European Christianity.

The pillars and pews were carved. The walls were painted with elaborate designs. The dome of the roof was gilded in layers. The altars were gold. Statues of bloody battles between saints and demons lined the walls. Nooks were filled with relics, and toward the back there was a mannequin in a glass coffin. The choir loft had been turned into a museum, including enormous old books illuminated on velum. Each pipe of the organ had been painted in the 1930s with cartoonish faces, Art Deco style.

It was like your grandmother's overcrowded knick-knack cabinet, where everything from the heirloom china to the snow globe she bought in Vegas is crammed onto one shelf, threatening to topple out at any minute.

In the center altar was a statue of the Virgin Mary holding a small but very adult-looking Christ child on her lap. Something about her seemed odd. I looked at the pamphlet I'd picked up at the door, which had been roughly translated into English. It said that the statue was one of the Black Virgins, made of ebony like the one back in Le Puy. In 1947, though, during a renovation of the altar, "they removed her blackness." I didn't even know how to start thinking about that, so I suggested it was time to leave the church of the sensory overload.

Eric and I had another quiet, solitary dinner of mediocre food. Though meals in Spain were cheap and plentiful, there was a monotony to the standard three-course *menu del día*: salad or lentils, chicken or pork or trout, ice cream or flan or fruit. And always, always *patatas fritas*. I didn't know it was possible to be tired of French fries.

I went to bed that night feeling "off," but I blamed the greasy dinner. I woke up in the darkest part of the night feeling *very* off. And very in need of a bathroom.

Out of the sleeping bag, past my snoring roommates, carefully opening the (squeaky, of course) door, down the charming but treacherous tile staircase, and into the bathroom . . . just in time.

That's all I need to say about that. It wasn't pretty.

Eventually, I made my way back to the bunk, back to sleep . . . only to wake up an hour later and do it all over again. And then again an hour after that. That charming staircase became my enemy, and the modern plumbing my only friend. And that nice thick mattress? I didn't spend much time with it.

In the early hours of the morning, when our roommates started stirring and pilgrim minds turned to spending a long day outdoors, away from all facilities, I woke up Eric and told him that we couldn't go.

He went to talk to the albergue owners. *Mi esposa está enferma.* My wife is sick. Was there somewhere in town where we could stay today?

The deep-voiced albergue owner took one look at me, pale and glazed-eyed and sitting not-too-close to his generous breakfast spread, and picked up the phone. Within five minutes it was arranged.

My memory of the next few minutes is fuzzy, but I know a young man in a pickup truck came and drove us to a tall, white building about six blocks away. I remember feeling silly that we didn't just walk such a short distance, but also not being sure I could walk.

By 8:30 that morning, we were in a clean, private guesthouse room, and I had my very own bathroom. While I rested, Eric went to the local *farmacia* to see what might help me.

The small storefront shops marked with green crosses were long since familiar to us. Even villages with just two or three streets had one, and sometimes two, pharmacies. When I asked a French pilgrim about it, he shrugged. "We have excellent health care, and the people of Europe are getting old." Pharmacies were where I bought topical ibuprofen gel, which I slathered directly onto my aching feet. And then, when I discovered that ibuprofen gel is alcohol-based and therefore dried out my feet until the skin cracked and bled, a kind pharmacist in Pamplona gave me medical-quality hydrating lotion. Pilgrims depended on the farmacias for knee and ankle braces, painkillers, and—as we learned that day—medicine for gastrointestinal problems.

I spent the day in bed, nibbling crackers, hydrating, and reading ebooks on my rarely used phone. Eric, trying to stay out of my way, wandered Los Arcos.

It was an unexpected rest day, but we still had two full days to get to Logroño, just twenty-five kilometers away. On Friday, I woke up weak and still feverish, but my stomach had settled enough for me to venture outside, as long as I didn't eat anything more complicated than plain bread. I walked without paying much attention to the scenery. I had vague impressions of more vineyards stretching over hills and the occasional stone castle or monastery in the distance. But mostly I concentrated on putting one foot in front of the other.

After fifteen kilometers we stopped in Viana and checked into the first private albergue we saw on the outskirts of town, which turned out to be one of those Camino-changing decisions for us. Almost everything that happened later hinged on Albergue Izar—a spacious, clean, modern townhouse with an open kitchen area and a sunny rooftop deck.

We were the first people to check in, and I collapsed into my bunk for a nap as soon as I saw it. I didn't even bother to shower, let alone think about laundry.

When I woke up, I noticed a young man sitting on the bunk bed opposite me, studying his feet. With a strong British accent, he introduced himself as Chris. He was recently unemployed, newly single, and at loose ends in life. The first time he'd heard about the Camino was only a few weeks ago, and he freely acknowledged he'd come looking for love.

"I met a girl in the albergue the first night," he told me. "We drank and talked all night. Fanny was beautiful and brilliant. My *soulmate*." He was practically swooning. "But then these," he gestured at his feet. "I have the most terrible blisters, and I can't walk, and she's gone ahead of me. I'm worried I'll never catch up." It seemed like bad form to ask why his soulmate wouldn't slow down a little to accommodate him, so I just listened as he told me he'd looked into getting a horse, an approved way to travel the Camino, to move faster without having to walk.

"It's pathetic, I know. I am, literally, chasing Fanny."

I eventually made my way up to the rooftop, where Eric was chatting with Mette, a delightfully pragmatic and cheerful Danish office manager who made me miss our Dane. Still weak, I mostly leaned back on a lounge chair in the sun and happily listened to them talk.

That night Eric made me a simple plate of plain rice and chicken. I ate slowly, carefully, while I enviously watched a gourmet dinner party evolve at the next table. A tall, bearded New Zealander named Rory was in charge, assisted by his girlfriend, Lis from the Netherlands. They'd assembled half a dozen albergue residents, including the hapless, limping Chris, and sent them shopping for random ingredients, which Rory magically chopped, sautéed, combined, and assembled into a feast. I wasn't surprised to learn that he was a professional chef in his normal life, working mostly in high-end resorts and private homes, while Lis managed the household or worked front desks. They traveled the world together.

Eric and I talked with them for hours that night after everyone else went to bed, and I laughed harder than I had since we'd arrived in Spain. Mette, Chris, Lis, Rory. If it took getting sick to find new Camino friends, I decided, it would be worth it.

I went to sleep happy, but in the dark of night, I felt the bed creak as Eric slipped out of the bunk above me and went to the bathroom. He came back, but was up again an hour later.

Enfermo, round two.

The next morning, as our new friends sipped their coffee and strapped on their packs, it was my turn to approach our host. *Mi esposo está enfermo.* Albergue Izar had a private double room, and I asked if we could move into it for a second night.

"Sí, no problem." Albergue Izar was run by multiple generations of the same family, who lived in private apartments next door. Within twenty minutes they had not only cleaned the double room, but they helped me carry in our things. We waved a reluctant goodbye to our new friends, wondering if we would see them again.

It was Eric's turn to sleep and read for the day, and my turn to wander a Spanish town. I poked around Viana's medieval buildings and narrow streets, and read the story of how Cesare Borgia, son of a pope and patron of both Leonardo da Vinci and Machiavelli, was murdered and buried here—first inside the stately cathedral and then, when his family fell out of favor, outside under the street, so everyone passing could walk on his remains. After time passed and emotions cooled, Cesare was finally moved to a nice, neutral place across the square.

The architecture was lovely, but I spent most of the day worrying about the future. We were supposed to be in Logroño, ten kilometers away, to meet Ian's bus that evening. Clearly, that wasn't going to happen. After that we had four days to get about 125 kilometers to Burgos, where Ian would catch a train on Thursday morning. Much of that seemed impossible now.

While I was sitting with my maps and trying to find a solution, I checked the secret email account we'd set up to stay connected with our traveling friends while still maintaining our "offline, disconnected" sabbatical. There was a new snag. Ian had missed a bus connection and wouldn't get to Logroño until noon Sunday. Well, that settled my first concern about how to meet him that night. But it made the larger reality more obvious. There was no way we could start walking in Logroño on Sunday afternoon, with Eric and me still queasy and Ian not Camino acclimated, and get to Burgos on Thursday.

We would have to skip ahead somewhere. It was time to swallow my "only on foot" Camino pride. "When in Spain," I muttered, as I hunted for the Office of Tourism.

On the Chemin du Puy almost everyone we met was a Camino purist: we all carried our packs and walked every step. While obviously there were exceptions, I felt like most of the GR65 people were there for the experience of the hike. Along the Camino Francés, I'd noticed, the exponentially larger number of pilgrims came with a more diverse set of purposes and expectations. The culture shifted to emphasize the destination of Santiago more than how anyone got there, and some people straight out told us they were in Spain to "experience" the Camino, not necessarily to walk it. On top of that, Spain drew thousands of pilgrims from around the world, who were often under tight timelines, with inflexible dates for their plane rides home.

So people hopped on buses and trains to skip over "boring" parts. They took taxis when they were tired or felt a blister. To be honest, I had been an incredible snob about this. I judged the "Camino tourists" harshly. This is supposed to be a pilgrimage, I thought. It's supposed to be hard.

"Walk your own Camino," the voice in my head would remind me. "That's right," I'd snap back. "*Walk* it."

But now here I was, standing outside a tourist office, desperate for a bus and panicking because the door said CERRADO. I broke another Camino rule and went to the internet for help, only to discover that I could make no sense of the Spanish bus system's website. There might be a bus from Viana to Logroño in the morning, but maybe it didn't run on Sundays. And if it did run, I didn't know where to meet it or if I needed to buy tickets in advance.

I had no one to ask. Our hosts didn't speak English. Our new friends from the first night were long gone. The new albergue guests were a team of loud, brash Italian cyclists who were riding the Camino on their state-of-the-art mountain bikes, supported by a van full of supplies.

"Let's see the Camino provide this time," I muttered as I sulked my way back to the albergue to see if Eric was awake. He wasn't, so I sat helplessly in the kitchen with my maps and guidebooks. The patriarch hospitalero found me there. He was a small, bald grandfather, an *abuelo*, with a cheerful smile and a kind voice.

"Su esposo?" he asked. I patched together my basic college Spanish to tell him that Eric was sleeping, that he was still ill.

"Will he eat?" I thought I understood.

"Yes," I said. I would make him food later. We had rice that would be kind to his stomach.

"No, no," the abuelo said. "When he wakes, you tell me. I'll make him a healing soup." He said something about "special herbs." I thanked him and went back to my worrying.

Eric woke up eventually and came to the kitchen. When the abuelo saw him, he beamed. "You sit. I will make you my soup."

It doesn't matter where you are. If a grandparent tells you to sit, in any language, you sit. We watched our host go into a closet and bring out a bundle of dried leaves. He fussed over the stove, brushed aside his own children when they came to him with questions, and half an hour later he set two bowls of salty, lemony, herb-filled rice soup broth in front of us. It was exactly the food that our ravaged stomachs needed. He refused any offer to pay him for the dinner.

It was time, once again, to reconsider my assumptions. I'd been sure that our Spanish hosts saw us only as transactions, another few euros. But this hospitalero went out of his way for us. We were more than just bodies in beds.

Reinforced by the food and Eric's language skills, I asked the abuelo about the buses. He shook his head. There were no buses on Sundays in Viana. But in Logroño, he said, the buses and taxis would run.

Eric and I consulted. His stomach was on the mend, and I continued to improve. We agreed we could walk a slow ten kilometers the next morning into Logroño, meet Ian, and then taxi or bus thirty kilometers ahead to Nájera. Then we'd be on track to start walking again on Monday. It still felt a little like cheating, but it was necessary cheating.

We both slept through the night, with no more stomach flare-ups. The next morning I got up, packed, and went downstairs before Eric. There was the abuelo. "No problem!" he boomed, in English. He was talking to the support vehicle driver for the Italian bikers, who I knew spoke neither Spanish nor English.

"No problem!" the driver boomed back.

I smiled and poured a cup of tea as the men kept talking, one in Spanish and the other in Italian. But when I heard "Americans" and "enfermo," I started paying attention. "Nájera!" the abuelo said.

"No problem!" the Italian said again.

Wait, what? I had several problems. I went to find Eric. "I know you're still sick and I'm supposed to be taking care of things, but we have a situation developing." When we reached the foot of the stairs, the abuelo waved us over. He introduced the Italian, who, he said, would take us to Nájera.

"No problem!" The Italian driver grinned.

"No problem!" The Spanish grandfather beamed.

We tried to explain that there was a problem, because we weren't going to Nájera. We needed to go to Logroño.

"No problem!" both men replied, and they picked up my backpack and carried it to the van. I heard the driver tell another Italian, "Nájera."

"Problem!" I kept squeaking. "Really, guys, we can walk to Logroño!" But honestly, Eric was still feverish, and I hadn't had a full meal in three days. And was it really cheating if we accepted the generosity of fellow pilgrims?

So in a rush of words and bags and confusion, we found ourselves in the back of a windowless van, surrounded by five dirty backup bicycles and a pile of duffel bags, driven by two men who spoke no English. It was only after we pulled away, with the abuelo waving proudly and still saying "No problem!" that we realized the real problem: our driver had no idea where Logroño was.

"Logroño?" the Italian man in the passenger seat asked, looking confused and pulling out a map.

"Logroño," I said firmly.

"*Dove?*" *Where?* The Italians, I realized, didn't know Spain any better than we did. They'd mapped out their route to the next place where they would meet their riders, probably fifty or sixty kilometers away, but they had no reason to know about a city just ten kilometers away.

The next few minutes were a comedy. The drivers left Viana and got on a highway of some kind. I had no idea if we were going the right direction. We all kept pointing to signs and reading them out loud to each other. Finally, there was an exit sign that said Logroño.

"Logroño!" all four of us shouted. The road took us to some kind of modern industrial park, deserted at 8:00 on a Sunday morning. The drivers asked us if this was where we wanted to go.

"Cathedral?" I guessed, scrambling for my guidebook. Tall churches were generally easy to find, and surely the Camino passed the cathedral. We could find our way to the bus station from there.

But in a city of 150,000 people, even finding the historic section required driving in a few circles. Finally, the buildings started getting older. The streets narrowed. "Sí?" the man in the passenger seat asked, waving out the window.

"Sí," we said. I had no idea where we were, but we would navigate better on foot than this wild ride.

The Italians left us by the side of the road, while we thanked them over and over, and they assured us "No problem!" The whole trip, including all our wrong turns, took twenty minutes. Two hours later, while we killed time in the city square, we saw two women who had left Albergue Izar on foot while we were sorting out the van question. They had just arrived in town.

TRIPLES

Once the Italians were out of sight, we headed for the tallest steeple we could find, and embedded in the sidewalk in front of it was a familiar bronze shell. The Iglesia de Santiago del Real was unlocked but empty this early on a Sunday morning. Even the devoutly Catholic Spanish, it seemed, were not morning people, and mass didn't start until 10:00.

I stopped to study the relief carving in the tympanum over the cathedral's main door and recognized Santiago Matamoros, or Saint James the Moor Slayer. Normally along the Camino, Saint James was portrayed as a pilgrim with a floppy hat, staff, and some kind of scallop shell. This James was kind and welcoming, although the logic of his appearance always confused me. Was he dressed to visit his own grave?

In Spain, however, we often saw another version of this disciple of Jesus. The Matamoros was always on a horse, sword drawn, and often depicted with a pile of bodies—or body parts—under his feet.

The image comes from the legendary battle at Clavijo between the Spanish Christians and Muslim invaders from the south.

Following the arrows to Cardeñuela

Things were going poorly for the outnumbered Christians until the miraculous appearance of Saint James, no worse the wear for having been dead for eight hundred years. With an enormous sword and an immortal horse, he led the Christians to victory against the infidels.

The story of the battle spread across Spain, cementing the Spanish commitment to their patron saint and unifying the northern Christians in their fight against the Moors. The only problem was that the whole thing never happened.

I don't just mean that a long-dead saint didn't appear on angelic horseback to slay an opposing army. I mean that *the entire battle was fiction*. There was never a battle near the town of Clavijo, and the two armies in the story never met. The whole tale was wartime propaganda. It took historians centuries to prove it, and by then the legend was too deeply ingrained, and the images and artwork too prevalent, to undo.

I squirmed under this depiction of the humble, martyred James turned into a violent, nationalist weapon. I wished it wasn't so easy to see modern parallels.

I pushed the thought aside before it could develop past the vague discomfort that usually came with the intersection of church and politics. It was time to find the bus station and try our hands at being Camino tour guides.

Eric first met Ian through parkour, which they both practiced and taught, and their friendship had expanded over years into motorcycles, sushi, and a love of cutting sarcasm. We saw each other often at home but had never traveled together.

Ian had been in Europe for a week already, touring Belgian monastery breweries with other friends, and he'd added a few days onto the end of his vacation to meet us for what he kept calling a "walkabout."

Despite that, I assumed that he had a basic understanding of what the Camino was. Ian's usually a very research-driven, plan-making kind of guy. So I was more than a little surprised when he got off the bus from San Sebastian with a carry-on-sized rolling suitcase.

"Don't worry," he assured us. "It's got backpack straps."

Well, okay. I wasn't sure how that would work, but I was prepared to let Ian walk his own Camino. We carried (and rolled) our things out of the bus station and to a waiting cab, which Eric had arranged to take us to Nájera.

It was a strange thing, after being surrounded by strangers in a shared experience, to suddenly sit down with someone from "before." Ian was so familiar, yet so foreign in this setting. He was "home," but we were not at home.

I found myself feeling self-conscious for the first time in weeks. What would he think of us? Had we changed? I was conscious of my frumpy, probably smelly trekking clothes and my face that hadn't seen makeup for forty-seven days. The people we'd met so far knew only this version of me. They'd never seen what I looked like in "normal" life, so couldn't compare it. Couldn't judge it.

Of course I knew that Ian wasn't judging me. But he brought a new perspective to the trip, and about how Eric and I had been living.

Half an hour later, the cab let us out on the edge of Nájera. It reminded me of a story Jan had told us back in Conques, about how he saw "fake pilgrims" getting out of a cab, dabbing mud on their boots, and posing for pictures as if they'd struggled to get there. Now it felt like we were the fake pilgrims.

But no. The sin was not in taking the cab, but in pretending they didn't. So when we ran into Rory and Lis, the Kiwi/Dutch couple with the amazing dinner skills, on one of Nájera's narrow streets, we fessed up immediately. They were, of course, gracious.

They invited us to join them in the albergue where they were staying, but that brought up a new dilemma. Because Ian was on the Camino for only a few days, he hadn't acquired a credential. That meant that he wouldn't be allowed to stay in any of the municipal or church-run albergues along the way, which required credentials to prove that people were walking the Camino. The albergues weren't for casual tourists on wine-tasting tours of the region.

Ian wasn't comfortable with the idea of sharing a room with strangers, so private albergues were out, too. That was fine; dorm life wasn't for everyone. But it meant that we needed a very specific kind of accommodation: a "triple," a private room with three twin beds.

We found the Office of Tourism, and Eric went in and talked with the women behind the counter while Ian and I waited outside. He came out with a reservation for a room in a private guesthouse, but he also mentioned that they'd called a few places before they found this, the last room available in the city in our price range.

We met our host at the bar he owned, and he led us to an unmarked door in a nondescript building a few blocks away. I started to worry when the musty smell surrounded me as soon as he opened the door. The feeling got worse as he led us through a dirty lounge and up a dark staircase, motioning to a tiny single bathroom down the hall. Through another open doorway I could see a room with two bunk beds, and a thin, middle-aged man in his underwear glowered at me.

Our host waved us into a room barely big enough for its two twin beds covered with dirty pink bedspreads.

"No, no," I said, or maybe it was Eric. "*Necesitamos un triple.*"

"*Sí!*" The man, who didn't seem all that clean himself, waved away our concern. He went to the two twin beds and shoved them together, until they were almost touching the far wall of the room. Then he bent down and pulled out a rollaway cot from under a bed, fought it until it stood upright, touching the beds, and waved. "Triple."

There was maybe six inches of clearance between the now-one giant bed and any of the walls. I looked at Eric. Could he fix this?

No. This was the only room available in Nájera. He nodded, and the man left, urging us to come to his bar for a good pilgrim dinner.

Ian tried to be a good sport. This was his first night with us, and for all he knew we spent every night in moldy rooms with paper-thin walls and bathrooms that were dirtier than we were. When we explained that this was, by far, the worst room we'd seen in forty-nine days, he relaxed a little. We explained what we knew about "sometimes you lose," and how by tomorrow morning we'd be gone and this would be a bad memory and a good story. And then we got out of the smelly, terrible room.

Many pilgrims say that Nájera is one of their favorite towns of the Camino Francés. The capital of the medieval kingdom of Navarre is a beautiful collection of red stone buildings, surrounded by towering sandstone cliffs. We climbed to an overlook point and explored a few shallow caves in the rock cliffs and then came back down to see the Monasterio de Santa Maria de Real.

There was a three-euro admission fee to see the monastery, and I swallowed a little more of my pride and shelled it out. We were tour guides as well as tourists here, and if that meant paying admission to see a church, so be it. We got our money's worth, pausing to read every inscription on the tombs of the Spanish nobility and visiting the cave where Sancho the Great's son once saw Mary, the mother of Christ.

After an awkward night spent in close quarters in the Camino's worst triple room, we set out the next morning to walk through the vividly colored red-dirt hills of La Rioja, the province of Spain best known for its wine. The paths were wide but made of rocky dirt, and we quickly discovered why our trekking backpacks, with all of their mesh panels and weight-shifting hip straps, are so wonderful. Ian's rolling suitcase had thin straps that would maybe be helpful for getting it through an airport, but they were not at all appropriate or even adequate for hiking twenty-one kilometers on unpaved paths. Eric and Ian eventually took turns carrying the heavy, awkward bag that bit into their shoulders and bumped against their tailbones, and by the time we reached Santo Domingo de la Calzada, they both swore they would never carry it again.

If Saint James had punished us in Nájera for our "fake pilgrim" day in a cab, in Santo Domingo he rewarded us for the extra labor of carrying a difficult burden. We easily found our spacious room, which we'd reserved the night before using Ian's phone, in a *pensión* just outside the old city walls. And when we set out to explore, we found the town itself was quaint, medieval, and built around a great story.

Like most good seven-hundred-year-old legends, the details vary, but here's the basic idea: a devout German couple was making the pilgrimage to Santiago with their eighteen-year-old son. When they reached Santo Domingo, a local girl took a liking to the young man, who, being a good Christian, did not respond to her flirtations.

Hurt and angry, she put a silver cup into his bag and accused him of theft. The town believed her, and they hanged the innocent boy. His parents, although they were sad, went on to Santiago, where they prayed for their son. On their return trip, they again stopped in Santo Domingo, this time to visit their son's body one last time. To their surprise, the boy was still alive, and still hanging from his rope. (At this point I get stuck on how they didn't notice that part before they left, but again, it's best not to ask too many questions about these stories.) In some versions of the story, the boy told them that Saint James himself was holding him and keeping him alive.

The parents rushed to the town's sheriff and demanded that he release their son. The good sheriff was just sitting down to a hearty poultry dinner, and he laughed in their faces. "That boy is no more alive than these chickens on my plate," he's reported to have said.

Yep, that's all it took. The roasted birds sprouted back their feathers and beaks, got up, and started walking around the dinner table. Properly chastened, the sheriff went to the gallows and released the young German, who was pardoned and allowed to go home.

The story spread, lending credibility (of sorts) to the Santiago pilgrimage and drawing more pilgrims to Santo Domingo itself. The church petitioned the pope to allow them to display two birds, a hen and a rooster, inside the church as a symbol of the miracle, and the request was granted.

This time I didn't hesitate to shell out another few euros to visit a cathedral. I wanted to witness firsthand the glass box, set high in the wall of the sanctuary itself, where two bored-looking birds pecked around. They're rotated regularly, I'm told, from the coop supported by a local albergue.

The chickens were fun, and the museum attached to the cathedral was full of the early icons and images that built the Christian story. But the real surprise in Santo Domingo's cathedral was up a spiral staircase at the back of the sanctuary. There was no sign, and I probably wouldn't have climbed it if I was on my own. But I was in the wake of two urban explorers, and they had disappeared around the corner before I could utter my first "we'll get in trouble" squeak.

We didn't get in trouble, of course. The stairs were open to the public and led to a few of the defensive corridors that surround the cathedral, which had doubled as a fortress and protected more than just the souls of its parishioners. Another set of stairs took us all the way up to a balcony on the roof. Santo Domingo's old city spread around us, its defensive walls now supporting a colony of storks.

We came down and snacked on cookies shaped like chickens, because commerce thrives on good stories as much as I do, and then over dinner set out the plan for arranging baggage service for Ian's terrible bag.

In both France and Spain there were luggage service companies that moved pilgrims' bags from town to town. The operation ran surprisingly smoothly. A pilgrim would pick up a company-provided tag in the lobby of wherever they were staying and write the address of the town and accommodation where they wanted the bag delivered the next day. They'd put a small amount of cash in the attached envelope and call the company to schedule a pickup. The next morning they'd leave their bag in the lobby. A driver would pick the bag up and deliver it to its destination, where it would be waiting when the pilgrim arrived on foot.

This whole enterprise says a lot about the level of trust on the Camino, and the relative safety of a pilgrim's personal possessions while they're there.

Eric and I decided not to ship our packs ahead with Ian's. The ten kilograms that had felt like a boulder to me the first week now nestled into its familiar place on my hips and shoulders, and I barely noticed it.

Well, I *thought* I barely noticed. With three people and only two packs, we agreed to rotate every hour, so that every third hour each of us could walk without one. And walking without a pack was pretty great. I could practically skip up hills. Okay, not that. But I was a lot faster. Which was good, because now I needed to keep up with two mountain goats.

We were a clique of three, meandering across a rolling countryside. We passed the enormous sign welcoming us to the autonomous province of Castile y León. There were fewer vineyards here than in La Rioja, and more fields of blowing grasses. Red poppies nodded to us from the bright green expanses, the contrast in color almost blinding. Crumbling ruins of hermitages and chapels hovered above us, carved dramatically right into the rocky cliffs.

We walked together and talked about serious things and silly things. We revisited the conversations about monasteries, dreamed about an actual Radio Camino podcast, and bantered in fake British accents for hours. The only thing we didn't talk about was what was happening at home. Eric and I had been strict with our "no email, no social media, no communication" rules, and Ian honored that we were still on sabbatical. Whatever the latest drama at work, or the latest gossip about friends, might be, it would wait until we got home.

We covered thirty-one kilometers faster than I'd ever walked that far before, with only two short coffee breaks. When we reached the tiny town of Espinosa, I was limping and ready to put my feet up.

But Espinosa was cerrado. This was, to say the least, unexpected. Eric had called the private albergue in Espinosa the night before to reserve our triple. He had spoken to someone who confirmed the reservation. Ian had sent his bag to that address. But when we arrived midafternoon, there was no one there, just a handwritten sign on the albergue door that said "Closed for rest."

They couldn't be closed. We had reservations! And they had Ian's bag! We knocked, first politely and then insistently. We called the phone number and heard it ring inside, unanswered.

And it wasn't just the pensión that was closed. I wandered through the town, which should have had a population of about forty, and noticed that the streets, pretty and shaded, were deserted. The windows in all the buildings were closed. Getting a little desperate, I knocked on random doors of houses. No one answered.

The entire town was cerrado, for rest. This was a possibility we'd never considered.

We waited for a while, tired and frustrated, to see if anyone showed up, but no one did. There was nothing we could do but walk to the next town, four kilometers farther up the road. We were a lot quieter that last hour. The guys graciously didn't point out when it was my turn to carry a pack.

The busy commercial road that ran down the center of Villafranca de Montes de Oca didn't seem appealing, but at least all of the heavy trucks passing through meant there were people. We followed a sign up a steep side road to the San Anton Albad, a luxury hotel built on the site of a former pilgrim hospital. The owner had once walked the Camino, according to the guidebook, and so also provided a pilgrim albergue on the property.

We staggered into a lobby too nice for our dusty appearance, and I fell into an antique chair probably older than my country. Eric and Ian handled negotiations at the desk. The albergue was full; we weren't the only pilgrims arriving that afternoon complaining that they'd planned to stay in Espinosa. But the hotel had a room available, and we could add a cot to make it a triple. There was also a pilgrim menu in the dining room that night and a full breakfast buffet.

Eric and I paid more for that room than we had the three previous nights combined, but we had few other choices. Also, the hotel was totally worth it. The rooms were well furnished, the beds comfortable, and the historical renovation beautiful. The real surprise for a backpacking pilgrim like me was that our bathroom not only had fresh white towels—a luxury itself for a person used to drying on a washcloth-sized travel towel—but also soap, shampoo, and even conditioner. I took a decadently long shower while the guys went in search of Ian's bag.

They'd called the baggage service company, which reported that they'd also been surprised by the closed town of Espinosa. The baggage driver had done the logical thing and brought Ian's bag to the next town, correctly assuming that's where we would end up, and left it at Villafranca de Montes de Oca's municipal albergue.

Ian and Eric tracked down the building a few blocks away, but the hospitalera at the door was anything but hospitable. She said, as far as Eric could translate, that she reserved beds for every bag that arrived, and she was angry that Ian was staying somewhere else. She demanded that he pay five euros for the bed he wouldn't use.

Eric tried to argue against the ridiculous claim. He pointed out that Ian hadn't requested the bag be sent here, and that every baggage transfer slip says in big letters that sending a bag does not equal a reservation, and that even if Ian wanted to stay she wouldn't let him, because he didn't have a credential. The woman wouldn't budge. She was going to hold the bag hostage until someone gave her money. So Ian handed over the ransom, got his bag, and they left with her still yelling at them.

By the time they got back, I'd found the hotel's well-appointed bar, complete with live peacocks in the garden and a hilariously melodramatic Spanish telenovela on TV. We all sank into the deep leather couches and sipped sangria while the stress and muscle pain faded away. Only the promise of food lured us out of those seats and into the dining room, where we were served an elaborate three-course dinner, with no patatas fritas in sight.

In three days we'd gone from our dirtiest, smelliest, most terrible room of the entire Camino, to the nicest, most luxurious. We'd also gone from a day without walking at all to our longest walking day. Saint James's rewards felt appropriate.

The next morning, we once again trusted Ian's suitcase to baggage service and passed through the heavily wooded de Oca mountains, where bandits used to prey on pilgrims, and then back into the open countryside. The conversation stayed light, the breaks stayed short, and by early afternoon we were in a private albergue in the tiny hamlet of Cardeñuela. It was a quirky building, all bright paint and big patios and small indoor spaces. We'd requested a private room with two bunk beds, and the room we were given was exactly wide enough for two beds—I had to turn sideways to squeeze between them. But it was clean, and the people were friendly.

While we lounged outside in the afternoon, one of the hospitaleros, who only spoke Spanish, came to find Eric. All he understood was that they needed someone to translate Spanish to English for one of their guests, who had a medical emergency. My husband, ever helpful if not exactly fluent, agreed to try.

It turned out the woman, an American, had fallen on the steep, rocky ascent after Atapuerca. She'd arrived at the albergue with a bloody face, and the hospitaleros insisted she go to the emergency clinic in a nearby town. Now the clinic was calling for help, because the woman spoke no Spanish, and they spoke no English. Eric pieced together that they needed to know basic medical information, like allergies, and he helped her get things more or less sorted out. The woman returned in time for dinner with a few stitches on her face, and I wondered again how the Black-Eyed B's were doing.

Burgos was only three hours away, but Ian's train the next day left at noon, so we left early, as the sun was just rising. The final kilometers into Burgos, a city big enough to have its own airport, inevitably took us through noisy, industrial, ugly suburbs. The Camino followed a major arterial road full of warehouses and traffic—hardly the inspiring ending I might have hoped for our friend's Camino adventure, but perhaps he already had enough stories to tell. Either way, we made it into the medieval, beautiful part of the city in time for a last leisurely breakfast together before Ian hailed a cab and started his journey home.

With five hundred kilometers of our own journey still to go, Eric and I stood under the white marble arch of the old city and waved goodbye.

And then, once again, there were two.

PART III

A GIFT TO THE SOUL

Morning sun pushes away the mist on the final climb to O'Cebreiro.

THE MESETA

With Ian safely on his way back to the States, Eric and I set out to find the biggest, cheapest albergue in the city. We arrived an hour before it opened but found a line of pilgrims already sprawled along the side of the building. These were the walkers who set out before dawn, I realized. For some, it was so that they could hike in the cooler morning temperatures. Others walked early so that they could get to the albergues first, do their laundry first, eat their dinner first, sleep first, and then do it all again.

Eric and I settled into line without saying much. Four days with Ian had been fun, but also a wall of words from the time we woke to the time we slept. Two natural introverts, we needed a quiet afternoon to recharge.

Eric took off as soon as we were checked in, saying something about shopping. I'd just finished the laundry when he came back. "It's a city. You'll like it," he said, before he climbed onto his bed to nap.

He was right. I felt at home in the narrow, pedestrian-clogged streets of Burgos. The city felt cosmopolitan, more formal than Pamplona but just as vibrant. I wandered, happily invisible in a crowd, through wide city squares where bronze statues and stone fountains shared space with acres of benches and signs promising free Wi-Fi. I had no reason to turn on my phone, no interest

Entering the Meseta

in shopping, and after a week of tourism I had no desire to pay for another crowded cathedral tour, so once I'd explored a little, I happily sat on a bench, eating ice cream and watching the crowds.

As the afternoon shadows started to lengthen, I went back to our albergue to check on Eric, who was still asleep. I took my journal to an outdoor cafe table, which is where Mette found me. The hours of solitude had revived me, and I was happy to see our Danish friend. My first encounter with her, when I'd still been sick in Viana, was a bit of a blur, but I'd walked with her for a while after our fancy hotel night in Villafranca de Montes de Oca and enjoyed her company.

Mette was exploring Burgos with another solo walker she'd befriended, a tall blond man with a beard and a straw hat, and we ordered a round of drinks. Nic was Swiss and comfortably fluent in English. He'd learned it, he said, by listening to Bruce Springsteen songs and watching American movies. He was about our age, married with a couple of kids at home. Walking the Camino had been a dream of his for many years, and now here he was.

Eric woke up and joined us as one small beer became two. We toasted our Camino adventures so far and talked about what we thought the Meseta would bring.

When people who've never seen it think about the Camino de Santiago, most of them picture the Meseta. While the Camino Francés crosses mountain ranges and hundreds of kilometers of rolling hills, the most popular photos always seem to be of the flat, dry, open plateau.

The Meseta is the bread basket of Europe, Spain's equivalent to the American Great Plains. The climate is ideal for sheep ranches and vast fields of cereal crops, which can create monotonous scenery. There are few towns or cultural distractions, and it's brutally hot in the summer and bitterly cold in the winter. Pilgrims either love it or hate it.

I'd heard people say that the Meseta was the most meaningful part of their whole Camino pilgrimage. Without all the distractions, they had time for their deepest reflections. On the other hand, I heard a lot of complaints about the monotony. Time-strapped or destination-oriented pilgrims often hopped a bus and skipped the Meseta altogether. One creative and blister-prone pair of Americans we met rented bicycles in Burgos and rode across the Meseta to León, sparing their feet and cutting the time in half.

I wanted to love the Meseta. It wasn't just because I reveled in the thought of a week without hills, though that helped. I wanted the Meseta to help me reconnect to a Camino rhythm. The past weeks had felt like a series of interruptions, first adjusting to crowds and shorter distances, then illnesses, and then the change in focus with Ian. I'd lost the quiet, predictable feeling of *walk, eat, sleep, repeat.*

The next morning Eric and I left Burgos at dawn. The path took us through a seminary campus and out of the city on a road lined with cottonwood trees, their "fluff" filling the streets in drifts that could have been snow if it wasn't a comfortable sixty degrees. We navigated a quiet residential neighborhood, turned a corner, and there it was: an unbroken vista of green and a single dirt path that stretched all the way to the horizon.

We'd found the Meseta.

As we started to descend to the plain, we ran into Mette and Nic, resting on a stone wall by the side of the road. We chatted for a while, but I was anxious to move on to the next village, where I was looking forward to coffee and a bathroom.

I could already tell the next few days would challenge my "pee with a tree" needs. Although there were ten times more people walking the Way of Saint James in Spain than in France—or perhaps because of it—Spanish towns rarely provided public WCs. Most pilgrims, including me, tried to follow a "rent a bathroom" model: we walked for a couple of hours and stopped at a cafe for a coffee and a chance to use the facilities, then walked a couple more hours and stopped again for a pastry or *tortilla patata* and a chance to use the facilities. It was a strange way to prop up the economy, but it worked.

Of course, there were times when the next town was just too far away. I still carried a few squares of toilet paper in my pocket just in case. And most of the men I met didn't bother waiting for a cafe to appear. For better or not, there are a lot of people doing their business in the olive groves and vineyards of Spain.

During our coffee/bathroom stop that morning, Eric met a French pilgrim who walked fast and was happy to answer my husband's many questions about linguistics. They took off together, and by the end of the day Eric knew the French names for more plants and crops than I could identify in English.

I intentionally slowed down and walked alone. Most of the time I could see them ahead of me, but instead of feeling abandoned or inept, I enjoyed the freedom of walking my own pace. The occasional pilgrim would pass me with a friendly "*Buen Camino*," and I would reply in kind, but otherwise, the open land was all mine.

I could just walk.

Our first night on the Meseta was about as different from Burgos as I could imagine. There was a single street with a collection of one- and two-story brick houses, a church, and a bar. Our private, recently renovated albergue had a well-watered lawn in the backyard, a vending machine with one-euro beers, and a full kitchen. It was an ideal setup for a home-cooked dinner, except that Hornillos didn't have a market, and we weren't carrying enough food for a meal. So after a lazy afternoon, we set out for the bar with Nic and Mette, who had caught up to us on the edge of town and were also staying in our albergue.

Unfortunately, there were more pilgrims staying in town than there were seats in the bar, and the dining room dished up the generic *menu del día* without hospitality while a line stretched out the door. I looked at the plate of unidentifiable meat and limp French fries and started to doubt my enthusiasm about the Meseta.

The next day passed much the same as the last, as we continued to follow the lone dirt road across endless expanses of open fields. The only breaks in the landscape came from the clusters of wind turbines in the distance.

There was no shade, but the temperature stayed cool enough to not be uncomfortable, and we walked with Nic and Mette for most of the day. Eric and Nic would go ahead, both of them comfortable at a faster pace, while Mette and I took our time behind them. We'd all meet in a town for a coffee/bathroom, and when we took off again, Nic would slow down to chat with me and Eric walked with Mette.

It was sometime that afternoon, two full days after he'd met us, when I said something that made Nic realize Eric and I were married. "But I never see you hugging or kissing each other!" he exclaimed, and I had to stop walking because I was laughing so hard.

Marriage on the Camino was a different kind of life, I told him. In the past two months Eric and I had spent more hours together than we ever would at home, and we relied on each other more deeply for companionship as well as basic practical support. At the same time, we slept on bunk beds and rarely had real privacy.

Being pilgrims on the Camino built our intimacy, I said, but most people appreciated that we weren't hugging and kissing in the common sleeping areas.

The hours passed quickly, and my feet were barely starting to protest when we passed under the arches of the crumbling San Anton monastery. There was a primitive albergue here, I'd heard. Unfortunately for us, it didn't open until June, which was still a few days away, so we continued to Castrojeriz, a sleepy village curled around the foot of a hill, under photogenic castle ruins.

We stopped at the first private albergue in town. Unlike the modern, almost Ikea-inspired dorm of the previous night, this was a worn-but-cared-for refuge in an old rowhouse along the main street. The hospitalero offered our group of four a private room on the lower level, with windows that opened over the neighbor's dirt yard. We threw some of our stale bread down to the chickens that lived there and watched them peck at the manna from heaven.

While my roommates went out to explore, I chose to nap. I didn't have high expectations for the dusty, monochromatic town. The distinctive *iglesia* we'd passed charged admission, and it was too hot to climb the hill to check out the castle ruins. But I woke up hungry and restless, so I wandered the streets, finding only clusters of unfamiliar pilgrims lounging in the sun.

Eventually I found Eric in a place called the Hospital del Alma—the hospital of the soul. I never would have noticed it in the row of identical sandstone houses, but something about the open door drew Eric in, and he'd discovered an oasis—an indoor version of the many shaded parks and open spaces we'd found in France, but with a distinctive hippie vibe that felt more at home in Spain.

There were odd altars and rustic artwork spread out through a warren of rooms, along with deep couches and shelves of books in multiple languages. A backyard full of sculptures led to a grotto in a rocky hillside. We caught glimpses of an older man moving through the yard, but he never approached us, and otherwise we were alone.

It took me a while to settle in this place. My American, full-speed-ahead, cynical side wanted to blow past it. My soul was just fine, thanks. I didn't need the ministrations of piped-in Gregorian chants, or wind chimes, or silence. Why would someone dedicate so much space to a place that had no obvious purpose? What did this "hospital of the soul" *do*, anyway?

But my pilgrim side operated at another speed. There was nothing else for me to "blow past it" to, because there was nothing more important that afternoon than to sit in silence with my husband and listen to the wind chimes while my body recovered from the exertion of the morning.

Eric and I had been throwing around the phrase "practice acceptance" a lot for the past few days—well, mostly he'd been saying it to me, usually when I got indignant about an inconvenience or disruption. "Practice acceptance," so far, had meant putting up with noisy neighbors and poor service and yet another plate of bland chicken. It was a legitimate and necessary reminder for me to live in peace with what I couldn't control.

As much as I pretended that I was living a spontaneous and present life on the Camino, the truth was that I kept trying to control and plan my experience. I kept reading the guidebooks and anticipating what I would do and feel. Yet no matter how much I planned, the Camino continued to surprise me with things like this place.

There was another side of acceptance, I realized, as I sat in the hippie meditation room in a tiny Spanish town in the middle of nowhere. There were plenty of disappointments that required conscious acceptance, but there were also gifts. Practicing acceptance meant sinking into this couch, sipping cool water provided by an anonymous stranger, and experiencing generosity offered to pilgrims of the Way, just because we were here.

I thought of the nuns in Estaing, now more than a month in the past, who had given us not only a bed and dinner, but invited us into their intimate moments of worship. I remembered the abuelo in Viana, just a week ago, who had shared his own special herbs and made sure we had a way to keep moving forward when we were weak. These gifts had pushed me into places where I wasn't comfortable.

Practicing acceptance was more than suffering disappointments. It was also about letting go of my deep desire to predict and prepare for what came next. It was being open to the unexpected, whatever form that took.

This wasn't a new revelation. I'd been working over this same idea, and relearning this same lesson, since the day we left Le Puy and found the Montbonnet gîte closed. And with 450 kilometers still to Santiago, I knew I would probably have to learn it again. But there in the Hospital del Alma, I unpeeled another finger from the need for control I held so closely, and then I sank back to listen to the wind chimes.

Sometimes, though, acceptance wasn't an option.

As we approached Fromista with Mette and Nic the next afternoon, I was playing the "where will we stay?" game. We no longer needed to make reservations for beds, but I'd learned it was a good idea to pick out a specific destination before we arrived in a town hungry (Eric), tired (me), and not emotionally ready to be directionless in a strange place (both of us). So every day during a coffee/bathroom break, I'd consult the guidebook and pick the albergue that sounded best. Sometimes my choice was based on the description or location and sometimes it was as arbitrary as the most interesting name. Then, when we arrived, Eric handled the face-to-face communication.

When I asked about our companions' plans for Fromista, they were vague. "We will see where you are staying," Nic said in his precise, contraction-less English. Mette agreed. I wasn't comfortable being responsible for the lodging needs of four people, but I couldn't think of a polite way to suggest that our friends should make their own plans, so I accepted it.

My first choice in Fromista was a private albergue on the out-skirts of town. On paper, it looked good, but when we got there, it felt dark and empty. Eric asked the man behind the bar to show us the rooms. They were dingy and windowless, and something about the place felt off. Our companions were noncommittal, but I met Eric's eye and shook my head, just a little. He under-stood and apologized to the man, gesturing to me as I stood in the doorway, frowning and playing the part of the hard-to-please wife. It was the first time we'd ever walked away from an albergue, but Nic and Mette followed without complaint.

Our next stop was a private albergue closer to town. It looked perfect on the outside, with a lovely walled terrace and soft grass that my feet begged to sink into. But I noticed a lot of signs posted about: NO shoes inside. NO laundry in this area. NO food in that area. NO lights on after this time. Every albergue had rules, and for the sake of a clean bed and shower I'd overlooked a lack of warmth plenty of times before. But when Eric, wary after our last experience, asked the man behind the desk if we could see the dorm room before committing, the hospitalero turned hostile. His albergue was full every night, he said, and he wasn't going to show us anything unless we paid him.

For the second time, we walked away from an albergue. For the second time, our companions followed without comment.

My patience was wearing out. I was tired. I was hungry. I wanted to sit down and take off my backpack. I wanted everyone to stop waiting for me to make decisions. But none of that would happen until I found a bed. I pointed across the plaza to a random building that said *hostal*. "There."

Eric, equally tired but willing to do his part in our travel dance, knocked on the door and spoke to the woman who answered, who was thankfully kind. She had only one room left with a *matrimonio* bed, she said. It was twice our normal budget.

"We'll take it," I said without consulting anyone. Eric and I hadn't shared a bed since Pamplona, two weeks earlier. And our friends needed encouragement to take their own initiative. It was easy to get caught in the pattern of trusting others to make decisions, but I wasn't a tour guide.

Of course, no one left Mette and Nic standing on the street. The hostal's owner called someone and located a nearby—and, to serve me right, more affordable—pensión with two single rooms. The four of us made plans to meet again for dinner.

A shower and rest improved my attitude, and a couple of hours later Eric and I were relaxing in the town square and hoping that my favorite Italian cowboy, a man we called Spaghetti Western, would come by. This had become a daily event and the high point of my afternoons for at least a week.

In the swirl of hundreds of Camino pilgrims, there are always a few distinctive characters that we all recognize and talk about. In France we had Jan. Strangers without a common language could say "Jan" and imitate his distinctive walk, his big bag, and his booming voice, and everyone knew who he was. The Dutchman gave us a shared experience.

We had lost Jan, but in Spain we had Spaghetti Western. I never learned his real name. I think that would have ruined it. He was tall and thin, with skin tanned like leather. He always wore white—tight jeans, button-down shirt, and wide-brimmed hat—with a purple scarf tied jauntily around his neck. He woke late and walked late, and always made an entrance into town after most other pilgrims were settled. Spaghetti Western smoked cigarillos while he walked, and he carried a pocket-sized radio that played, of course, opera. He didn't bother with headphones.

"*Buongiorno, signora,*" he would boom every time he saw me. He made each word at least four syllables. That afternoon, for some reason, he singled me out for more than a "good day." "You are American," he said. He asked where I lived and what I did for work.

Not sure how well "publishing consultant" would translate, I simplified. "I help people write books."

"You're a writer," he boomed. "You will write a book about me someday."

I assured him that I would, and he swaggered on. From then on, when he saw me, it was "Buongiorno, Signora Writer."

That night Mette seemed distracted, sometimes on the verge of tears. Her shoulder was bothering her, she said. Remembering the nights when my pain stayed near the surface, I tried to distract her by talking about the happiest thing I could think of: storks.

Our friends thought it was funny that I was so fascinated by the birds. "In Switzerland, we tell our children that storks bring new babies," Nic told me.

"Oh, we have that story, too," I assured him.

"But you told me you have no storks in America. How can they bring babies?"

Huh. I'd never thought about that. "Well," I told him, "we've never seen Santa Claus or the Easter Bunny, either, but we believe they bring presents." That started a conversation about other holiday traditions, and I felt like the tension from the afternoon had cleared. But at the end of the night, when Mette suggested that we exchange email addresses, I suspected this was the last time we would see her.

Eric and I walked by ourselves the next day, taking a shaded variant route that curved away from the *senda*, the main trail that paralleled a major roadway. We ran into Nic that evening in Carrion de los Condes and realized that none of us had seen Mette. Later, she sent an email saying she'd walked out of Fromista but was in so much pain she had to stop. Her Camino was over. She took a cab to León, where she stayed for a few days, and then went home to Denmark. It was a healthy decision for her, but another abrupt goodbye for the rest of us.

Nic had checked into a private pensión in Carrion, while Eric and I made up for the previous night's splurge by checking into the town's main albergue, run by a group of kind Catholic nuns and supported by friendly American volunteers. The building was crowded, and for some reason that afternoon the pilgrims seemed especially thoughtless.

This was something I'd noticed a few times before in the larger albergues. The more people there were in a space, the less we all seemed to be aware of one another. Eric was in the kitchen when a young man breezed in and lit his cigarette on the glass-top stove burner. A woman in our room lay on her bed and talked loudly on her phone until well after 10:00, while others were obviously trying to sleep. People turned on lights, left doors open, cut in line, left a mess, and woke everyone up by packing noisily long before dawn.

In the smaller albergues, which were often privately owned, pilgrims seemed more respectful of one another. Maybe it was because in smaller groups each person's behavior was more obvious. Maybe the private owners were more involved in keeping order. Maybe it was because we had more opportunities to interact with everyone and see ourselves as fellow human beings. But after Carrion de los Condes, Eric and I always tried to find the private albergues; the extra euro or two we spent per night was worth it.

From that point on, Nic and Eric and I were a Camino family of three.

Walking, for me, became an almost pleasant experience. We established a pattern. We'd often split apart during the day, or two of us would walk together while one went ahead or lingered behind, catching some solitary time or talking with someone new. Every afternoon, we'd meet in our destination town, usually a sleepy, remote village where there wasn't much to do except drink *tinto de verano*—red wine and lemon soda, kind of a simplified sangria—and share stories. Nic was a natural entertainer, aware of both how to tell a good story and when to ask a question to draw out another person. We learned a lot about one another in a short period of time, while the landscape of the Meseta shifted from greens to browns and the fields of poppies gave way to dusty pastures for distant sheep.

We were with Nic and Vivianna, a young Korean exchange student who could shift from fluent English to Spanish to Korean without taking a breath, when we arrived in Bercianos de Real Camino—a tiny, sunbaked village where many of the houses were made from mud and straw. Once we were settled in our albergue, I decided to walk around town and see what was there. The others wisely stayed in the shade of the albergue courtyard.

The town was deserted and felt like one of those dream sequences in the movies where a person walks down the middle of an empty street, hyper-saturated with color but completely silent. There was even a tumbleweed drifting across the road.

The only human I saw was an old woman, wearing a traditional black dress and headscarf, sitting on a bench outside an open door. She never moved and never acknowledged me. She didn't even blink when I walked by. The more I think about it, the more I wonder if I imagined her. The Meseta is that kind of place.

All told, it took us eight days to cross the Meseta, at a steady but not grueling pace. We met people who did it much faster, sometimes walking through the night to cover more kilometers. But our pace suited us. It gave us time to experience corners of life in Spain's "flyover" country and to linger over long conversations. We heard stories from around the world and probably drank our body weight in cheap beer and sangria.

We rediscovered our Camino rhythm. I can't imagine why anyone would choose to skip it.

DESAYUNO, DESAY-DOS

The Meseta ended as abruptly as it began. One day we walked with Nic across kilometers of open space. The next morning we pounded the pavement past car dealerships in the suburbs of León. We all were sleep deprived after a rough night in a hot, stuffy albergue, where the man in the bunk two feet from me talked in his sleep. At 2:00 in the morning he'd suddenly shouted, in English, "Well, I'll find someone else then!"

Snoring, by then, was to be expected. We slept in rooms of between ten and fifty people, many of them past middle age. We were in unfamiliar and often uncomfortable beds, with minimal pillows. Most of us enjoyed the complimentary tinto that accompanied every pilgrim dinner. So we all, including me, snored in an asynchronous chorus throughout the night.

Later, I walked for a couple of hours with a woman who complained about the snoring. Just to be clear, she complained a lot. To neutralize her, I made my "everyone snores" case.

"Not me," she said. "I never snore."

"Well . . . " This came from another pilgrim in earshot—a kind, always positive person who'd shared many rooms with this woman. "Actually, you do. Most nights, in fact, after you've been asleep for a while." The complainer was aghast and defensive, but she couldn't dispute the testimony. She immediately changed the subject.

So yes, everyone snores. Some lighter sleepers wore earplugs to cover the sound, but after long days in the sun and a lifetime of living in noisy cities, it rarely kept me awake. Shouting in the middle of the night, on the other hand, was both unusual and really hard to sleep through.

Understandably, then, our group of three was tired and cranky as we navigated the busy outskirts of León. It took most of the morning before the cars disappeared, the streets narrowed, and the older, pedestrian-friendly heart of the city surrounded us.

León is not the biggest or the oldest city on the Camino, but my first impression was that it was the most *alive* city. Tourists and locals mingled. Rowdy groups of bachelor and bachelorette parties wove among pilgrims with backpacks and dozens of women in improbably high heels who navigated the cobblestone streets without a single turned ankle.

I soaked it all in as we approached the Plaza Regala and the visual centerpiece of León, the soaring cathedral. We gaped at it from the outside, but it wasn't time for sightseeing yet. First, we needed to clear the daily hurdle of finding a place to stay.

It was an important night for our little Camino family, and not only because it was a Friday in a tourist-filled city. Though no one had said it, we knew it was likely our last night together. Eric and I were about to make the mental shift back into tour guide mode, preparing for the arrival of our second American guest the next day.

We'd met Emily through her work as a physical therapist and then bonded over her fast-talking New Jersey style and love of impulsive adventures. I'd casually thrown out my "so come visit us in Spain" offer just two weeks before we left the country, and she jumped at the idea. Her cousin Heather lived in England, and Emily worked out a plan for them both to join us for a few days, while also catching up with each other.

Eric and I would take Saturday as a rest day to await their arrival and explore the city with them, so we wanted to splurge on a hotel room where we could sleep late. Nic, as always, was content to tag along wherever we went. By this point I was used to making plans for three, and I half wondered if he would linger in León the next day with us as well.

Finding a private room in a city, though, turned out to be difficult on a summer weekend. We went to the Office of Tourism, but for the first time in our experience, the staff wouldn't help us make a reservation. The woman behind the desk handed us a map with all the pensións and hostals in the city, but she refused to call anyone on the list to ask about availability. Perhaps that was the policy in León, or maybe she just didn't want to.

This was one of those times when it would have been handy to break our no-phone rule and do some internet sleuthing. Surely there was an app for that. But the old city area was small, and we had a map. We agreed to try it on foot first.

No one answered the bell at the first pensión, and the second reported they were fully booked. On our third try, we lucked out. We found a tall, narrow hotel tucked into an alley half a block from the cathedral, with both a single room for Nic and a matrimonio for us. We went our separate ways to clean up and settle in. Eric doesn't get energized by cities the way I do, so he stayed in the room while I explored. Down a narrow street and past the ruins of the original Roman city walls, I found the Basilica of Isidoro, where people worshiped and prayed under pastel-painted Romanesque arches and simple architecture. A brochure said that parts of the building were original to the 1056 construction. A few blocks away I found the Casa de los Botines, a mansion designed eight hundred years later by Spain's favorite modern architect, Antoni Gaudi, for a family of shoe manufacturers. In between were museums, cafes, and parks where food and craft vendors were setting up stalls for some kind of party. I decided I could spend a week in León and not see everything there.

It was late afternoon when I ran into Nic and stopped to join him for a drink, which became two. He seemed pensive. He told me he didn't have time for a rest day, so he would leave León in the morning. We both knew that meant we were saying goodbye. With our American friends in tow, we wouldn't be able to catch up to him.

I hated to see him go, but at least we still had one more night to spend together. When Eric came downstairs, we all enjoyed a fancy dinner at the outdoor cafe under our hotel. Nic ordered *pulpo*, the specialty of the region, and they brought him what appeared to be an entire octopus, head and all, on a plate. We weren't sure if we were supposed to eat the head, but the legs were delicious.

We said goodbye with long hugs, hearts full of gratitude, and no promises for the future. As I expected, we didn't see Nic again.

Eric and I slept until the decadent hour of 9:00 the next morning and breakfasted like true tourists on strong coffee and churros before it was time to be pilgrims again. We gathered our things from the hotel and went to check in at the city's primary albergue, run by an order of Benedictine nuns. Emily and Heather were both budget conscious and game to share rooms with strangers, and they could get Camino credentials from the Benedictines when they arrived.

When we handed over our credentials to be stamped, the albergue volunteer looked at us. "Are you married?" I thought he was just being polite, but it turned out that the Albergue Santa Maria, like the convent back in Estaing so many weeks ago, organized its guests. There was a dorm for men, one for women, and one for couples traveling together.

Once the daily chores were done, we lazed around the cobblestone square until Emily and Heather arrived. When they were settled in the women's dorm, the four of us set out to see the city, starting with the cathedral of León and its almost twenty thousand square feet of stained glass.

I barely felt my old "don't pay to see a church" reaction, because there was little that was churchlike about the Cathedral of Santa Maria, with its ticket booth and mobs of tourists milling around, listening to self-guided audio tours in multiple languages. It was more like a museum of medieval art and architecture that happened to have a religious theme. And it was magnificent art; the elaborate windows alone were worth the price of admission.

Back on the streets of León, we found ourselves caught in the revelry of a Saturday night. A marching band competition filled a square first built by the Romans. A few blocks away, young men and women in baggy sweatpants gave a drum-accompanied demonstration of capoeira, a Brazilian martial art, while across the street couples in black ties and formal dresses assembled in front of the cathedral, now closed to tourists, for a series of what must have been incredibly short and expensive weddings.

When the noise got to be too much, we wandered back toward our albergue, only to discover the square in front of it had been transformed into an outdoor *fútbol* party. All afternoon we'd seen groups of enthusiastic sports fans roaming the city, getting ready to watch Barcelona's team play an important match. Now our cobbled square, which had been empty throughout the afternoon, was filled with tables and chairs, all pointed toward the big-screen TVs that resourceful bar owners set up in their windows.

We joined the rowdy crowd, cheering for Barcelona over Italy, while a few yards away two older nuns in wimples moved from window to window in the convent, hanging red and green buntings from the windows. The next day, someone said, was the Feast of Corpus Christi. There would be a parade and a festival in the church, if we wanted to stay.

No, I thought, one rest day here was enough. I loved the energy of León and the mashup of old and new around every corner, but it was time to walk again. Later, as I lay in bed under an open window and listened to the city's energy, I realized this was our sixtieth day on the Camino. Walking twenty-five kilometers a day was normal now, and the holes in my shirts and my shoes were well earned. I was a Camino pilgrim, and that magnet pulling me west was strong.

I woke at 5:00 the next morning to the happy songs of a drunken reveler singing rowdily outside. Two hours later, the fútbol fans were all in bed, and the golden dawn belonged to pilgrims. Our group of four wound through León as sunlight reflected off the recently washed streets. We paused to pay our respects to the statue of the Camino pilgrim outside the famous Parador Hotel and then navigated another set of less-than-lovely suburbs. Soon enough, the land opened up, and we walked over rough dirt tracks through scrubby fields. It wasn't the most beautiful part of the Camino, but the walking was easy, and Emily and Heather's family gossip easily carried us the twenty kilometers to Mazarife.

Our Camino pace was changing again. Heather would walk with us only to Astorga, about fifty kilometers from León, but she had three days to cover the distance. Rather than walking for two days and then taking an unnecessary rest day in Astorga, we all agreed to keep our daily distances short and linger to explore the country along the way.

That's how we ended up approaching Mazarife just as the explosions started. At first, I thought they were gunshots. Was someone hunting in June? My second guess—or maybe someone else suggested it—was that a farmer was shooting blanks in order to frighten birds off the crops. That made more sense, and I just hoped we didn't look like birds.

As we checked into our small albergue, our hospitalera mentioned that the Corpus Christi parade would start after the noon mass. None of us knew what Corpus Christi was about, but we were game for a parade. So once we showed Emily and Heather how to "do the things," and all our wet clothes were hanging on the outdoor lines, we set off to explore.

We found the church set above the small town square, a modest building with three giant stork nests in the belfry. There were a few other people lounging or leaning in the limited shade. They didn't say anything, but there was anticipation in the hot summer air.

Shortly after we arrived, a solemn-faced band of men and women with bagpipes and wind instruments assembled and waited. They wore traditional dress, the women in long skirts and head scarves, the men in vests and jaunty red cummerbunds. Finally, the bells in the tower began to rock, just a little at first, and then with such vigor that they spun all the way around in noisy celebration of . . . well, whatever Corpus Christi celebrated. The storks flew away. The church doors swung open, and the parade started.

First there were about a dozen children carrying a litter with a statue of baby Jesus. Then four women, in perfect Sunday dresses and heels, carried a litter with a statue of the Virgin Mary. Then the priest, swinging his censer, led four men carrying a litter with a crucified Jesus. The rest of the congregation followed, all wearing their Sunday best. The band moved in to take up the rear.

A man walked in front of the children, and I saw that he was holding a long tube. He fiddled with it, and then *boom*, we had found the source of those explosions. Fireworks. In the middle of the day. In the middle of a crowd. In the dry heat of summer. In a town that seemed to be largely made of wood. Safety codes here were obviously different.

The band played, and the parade moved off. Somehow, it felt rude to follow them. A religious celebration was no place for tourists. So instead we retreated to the shade of the local bar and ordered a pitcher of sangria, which we shared with a couple of young Dutch pilgrims. One, an attractive twenty-something policeman named Arjan, confessed that he was putting maxi pads in his shoes to soak up the sweat and prevent blisters. I couldn't decide if that was horrifying or brilliant.

We lost track of time and arrived a few minutes late to our albergue's communal dinner, taking the last scattered seats at the long table. These group meals didn't happen often in Spain, but Eric and I always sought them out when we could. There was no better way to meet new pilgrims than over a shared meal.

I found myself seated in a corner, chatting with two friends from Idaho who had just started their Camino in León and were full of questions. Emily and Heather, at the other end of the table, found their own interesting Camino stories, and a few seats away Eric engaged with a middle-aged French couple. Even without much recent practice, his language skills were so good that I overheard him attempting to explain the American health-care system. For someone who never traveled internationally, my husband turned out to be the ideal companion to take to the Continent.

After dinner, we lounged on the grass outside, not yet ready for bed while the sun was still in the sky. Just as the last rays disappeared on the horizon, a shepherd on horseback, carrying an umbrella, guided his flock past our albergue yard and home for the night. We took that as our sign to take ourselves off to our bunk beds as well.

Our walk the next day was even shorter, just fifteen kilometers, but we kept our pattern of waking and walking by 7:00 to beat the

The jousting bridge of Hospital de Órbigo

heat, and we were in the open countryside, with no one else in sight, when the sun rose behind us over the mostly flat fields of Castille, turning the sky into a palette of colors.

The albergue, like most, hadn't offered breakfast, so we walked until we came to an open bar and stopped for a leisurely coffee/ bathroom break. At our current pace, we realized we would reach Hospital de Órbigo by 10:00, which was much too early. So about an hour after breakfast, when we passed through another village and saw another open bar, we stopped again to eat pastries and drink more coffee.

If *desayuno* is the word for breakfast in Spanish, we decided that this second breakfast must be *desay-dos*. (You'll have to know a little Spanish to get that joke. And I should confess that none of the Spaniards ever thought it was funny.)

The whole day was full of jokes and fun and play. Entering Hospital de Órbigo, the Camino crosses a seven-hundred-year-old, two-hundred-meter-long stone bridge. Its twenty arches mostly rest on bare ground now that a dam blocks much of the Órbigo River, but the bridge survives because of the Camino-worthy legend attached to it. We took turns reading it to one another with great drama and relish.

In the fifteenth century a knight named Don Suero de Quiñones fell in love with a lady who unfortunately did not return his affections. Don Suero, who should have gone on to become the patron saint of emo, displayed his heartbreak by donning an iron collar every Thursday to show himself a "prisoner of love." (That "every Thursday" part gets me every time.)

But a weekly collar wasn't enough to get over the lady's rejection, so Don Suero also announced that he would joust any knight brave enough to fight him on the long bridge of Hospital de Órbigo. When he won three hundred lances, he said, he would remove the collar and be free of his affliction. But Don Suero didn't really intend to fight all three hundred jousts himself. Because there are bros in every century, he managed to convince nine of his closest friends to fight in his place sometimes— probably on Thursdays, when he was hampered by the collar.

The contests commenced, but it took more time than expected to find enough worthy opponents. Plus, of course, Don Suero and his pals didn't win every joust. The ten knights combined had broken fewer than two hundred lances when the judges, at the king's order and probably because the jousts were about to impede the annual cattle drive through the city, announced that the contest was over and Don Suero was the winner. They ceremoniously removed the knight's collar and sent him far, far away—on a pilgrimage to Santiago, of course.

In his honor, all afternoon Emily and I galloped up and down the bridge and "jousted" at every opportunity. After we wore ourselves out, we picked up picnic supplies and went to the river, where I cooled my tired feet and Heather tried to swim, even though the water was barely shin-deep.

Later, while we lounged in the sun, I saw a familiar face on the bridge above us. I'd met the young American in León when I was with Nic and then ran into him again the next day with a few other acquaintances. I remembered he was from the Midwest, but I couldn't remember his name.

"Wisconsin!" I called, and he turned, surprised.

"Seattle!" I pointed at myself, and he came over to swap stories and catch up. Our chat lasted through drinks and then dinner. Wisconsin was an interesting kid. On the one hand, he was a normal, flirty, reckless American college student who bragged about staying out partying all night and then walking forty or even fifty kilometers the next day. On the other hand, he was a true believer. Deeply Catholic in a way I didn't know that twenty-something Americans still could be, Wisconsin was walking to Santiago because he believed in the blessing of Saint James. He believed the miracles—the chickens coming to life and the modern statues that bled tears—were real. He believed it all. He was genuine with his faith and had a ready answer for every question, even if it was "we don't have to understand; we have to believe."

His easy answers seemed to irk Heather, who quizzed him relentlessly about his upbringing and how he reconciled some of his more mystical beliefs with modern science. I wasn't sure if she was toying with him or really wanted to unpack the religious side of the Camino, so I sat back and watched the conversation happen.

In between the fun and silliness of the past few days, Heather and Emily had made me think about the Camino in a new way. Until they arrived, I hadn't really considered how the Way of Saint James, with all of its image-heavy Catholic churches and Christian icons, would be different for my Jewish friends, who arrived in Spain without a lot of what Eric would call "Christian priors."

While they were with us, I was hyperaware of things I'd taken for granted before, like the roadside crosses and images of Jesus everywhere. Both Emily and Heather took the religious icons of the Camino with grace and curiosity, but there were some stories that we all were ill equipped to interpret.

We stayed up late that night with Wisconsin, drinking vending-machine beer and talking about miracles (Heather and I) and practicing headstands and acro-yoga (Emily and Eric). We didn't get much sleep, but we had only a short walk the next morning to Astorga.

This was our last day with Heather before she flew back to England, and we arrived in the city early enough to sightsee. The cathedral was closed, but Heather and Emily and I toured the Episcopal Palace, designed by Gaudi and now a museum of the Camino story. We admired the stained-glass windows and gaped at some of the depictions of early medieval saints. The story of medieval Christianity wasn't all resurrected chickens and lovesick knights. There were plenty of martyrs dying violent deaths and, it seemed, even more artists who were happy to tell their stories.

As we walked back to the albergue, we noticed that the sky that had been blue and summer-warm all week had turned gray, and there was a chill in the air. Our easy days of short walks and second breakfasts were over. There were storms on the horizon.

STORMS

I was still in León when I first heard about Denise Thiem. "Do you know about the American woman who disappeared?" our friend Rachel, a Canadian pilgrim walking alone, asked. "She was on the Camino, and now she's gone. The path from Astorga isn't safe for women."

My inner skeptic perked up. A missing pilgrim? That sounded like a Radio Camino legend, passed along the gossip network and growing more dramatic with every telling.

I had reasons for my disbelief. Just days after Eric and I left Le Puy, a fellow walker whispered that the elderly woman we'd met in Saint-Privat-d'Allier, the one who refused to let anyone at the dinner table speak English, had been beaten and robbed on the trail. I wasn't sure what to think at the time, but two weeks later the woman popped up at the gîte in Lascabanes, looking fine. I couldn't ask her about the story, of course, because she still refused to acknowledge anyone who didn't speak French, but I saw no signs of injury, and she carried the same pack I remembered from our first meeting. Radio Camino had that story wrong.

Now the rumors flew again. Rachel told me she was considering taking a bus from Astorga to Ponferrada, skipping a part of the trail she'd been looking forward to. And she wasn't alone.

A steep and rocky climb out of Rabanal

While I was watching a Corpus Christi parade and play-jousting on a medieval bridge, it seemed like everyone else had started looking over their shoulders, suspicious of every quiet stretch of trail. Denise Thiem's absence became a part of all of our journeys. I started to hear stories about others who had abandoned the Way altogether, afraid for their safety. In Astorga we met an American named Roy, who told us he planned to delay his pilgrimage to join a community-organized search party.

I broke my no-internet rule to check the news and found that this time Radio Camino had the facts (mostly) right. An American woman traveling alone had disappeared on Easter Sunday, the same day that Eric and I flew from Seattle to Paris. She'd last been seen in Astorga, and with prodding from her worried family, the media had started posting attention-grabbing headlines about the "dangerous for women" section of the Camino.

To me, the reports seemed sensationalized. There had been no incidents since Ms. Thiem's disappearance, now months old, and even that was wrapped in more questions than facts. Based on the information publicly available at the time, I told Eric, it was also possible that there'd been an accident, or even that Ms. Thiem had voluntarily walked away from the Camino without telling anyone. (At least, that's what always seems to happen in novels.)

It's hard to admit all of this now, because I was wrong. Denise Thiem's story doesn't have a happy ending. In September 2015, months after Eric and I had returned to Seattle, police found Ms. Thiem's body and arrested a local man for her murder. In 2017 he was convicted of the crime and sent to prison. Radio Camino hadn't known the facts, but unfortunately had predicted the outcome: Denise Thiem was a victim of a random, tragic act of violence, the kind that gives us all nightmares.

On the Camino, crime of any kind is rare, and violent crime is almost unheard of. As a woman, I knew I was safer on the Way of Saint James than I was in my own neighborhood in the States. But that summer, when Heather asked Emily, Eric, and me to make sure we stuck together for the next few days, I agreed. Even if I was skeptical of rumors, I reasoned, it was smart to be aware of my surroundings.

In the end, our promise didn't matter, because the Camino had other plans for us. Roy's search party never happened, and Eric and Emily and I never had an opportunity to be out of each other's sight on our long walk to Rabanal.

That night in Astorga, we all awoke to the crack of thunder at 3:00 a.m. No one said anything, but I could hear the change in breath as the ten pilgrims in our room listened to rain pound the single-pane windows.

Despite the storm, at 5:00 our roommates started banging around in the dark, rustling bags and ponchos and bouncing flashlight beams. I kept my head on my pillow and my eyes stubbornly closed until 6:30, when we were, as always, the last ones left in the room. It was still raining, but there was nothing to do but gear up and go. Like American mail carriers, we would not be defeated by wind, or rain, or darkness.

Once again, we packed anything paper or electronic into plastic bags and then tucked those deep inside our trash bag–lined packs. We enjoyed one last café con leche with Heather before she left for the train station and then covered ourselves with jackets and hats, hoisted our rain cover–encased backpacks, and took stock of the situation. The rain had slowed to a steady, cool drizzle that felt familiar to the three Pacific Northwest residents.

"This isn't so bad," Eric said as we dodged puddles and started to follow yellow arrows around corners and down the narrow city streets. "It's just like Seattle."

The Spanish rain gods apparently didn't appreciate the comparison. He'd barely finished the words when the sky opened and the drizzle became a biblical-proportion deluge. Everyone scampered through sheets of water toward whatever shelter they could find. We huddled under the overhanging roof of a nearby shop, but it was already too late. My shoes were full of water, and the rain dripped down my jacket sleeves and soaked my socks. My hair dripped into my eyes.

There was no way to beat this rain, so we walked through it, squinting to see through the downpour.

A few days before, when the weather was warm and the stories were flowing, Heather entertained us with how she'd learned the subtle differences between American English and British English. The word "pants," for example, in the US means the same as trousers, dungarees, or slacks. In the UK, though, "pants" is another word for underwear. Heather had gotten some strange looks while shopping until she learned that.

By the time we reached the outskirts of Astorga, my pants were wet by anyone's definition. I felt like I had stood, fully clothed, in a shower for an hour.

"At least it can't get worse," Eric announced. A few seconds later, the Spanish rain gods sent lightning and hail.

We informed Eric he wasn't allowed to talk about the weather anymore.

The hail passed quickly and the lightning trailed off, but it rained steadily for the entire morning as we joined a line of hooded pilgrims slogging over a highway, past the end of the pavement, and up a dirt road that climbed, gradually, toward the mountains.

Forget what they say in *My Fair Lady*. We'd reached the end of the plains of Spain, and the rain was definitely still falling.

Emily and Eric had a splashing good time. I tried to join the fun, but my attitude could only be generously called resigned. We passed through a few small villages where the bars did brisk business with pilgrims trying to get out of the elements. We stopped once but discovered that getting out of cold, wet rain gear (and then back into it) was harder than just staying wet and moving forward. So we kept walking, squishing forward into the hills.

The rain let up just before we arrived in Rabanal. I was footsore and out of practice with such a relentless pace, but it was hard to stay miserable when we walked into a fairy tale.

I'd come to expect a certain look from Spanish towns. Smooth walls, either whitewashed or light stone, red-tile roofs, wide streets, and open spaces. Rabanal was something entirely different. The town was set on a steep hillside, the buildings all made from the rough gray stone of the surrounding mountainside. Monks in long black robes walked purposefully along winding streets shrouded in fog. The whole place felt ancient and sleepy, and I had my first glimpse of the Celtic influence on this part of Spain.

It was exactly the kind of place I wanted to be on a cold, wet afternoon.

The first order of business, as always, was to find a place to stay. Refugio Gaucelmo, according to the guidebook, was run by British volunteers and open only to "bona fide" pilgrims who arrived on foot and carried their own bags. There were no baggage service deliveries here. This was our kind of place.

We found the albergue in the old parish house, next door to the monastery bookstore and across the street from the crumbling local church. The gate was closed, the opening still an hour away, and there were just two bags in line ahead of us. Many "bona fide" pilgrims, it seemed, were not walking to Rabanal in weather like this.

We briefly pondered the wisdom of spending another hour in wet, chilly clothes. Should we find another place? But the rain had stopped, and we could see a courtyard and a garden through the gate. Emily hadn't experienced a donativo run by volunteers yet. We would stay.

A few more people trickled in to line up behind us, and eventually a very British woman who bore more than a passing resemblance to Dame Judi Dench came to the gate and allowed us to move inside, where it was dry. As we shed our wet shoes and socks in the entranceway, she told Eric that he had "gorgeous-shaped toes."

The building was a maze of stairs and balconies and low doorways designed for concussions. There was a serviceable, practical dormitory for about twenty pilgrims and an overflow dorm in a stone outbuilding that I suspected had once been a barn. The volunteers told us the sloping yard was usually lovely for their afternoon tea service, but today they'd have to move it to the common room. Because of course the British Confraternity of Saint James offers afternoon tea.

I wanted to see more of the town. I wanted to eat. Instead, we did the responsible thing and unpacked, showered, dried the things that were wet, and washed the things that needed washing. And then, finally, it was time for soup.

I'd done a bit of exploring (okay, bathroom-hunting) while we waited for the Gaucelmo to open and had stumbled across The

Bar. Now I dragged Eric and Emily back to see the thick stone walls, low-beamed ceilings, huge fireplace, and *soup*—hearty, hot seafood and vegetable chowders designed for rainy days. The three of us settled on stools at a wooden table with a bottle of local wine, a loaf of crusty bread, and generous bowls of the best soup I've ever had. We watched two older women, locals in long wool dresses and sensible shoes, climb up onto bar stools almost as tall as they were to gossip over glasses of beer. We watched new waves of pilgrims, still dripping and squishing, arrive. I felt delightfully at home.

But the previous late nights, the storm-interrupted sleep, and the hours of being cold and wet caught up with me, and when we were done eating, I needed a nap. So I didn't actually witness what happened next, although so many people told me about it that I feel like I did.

Eric and Emily had gone exploring. The rain was over but the air was still damp and chilly, so when they discovered oranges and cinnamon sticks in a tiny local market, as well as cheap bottles of wine, Eric's plan was born.

Back in the albergue kitchen, they found more spices and a saucepan, and started to simmer a batch of hot mulled wine. The aroma drifted through those twisted hallways and staircases, and pilgrims, young and old, started to drift toward the kitchen. I imagine them like cartoon characters, floating along the waves of delicious scents, led by their noses. Eric and Emily, true to their natures and the spirit of the Camino, hosted quite a party in the Gaucelmo kitchen that afternoon, going out twice more to buy more wine and oranges.

By the time I woke up, the whole building had become friends. The wine was the talk of the night, and the story traveled with us for days. "Mulled wine is usually a winter drink, a holiday drink," someone said. "But it was as cold as winter that day, and they made it feel like a holiday."

I missed the wine but did make it to the afternoon tea gathering, where I met Eric and Emily's new friends. After that, we all went across the street for what was described as an evening service of Gregorian chants in the chapel. The program turned out to be less CD-quality Gregorian and more four German monks with average voices singing in Latin, but my enchantment with Rabanal refused to fade. The church building, crumbling around the edges, felt medieval in the candlelight, and the whole event had a solemn, reverent feel.

The day that had started with rumors of violence and an actual attack by Mother Nature turned into one of the best days of my entire thousand-mile Camino.

We climbed the steep path out of Rabanal the next morning as the world around us shimmered with the previous day's rain. Eric paused to pet a friendly cat among the ruins of Foncebadón, a town that had almost disappeared but was slowly reemerging as a pilgrim stop. We climbed past remnants of old farms and a pasture of cows that seemed to be guarded by an excited horse, wearing a bridle but not tied or fenced in. We later met a pilgrim who'd left earlier than we did, and who was climbing the hill after Foncebadón when he heard the sound of horse hooves galloping behind him. He got to the side of the trail just as the horse emerged out of the mist and raced past, like a scene from a movie.

It was midmorning when we reached the Cruz de Ferro, the Iron Cross, which at 1,505 meters above sea level marks the highest point of the Camino Francés. The cross itself, I was surprised to realize, was small, but it sat on a tall pole, which gave it gravitas.

So did its history. A cross had been here, in some form and size, since the Roman era. Some believe it marked the border between two territories, while others say that the original cross was placed on the mountain by Gaucelmo, the abbot whose name graced the albergue, as a way to guide pilgrims through a difficult stretch of trail that could be lost in winter snow. Whatever its original purpose, the Iron Cross is now an iconic stop on the modern pilgrimage to Santiago. There is a tradition that pilgrims carry stones from their homes to leave at the base of the cross, symbolizing burdens that they leave behind.

Somehow, despite all of my lists and overpreparation, I'd forgotten to bring a stone from Seattle. I suspect that even if I had, I would have sacrificed it by the side of the road back in L'Aubrac. Still, it seemed appropriate to stop at the cross for a few minutes, shed our packs, and look around. I admired the view over the valley and waited to see if I would feel some experience-defining emotion or revelation. It didn't come.

People weep here, I knew. They pray. They find new purpose for their lives. I am just not one of those people. My Camino moments all happened in the places that are barely mentioned in the guidebooks—the quiet chapels or cathedral rooftops.

Honestly, the best thing that happened to me at the Cruz de Ferro was running into Chris, the British pilgrim Eric and I first met in Viana, where he morosely considered hiring a horse to help him "chase Fanny." Now Chris was grinning, and it had nothing to do with Fanny. "I've met a She Wolf," he declared. Somewhere on the Meseta, Chris had found the love he sought with a "fierce" Hungarian named Lizzy. They were walking the Camino together now, hand in hand. I congratulated him on his own Camino Miracle.

Eric and Emily and I continued through the hills, which took their toll on my body. I was spoiled after two weeks on relatively flat ground, and not ready for the rocky, uneven footpaths we now followed. Even so, I noticed that the physical discomfort didn't throw my mind into the spiral of failure that I'd had in the beginning. Yes, it was hard, but this Camino was still fun.

Midmorning we passed Manjarín, the famous donativo albergue run by the quirky character Tomás, who has declared himself a modern Templar knight caring for pilgrims. We caught a glimpse of him, in a white robe with the red cross of Saint James, puttering in his warren of buildings, but it was too early to stop.

After winding through the hills for another hour, the path began its steep descent toward Molinaseca. It was brutal. I minced and picked my way slowly down nine hundred meters of elevation in less than three kilometers while Eric and Emily sped ahead. It was the longest, hardest day we'd had in a while, and we were all tired when we arrived in Molinaseca, only to discover that the albergue was another kilometer on the other side of town.

Once we found our beds, though, we discovered that we weren't too battered or bruised to stagger back to town, looking for snacks and refreshment. We ended up, as we usually did, at an outdoor table of a tiny bar. The bartender brought free tapas with each round of tinto de verano or *cañas*, the small beers that were probably a third of an American pint. With each round the quality of the tapas improved: Spanish ham on bread, or slices of cheese, and eventually cups of homemade gazpacho.

We were a couple of rounds in when Dennis came by. We'd first met the tattooed Dutch pilgrim in Rabanal over mulled wine and British tea. He told us he was on a six-month paid sabbatical from his job as a border patrol agent, which seemed generous even for European holiday standards. His employer had a program, he said, where if a person worked overtime they could bank the hours and take them as paid time off later. So Dennis worked two hours of overtime every week and banked the time *for twenty years*. He told us he didn't really notice working a few extra minutes a day when he was already on the job, especially not when he could see the hours adding up. Now, he was on a six-month adventure. He'd walked from the Netherlands to Germany to attend a music festival and then he'd tackled the Camino Francés. After that, he was planning to take his girlfriend on a long vacation in Portugal. After that? Who knew?

I asked Dennis what a border patrol agent in the Netherlands does in the age of the European Union and the Schengen zone. It's not like anyone was checking passports at the border. "Mostly human trafficking," he replied. Criminals smuggled in women and children from Asia and Eastern Europe to work in prostitution. At that, we ordered another round and toasted him, declaring he deserved every day off he could get.

Dennis was great company, and the cañas and tapas kept coming. The afternoon slipped by, until we realized that we were almost late for the communal dinner at our albergue.

The dining room was noisy and friendly. I sat next to a Christian pastor from Georgia who was walking the Camino with his teenage son. I concentrated on speaking clearly and not too dramatically, as I'm prone to do after a few drinks, and I let the giant plates of spaghetti soak up the beer in my gut.

As soon as it was polite, I excused myself to crawl off to bed and sleep it off. But as I headed for the stairs, a couple of retirees we'd met earlier that afternoon waved me over. They were British, and they'd mentioned earlier that they wanted to hear about our experiences walking through France. They'd already bought a bottle of wine and set out glasses for us. What could we do?

It was almost 11:00, long past my pilgrim bedtime, when I finally fell into my bunk, and it was hard to get up the next morning. But we were just seven kilometers from Ponferrada, where Emily would catch a midday train to start her journey home. Eric and I had already decided to make it a short day as well, mostly so that we could explore Ponferrada's Templar castle.

By this point we'd seen plenty of castles from a distance, but the Templar monument was open to the public, and it could have been the model for every toy castle from my childhood, with round towers, square battlements, and a drawbridge over a moat.

The three of us walked to Ponferrada and ate a fortifying desayuno while we waited for the castle's ticket office to open. The staff let us stow our backpacks behind the front desk, so we spent the next few hours unencumbered, climbing the battlements and exploring the extensive grounds and historical exhibits.

While the outside was perfectly preserved, the inside was mostly open, with a few scattered ruins and plenty of informational signs to help us imagine what things had looked like in the twelfth century. We lingered over the collections of illuminated manuscripts and tried to imagine the patience and focus it would have taken to create them.

All too soon, it was time for Emily to leave. Her visit had been delightful and exhausting, a vacation within my Camino. I waved as she walked away, then turned to Eric and said, "I really need a nap."

TO GIVE AND
TO RECEIVE

After Emily left, Eric and I made our way to Ponferrada's large donativo albergue, housed in a former convent. Once settled, we each found quiet corners to sleep and catch up on our journals. Writing down the events of each day, I'd discovered, was the only way to keep track of all the new places and people and memories.

At some point in the afternoon I wandered to the entrance of the albergue to look around for likely places for dinner. There were no cafes or restaurants in sight, but there was an older man standing just outside the gate, holding the hand of a girl who looked about eleven.

"Excuse me," he said, in English. "Are you American?" When I said I was, he asked if I would talk to them for a little while. He was trying to help his granddaughter learn English and wanted her to chat with people who were fluent.

The girl looked mortified, but of course I said yes. Everything about being eleven is mortifying. We talked about Seattle and New York City. She asked me how much a cup of coffee cost where I lived, and I asked her where she went to school.

Her grandfather seemed comfortable with English, and I asked him how he'd learned the language so well. He'd worked in Australia for an American coal company for a few years, he said, after the mines here closed in the 1980s. Ponferrada, I remembered reading, had been a mining town since the time of the Romans. There was still a working-class feel to the place, and the next morning Eric and I followed the Camino past graffiti-covered apartment buildings and a power plant surrounded by barbed wire before we emerged back into the more familiar dirt tracks and vineyards.

We were on the dry side of the mountains that surrounded Galicia, and the weather was perfect: still cool enough for comfortable walking but warm enough for people to enjoy being outdoors. In one town an older man stood on the steps of a modern church, waving down anyone with a backpack. "Sellos!" he called. Of course we stopped to get a new stamp in our credentials.

In the next town another man waved us into a small chapel marked SAN ROQUE. We hadn't seen our favorite saint, with his faithful dog and attractive thigh, for a long time, so we stopped again. This building, it turned out, was more of a museum than a church. It was packed with odd religious icons—from a statue of Jesus with real human hair to a Barbie doll dressed as the Virgin Mary. We looked around, trying to keep straight faces as we studied the Renaissance angel holding what looked like a piranha, while our host kept up a running monologue in Spanish.

Although we were no longer entertaining guests, Eric and I walked together all day, swapping ideas. After almost ten weeks I was happy to note that we hadn't run out of things to talk about. If anything, the unbroken time gave us a new language of shared stories and experiences that most couples in the midstream of their marriages don't have, and it reminded me again that I was madly in love with this man. Even more than that, I was glad he was my friend. He was funny. He was interested in everything. He was kind. Plus, I had to agree with the rest of the women on the Camino: he was a pretty good-looking guy.

Dropping our normal lives and distractions and setting out on foot for three months had been a risk, perhaps. But it was paying off in spades.

All in all, I was feeling hopeful and optimistic as we approached Villafranca de Bierzo that afternoon. My only nagging concern was that I didn't know where we would stay. There were popular municipal and private albergues on the outskirts of town, but neither felt right. Should we venture into town and see what else we could find? If it didn't work we'd have to backtrack, which was never fun.

I was still waffling when I noticed one of the ubiquitous flyers posted along the edges of the Camino path. We were used to those kinds of signs by now. Enterprising Spanish business owners knew exactly where to find their customers and had a good sense for what would catch our attention. This particular sign was for a new albergue, San Nicolas, and there was a photo of twin beds. "No bunks," the sign said, just to make it clear.

When was the last time we paid albergue prices and got to sleep in real beds? I knew where we would stay. The only issue was how to get there. There was no address on the flyer, and the albergue wasn't listed in our guidebooks. My best guess was that something called San Nicolas would probably be near the Iglesia San Nicolás, in the heart of the town. So that's where we headed.

We reached the center of Villafranca and found a busy plaza. The weekly outdoor market was in full swing, with blocks of tents and vendors selling everything from plastic flip-flops to loaves of bread bigger than my backpack. There were cafes serving pulpo and lovely old buildings everywhere.

Even better, when we reached the church, we discovered one of those Camino surprises: the albergue wasn't just *near* San Nicolas. It was *in* San Nicolas. A group of private owners had recently bought the seventeenth-century convent and pilgrim hospital attached to the church and were in the process of turning it into a full albergue and hotel. They'd opened the first rooms just a few weeks before.

The building was huge, with wide, bright hallways around an enclosed cloister that opened to a manicured courtyard. For eight euros each, Eric and I got twin beds in a spacious corner room with a private bathroom, high ceilings, and only one roommate— an American named Chuck.

Chuck was friendly and confident, a competent backpacker who liked to tell stories about all the places he'd been. But that night, in our quiet room, he stopped breathing.

Crossing the rolling hills and vineyards of Bierzo

I'd never heard someone with sleep apnea before, but it was hard to miss. Chuck snored loudly enough to wake even a deep sleeper like me, and the sounds bounced off our spacious but bare room. Then there was nothing. No sound. No breath. The seconds stretched, and just as I started to really worry, he let out a gasping, choking inhale, as if he'd broken the surface after a long dive underwater.

And then the whole cycle repeated.

I finally fell asleep, and the next morning Chuck was gone when we got up. Eric, who had also been awake to hear what happened, wanted to track him down to tell him. I disagreed. It felt rude to confront someone about a health issue they couldn't control. There was a general pilgrim code of privacy, I argued. We all slept in rather intimate quarters, but during the day we mostly pretended that we hadn't seen each other in our underwear.

But Eric kept worrying that Chuck didn't know about his problem. We'd talked to him enough to know that he was a single, churchgoing conservative. He probably didn't share a room with anyone at home, Eric reasoned. What if no one else on the Camino had mentioned what they heard? It could be deadly.

We went back and forth as we walked out of the city, but when we happened to run into Chuck on the trail, the Camino seemed to make our decision for us. Eric explained what had happened the night before, and Chuck was stunned. Eric was right. No one had told him. Sometimes being pathologically helpful is, well, helpful.

As we parted with Chuck, we faced another decision. There are three Camino routes out of Villafranca de Bierzo. The one that most pilgrims take follows the paved road along the river valley, on a relatively gentle incline. A second, "remote" route climbs into the hills to the south of the river and winds up and down, without any services, for twenty-six kilometers. We dubbed the third, scenic route "the compromise." Just past the town it shoots up four hundred meters into the hills on the north side of the river, then follows a fairly flat and natural trail along the ridgeline. It weaves in and out of chestnut orchards, with a view over the nearby hills and an opportunity to catch the morning sun.

This, of course, was the path that we chose. Who had I become, I wondered, that I would voluntarily add an extra three kilometers of walking, not to mention an extra four hundred meters of climb and descent?

But the extra effort was worth it. For three hours we didn't see another pilgrim, and we mostly walked separately from each other, soaking in the quiet beauty of the morning sun burning off a thick dew. We watched old men tending their gardens and listened to the birds. I was glad we'd done it even as we slid down the steeper descent back to the valley floor in Trabadelo, where we had a hearty second breakfast before starting the real work of the day.

The Camino eventually breaks from the river valley in order to climb to the town of O'Cebreiro, which sits atop a mountain at the end of a notoriously difficult ten-kilometer ascent up rocky trails. It would be a challenging, but not impossible, walk from Villafranca de Bierzo, even with our scenic detour.

According to the map, though, there was a better option. Halfway up the O'Cebreiro climb was a tiny hamlet called La Faba, with an albergue run by the German Confraternity of Saint James. We could stay there and break the ascent into two days. Plus, I told Eric, I always liked albergues run by those who loved the Camino so much they came from other countries to support it.

This was a thing I'd noticed about the Camino—walking the Way of Saint James often left a person not only with a sense of personal accomplishment but also a deep sense of community that often led to a desire to serve. At least half a dozen countries supported associations or confraternities of Camino supporters who provided donations and volunteers to work in specific albergues. British volunteers cared for us in Rabanal. The American Pilgrims on the Camino placed volunteers in Carrion de los Condes and Ribadiso. The French and Spanish Camino associations each supported dozens of gîtes de pèlerins and albergues in their home countries. And the Germans served the Camino in the tiny hamlet of La Faba, which they chose because of a centuries-old German poem that eulogized pious German pilgrims who died on the way to Santiago. One of the lines essentially translates to "The sons of Germany are buried in La Faba"—a phrase that they still replicate, rather morbidly, on their credential stamp.

The climb was as steep as advertised, and the rocks were slippery in a light but steady rain. I was happy to leave the trail halfway up and take a dirt track, no wider than a person, into La Faba.

The village turned out to be everything I'd hoped for. The hamlet was hardly big enough to be considered a village, with a population of just thirty-five people. There was a market the size of my sofa and a single cafe, both of which appeared to be sustained by passing pilgrim traffic. The albergue at the end of the single, tree-lined dirt road had been renovated from the village's former rectory and stood next to the town's tiny church. There was no priest here anymore, but the doors were unlocked during the day.

We arrived before the albergue opened and set our bags down to hold our place in the line of people slowly arriving. The rain was still falling, so Eric and I ducked into the church, a single room with stone walls and just a few windows set into deep casements. The air here was noticeably warmer than outside, heated by the bank of prayer candles left, presumably, by previous pilgrims. While I explored the guest book, with contributions mostly from French pilgrims, Eric bought and lit another candle to warm whoever came after us.

At the designated time, two young German volunteers unlocked the albergue door and, with admirable efficiency, stamped credentials and assigned beds. After that, there wasn't much to do except get in each other's way. The albergue had wide lawns, but it was still raining, and there was little common space indoors except the tiny kitchen.

Seeing an opportunity for another mini-party, Eric ventured to the market for supplies to make mulled wine, the antidote to a chilly, wet day. But magic, like lightning, doesn't strike the same place twice. Our fellow pilgrims in La Faba didn't seem interested in wine, and we were eventually crowded out of the kitchen by a group of six Spanish pilgrims who spread out over the only table to make themselves a three-course dinner, and who took my seat whenever I stood up. Not everyone, it seemed, wanted a community.

Eric retreated to the covered porch with François, a retired Frenchman who wanted a warm beer and a bit of quiet. They chatted for several hours, until the cafe opened and we could escape for dinner, and then, tired from the rain and the climb, to bed. Eric, as always, took the upper bunk, and I settled into the space below him.

Sometime later, in the dead of night, I felt someone standing just inches from where I slept. It was one of the German volunteers who managed the albergue, and she was whispering with Eric. Someone was sick in the other dorm, she said, but he spoke only French, and she couldn't decide how serious it was. Could Eric translate for her? We later figured out that she'd heard Eric speaking with François on the porch and assumed he was fluent. Of course Eric went to be helpful. It turned out that the young Frenchman wasn't sick; he was drunk. It was tinto he was coughing up, not blood.

Once that was sorted, the rest of the night passed easily, and there was coffee in the morning to fuel us for the last five-kilometer climb to O'Cebreiro.

As we walked, the morning mist filled the valley below, and the sun glistened on the yellow flowers and sage all around us. Mountains and valleys extended in every direction, and I was filled with the deepest sense of gratitude for being awake and present at 7:00 in the morning, climbing a small mountain somewhere in Spain. Even as I dragged my body up, meter after meter, there was nowhere else I wanted to be.

Me, awake at dawn and happy to be climbing? This Camino really was changing me.

We had reached Galicia, the final province of our walk across Spain, with its Celtic roots and damp climate that felt like the Pacific Northwest. O'Cebreiro, normally a bustling tourist town, was still asleep and shrouded in fog when we arrived a little after 8:00. It could have felt mystical, but Eric kept ruining the mood by singing the tune of "Oh, Susannah" (*O'Cebreiro, don't you cry for me . . .*).

It was hard not to let our thoughts and conversation drift toward the future. Eric had started dreaming about home and work. I was distracted with worries about what we would do when we reached Finisterre, and how we would get back to Paris for our flight home. Since we hadn't known when we would finish, we hadn't made any arrangements. But the Camino continued to draw us back.

We were walking through the highest altitudes of the Camino, even higher than the Pyrenees crossing, and passing through villages made entirely from the same shale and rock that were under our feet. The scenery—not to mention the steady ascents and descents—demanded our attention.

As we came around another bend in the winding dirt path, we ran into two familiar and welcome figures. Rory and Lis, the New Zealand/Dutch couple, were coming out of a small market to watch a farmer drive a herd of cows through the middle of town. We'd bumped into them a few times since the night of the abuelo's herb soup in Viana, often stopping for a drink or a chat. We liked spending time with them, but they'd attracted a group of followers who seemed happy to rely on Rory's cooking skills and Lis's ability to organize rooms in out-of-the-way places. These were two people who knew how to lead, and for better or worse, they'd collected a group of people who liked to follow. I didn't want to become another burden, so we tended to meet, visit, and then move on.

That morning was no different. We walked together for most of the morning, trading stories and Radio Camino gossip. The road continued to climb, until we finally reached Alto de Poio, at 1,330 meters. This, finally, was the point where we could assure ourselves that it was all downhill from here. When Rory and Lis and their Camino followers stopped for a snack, Eric and I decided to keep going. It was getting late, and we planned to cover another ten kilometers to Triacastela.

But the rocky path left my feet sore, and the interrupted sleep in La Faba made Eric tired. When we reached Biduedo, a tiny village of maybe half a dozen houses along a single, curving road, we decided it was time to listen to our bodies and stop. There was a small pensión with an available private room, probably our last before the push to Santiago. We gladly handed over our money and settled in.

The only place to hang our wet laundry was a line in a cow pasture covered with fresh manure. While I was wrangling safety pins to keep our clothes from falling into the muck, I watched a van pull up to the park next door. Two people began to unload what appeared to be a full catered meal.

I'd seen vans like this before, with their ironic tag line: "The best way to see the world is on foot." They supported the organized tour groups who, for lack of a better word, "sampled" the Camino. A van would drive a dozen or so tourists to the beginning of a particularly scenic part of trail, and they'd all get out and walk a few kilometers before piling back into their motorized carriage to zip ahead to the next town.

I was feeling judgmental as I stood there, hanging my well-worn underwear over giant cow patties, while people in top-of-the-line hiking gear indulged in a catered spread of fancy cheeses, seafood, and vegetables. But then we started talking.

The group was mostly British and Australian, and somehow it came out that Eric and I had walked from Le Puy (well, except for that one day with the mountain-bike van/cab). The tourists wanted to hear all about our adventures. They waved to the food and told us to help ourselves while they peppered us with questions.

At first, I shied away, not wanting to be an extra attraction on their tour—meet the crazy couple who will walk a thousand miles!—but the people were surprisingly nice, and it was hard to pass up an opportunity to tell our stories or eat their smoked salmon spread. I found myself waving a piece of cheese as I made a rather passionate case for why they should ditch the tour group next time and come back to just walk. I told them about the surprises of the Camino that weren't in any guidebook—the tiny chapels and dew-covered fields. I told them about meeting people from around the world and, waving at my own less-than-athletic frame, assured them that if I could do it, so could they.

I don't know that it made much difference, but when they climbed into their van and drove off to the next attraction, at least they left us the remains of their lunch, which we shared with the straggling, weary-looking pilgrims still coming down the path.

The story of the Americans who'd been walking for seventy days carried over to our fellow albergue guests. There were two other groups in the pensión that night—two Irish couples walking together, and an American mother-daughter pair—and we found ourselves answering questions and sharing more of our story. The Americans were great company, interesting and down-to-earth. They hadn't resorted to buses, but they'd biked across the Meseta and then they conquered the climb to O'Cebreiro on horseback, guided by an entrepreneurial Spanish farmer who lived at the bottom of the incline.

The Irish couples also seemed nice, asking questions and flattering us for what we'd done. But when it was time for dinner, which we all ate in the pensión's dining room, we saw a different side of them.

A young, sullen-seeming server who spoke only Spanish offered us the standard three choices of *menu del día*, but she wasn't interested in accommodating more than that. No, there were no printed menus. No, there were no substitutions. No, that beverage was not available.

"Well, we know 'charm' isn't your middle name," one of the Irishmen said, while she was standing right in front of him. His companions laughed, and he turned to me—the veteran pilgrim celebrity for the night—to share their joke, but I turned away. I'd seen her wince a little; even if she didn't understand the language, it was clear she understood the tone.

Yes, service on the Camino came with a wide range of attitudes. This wasn't the first server I met who believed that "no" was the easiest answer. But as I watched her balance the various needs of eight awkward foreign tourists, I tried to imagine what it would be like to do this same thing, day after day.

If our waitress was surly, perhaps she had a reason for it. Pilgrims are always in motion, experiencing new things and creating new memories every day. Our questions and needs were still new to us, but she'd heard them a thousand times before. It must have been an exhausting way to make a living.

I finally understood why my own impatience bothered Eric so much. There was a balance, somewhere, between not being taken advantage of and not taking advantage of others. Of serving the Camino, as well as expecting it to provide. These thoughts tumbled in my mind the next morning as we set out again in the early dawn light. There was a cloud bank in the valley below us, with the pinks and blues of dawn above it. All I wanted was to live another week just like this last one in Spain.

However, things were about to change.

THE LAST
ONE HUNDRED

Radio Camino had been talking about "the last one hundred" for weeks. To earn a Compostela, Santiago's Pilgrim Office requires proof that a person walked at least the final one hundred kilometers (or biked two hundred) to the cathedral. The draw of the Compostela certificate means that the crowds increase exponentially in Sarria, the closest city to the hundred-kilometer mark. In fact, more than a quarter of all pilgrims who reached Santiago in 2015—more than sixty-seven thousand people—started walking in Sarria. (By comparison, thirty-one thousand started in Saint-Jean-Pied-de-Port, and I thought that was too crowded.)

The closer we got to Santiago, the more often conversations among pilgrims turned toward the chaos that would befall us. The prices would go up. The rush for beds would be worse. The crowds would be impossible. As we crossed Galicia and approached Sarria, I started to hear a name for the late arrivals: *touregrinos*.

The apprehension reminded me of the dire warnings we'd heard as we approached the French border with The Dane, Marieke, Jan, and the rest. I'd been through this culture shock before, and now when someone said everything was about to change, I believed them. But this time, I had a plan.

The clock was ticking, and Santiago was almost in sight.

Five Days to Santiago

Eric and I descended through the cloud bank from Biduedo and approached Sarria cautiously. We didn't want to stumble again into the middle of a city crowded with new walkers. About a kilometer before the bridge to Sarria, we came across a private albergue that advertised a communal pilgrim dinner, small rooms, and a private backyard. The owner also owned the bar next door, where we could linger over afternoon refreshments while looking for our friends among the passing walkers. It was perfect.

Once we were settled and the laundry was on the line, I considered going into town to look around the old quarter, but I couldn't find the motivation. Plus, I rationalized, I still needed to figure out where we would go when the Camino ended. So I spent the afternoon in a lounge chair behind the albergue with a map and a forbidden internet connection, trying to understand the convoluted railway systems of Europe.

We gathered for dinner that night with four pilgrims who were also avoiding the center of town. I'd never met any of them before, and they didn't make much of an impression. Our host, on the other hand, was a character. He filled us with red lentil soup, a hearty salad, a delicious tortilla patata, and a *tarte de Santiago* for dessert. We'd been seeing this special almond cake more as we moved west. It was heavy and dense—I learned later that the best recipes are simple, made only from ground almonds, sugar, and eggs—and adorned with a powdered sugar stencil in the shape of the cross of Saint James.

When he saw that Eric liked to eat, our host pressed seconds on him with every course. After the meal, he pulled out a bottle of homemade grappa—a liquor so potent it makes wine seem like grape juice. I sipped mine but passed it to Eric to finish when the alcohol kick gave me the hiccups. Then our host pulled out a second bottle of a blend supposedly made by his grandmother and set it on fire to show us how the alcohol burned. And then he poured Eric another glass.

Four Days to Santiago

Not surprisingly, when we woke up the next morning, my dear husband was feeling under the weather, or at least under the grappa. But we pressed on, through Sarria—quiet at dawn—and then back into the countryside of Galicia. We passed through groves of oak and chestnut trees and a series of small towns where the bars all did brisk business. There were noticeably more people on the road.

Actually, that doesn't begin to describe it. The Camino path out of Sarria felt like we had joined the kind of swarm I usually equate with a crowd moving toward a concert or sports stadium. The hundreds of pilgrims I'd finally gotten used to were now thousands. (That's not an exaggeration. The Santiago Pilgrim Office issued three thousand Compostelas the day we arrived.)

There were school groups of rowdy teenagers clogging the path, flirting and singing and yelling to one another. There were fashionably dressed Spanish adults carrying day packs. There were families with strollers. Our ragged group of veterans, with dirty boots and worn clothes, stuck to the edges of the road and tried to ignore them all.

At every stop there was someone we knew. The two friends from Idaho we first met in Mazarife were soldiering on, despite blisters; we seemed to cross paths with them two or three times a day, regardless of how fast or far we walked. Hans, a serious German we met in Estella, was walking with his wife, Gertrude, and Eric kept calling them Hansel and Gretel. Kim and Sarah, the American mother/daughter duo we met in Biduedo, took their time walking and arrived late most afternoons, always with smiles. We didn't have a specific Camino family the way we did in the final days of France, but we had friends all the same.

With an early start and more experience than most, we moved at a steady five kilometers an hour and soon outdistanced the crowd. Eric and I walked together all day; the chance for peace and solitude was past, and the chance of losing each other among all the people was high.

We crossed the long bridge into Portomarín just after noon. This was the first part of the plan: stay ahead of the swarm.

The Portomarín bridge, unlike so many we crossed, was modern, with two lanes for cars and a narrow sidewalk for pilgrims, as well as splendid and vertigo-inspiring views of the Mino River reservoir below.

Climbing the long stairs into Portomarín

Portomarín itself was also modern, at least by Camino standards. The town had existed since Roman times in the valley below us, but the completion of a new dam over the Mino in the 1960s created a reservoir that flooded it. Before that happened, engineers carefully disassembled the historic buildings, including the blocklike cathedral, and moved them all to a new town built higher on the hill. If you look carefully, I'm told, you can still see faint numbers penciled onto some of the bricks of the cathedral, showing the builders how to reassemble it.

Eric and I climbed a final set of stone stairs to get to the town, which felt a little like insult-upon-injury on a hot summer day. Once we arrived, it was time to initiate the second part of our beat-the-crowd plan: instead of turning toward the center of town, where most albergues were clustered, we walked away from it to find an albergue on the edge of town. We were rewarded with a private cubicle, separated by a curtain, and a leisurely lunch with Hans and Gertrude, who'd had the same idea.

As the sunny summer afternoon spread before us, Eric and I ventured back to the lake-like river and soaked our tired feet in the water while we watched the long line of late arrivers stream across the bridge above us.

Three Days to Santiago

We left Portomarín while dawn mist still hung over the reservoir and spent the day walking through eucalyptus groves and cow pastures. Whenever we came across a herd on the road, always guided by a farmer or two, I reminded Eric not to get trampled.

The paths beneath our feet were rocky, and the houses, barns, and even the fences we passed were made of local slate and Galicia's rough granite. We started to see *horreos*, which I thought at first were backyard altars or chapels, because of their often elaborate crosses and roof spires. Their real purpose was far more practical: these were granaries, ventilated through slits in the wood or stone walls and erected on stilts to keep rodents out.

Even the Camino itself was marked with granite bollards, which featured the familiar yellow arrows and a more-or-less accurate countdown of the distance left to Santiago. We watched the number of kilometers drop through the double digits, from ninety to eighty to seventy. But as afternoon approached, we made a mistake. Instead of stopping at one of the albergues on the outskirts of Palas de Reí, we followed the path into the town center and then realized we'd left ourselves with no good options for the night. The town was modern and noisy, with car-clogged streets and uninspiring albergues. We reluctantly checked into a modern place with inspirational quotes on the orange walls and Ikea furniture in the lobby.

Our roommates were an adult family of touregrinos. They had trouble dragging their full suitcases, clearly transported by baggage service, into the room, and later I saw the women in the bathroom with full-sized hair dryers, makeup kits, and lingerie. They stayed out until midnight and carried on full-voice conversations when they came back, ignoring us trying to sleep just three feet away. Then at 5:00 the next morning, they zipped and crinkled and whispered and packed again.

Lesson learned, we pressed on.

Two Days to Santiago

It was impossible to think about anything but Santiago.

Eric and I cruised over rolling hills, sweating in the bright sunshine. After La Faba the fabled rain of Galicia never fell on us. Instead, we found ourselves on the brink of summer, the frosty mornings of France a distant memory.

With the lesson of Palas de Reí behind us, we walked fast and with a purpose: we were headed for a municipal albergue in the hamlet of Ribadiso. Yes, we normally avoided municipally run albergues in Spain, for reasons already explained, but this one had been recommended by several people and was supported by the American Pilgrims on the Camino. Also, I suspected that most of the touregrino swarm would blow past it and go to Arzua, the bigger town three kilometers farther.

The bet paid off. First, because I was right. Most people, including our roommates from the night before, crossed the stone bridge over the River Iso and barely even looked at the cluster of buildings hugging its edge. And second, because Ribadiso was a final gift from Saint James.

The albergue was built around what had once been a pilgrim hospital. The two dormitories were low and made of stone, cool against the summer sun and probably cozy on rainy days, with an extensive modern bath and shower facility in a separate building. Another building, also stone, contained the office, a common dining and kitchen area, and an apartment for the live-in volunteer.

Eric and I were, as usual, among the first to check in. A stoic-faced municipal employee took our money and stamped our credentials, then an American volunteer stepped in to warmly greet us and help us get settled. It was an arrangement that seemed to work well for everyone, especially pilgrims.

There was no town in sight, but there was a bar/cafe, and there was the Iso, which was more like a knee-high stream than a river. Eric and I couldn't resist stripping off our walking shoes and smelly socks and wading into the cold, soothing water. More pilgrims joined us as the afternoon wore on.

I finally dragged myself away from the water to shower and wash my clothes, which I hung on a line a few feet away from a group of cows that had wandered into the albergue yard. Eric continued to poke around the edges of the stream like a kid at play and came across a mongoose. Not far away, an Italian pilgrim sunbathed topless in the grass, distracting the neighboring farmer as he tried to drive a tractor in straight lines to harvest hay.

We eventually ambled to the bar next door, where we shared afternoon drinks with an international group of veteran pilgrims: a vivacious Korean American from California, a Spanish sailor who crewed the yachts of the rich and famous, a Japanese university student, a shy young Korean who spoke no English, a German Mexican, and a Czech German. It was a rowdy, happy group. At one point someone called a friend at home, and we all wished them happy birthday in our native languages.

While chickens ran around underfoot as if they were city pigeons, Eric and I table-hopped and shared dinner with an older Italian couple we'd met in Portomarín. They spoke almost no English and even Eric couldn't fake much Italian, but they were warm and friendly and pantomimed for us stories of their travels.

When I wandered back to the albergue in the gathering twilight, two pilgrims were playing guitars on the lawn outside and a group had gathered around them. I lingered, singing along when I knew the tune, until the sun went down.

Nothing in Arzua could have compared with the mix of cultures we found that night, as we all held tightly to the final moments of this crazy thing that we'd done together.

One Day to Santiago
When we walk tomorrow, it will be into Santiago.

We left Ribadiso in golden morning light that bounced off wildflowers and filtered through the slatted walls of horreos. The morning was full of eucalyptus trees and pastures, but as noon approached they gave way to towns and suburbs. This was the edge of the Santiago metropolis.

Our destination for the night seemed to have three names. There was Pedrouzo, the town, and O Pino, the municipality, and Arza, the parish. I had no idea what the difference was, and no one else seemed to know either. But there were plenty of services, and it was in a good place to begin the final morning push.

When we arrived at noon, the line for the municipal albergue already snaked around the building, but we easily found two beds in a private albergue a few blocks down the road. It lacked personality, but there was hot water and a patio where we could hang our laundry, so it would do.

Basically, everything about that last night was *fine*. We once again sat at a bar table near the Camino path and chatted with anyone familiar who came by. None of us could talk about anything but Santiago, so that's what we did.

Four Hours to Santiago
Every day at noon there is a special mass for pilgrims in the Cathedral of Santiago. Radio Camino said that if we wanted to get seats, we needed to be there by 11:00. To give ourselves plenty of time to cover the last twenty kilometers, Eric and I decided to leave Pedrouzo/O Pino/Arza at 6:00 a.m., an hour earlier than usual.

Our roommates had other ideas. The alarms in the dorm started to go off at 4:30. By 5:00 the noise of everyone around us packing to go was impossible to ignore. So even I gave in and got up, and we were on the road by 5:30. The sky was still totally dark, and for the first time we needed our headlamps to guide us out of the town and through the eucalyptus groves.

We were surrounded by the shadows and murmurs of fellow travelers we couldn't see. There were people everywhere, and even in the dark it was hard to miss the excitement in the air. For most of them, this was the final push.

We all walked fast that morning. Eric and I skirted an airport and several modern suburbs before we found an open cafe for desayuno. We ran into Hans and Gertrude as we were leaving and walked with them for a while.

Somehow between our conversation and the surging antici-pation of the crowd around us, we walked right past Monte del Gozo, the last of the iconic Camino sights, without realizing it. Historically, this was the hill where a pilgrim could first see the city of Santiago spread before them, the spires of the cathedral visible ten kilometers away. The whole hilltop has been flattened now, and the only thing I noticed as I passed was a statue of Pope John Paul II, commemorating a visit he made to the holy city.

We lost Hans and Gertrude as the swarm carried us into the outskirts of Santiago. We tried to ignore the Italian tourists in matching blue scarves who emerged from a tour bus to walk in as if they were pilgrims, but they surrounded us. To escape them, we slowed down and struck up a conversation with a group of Americans who turned out to be seminary students preparing to join monasteries.

Radio Camino had been buzzing for days about the attractive young monks-in-training, but this was the first time we'd met them. We crossed the city line of Santiago with Mark, a twenty-two-year-old on the verge of committing his life to a monastery in North Dakota. He told us he'd left his faith for a long time to pursue Satanism, had recently returned, and had chosen his future monastery carefully based on the personalities of the monks there and the spiritual groundedness of the place. He was a little concerned about it being in such a remote location, but that was where God called him.

I had so many questions, but there wasn't time. The clock was ticking, and our attention was on the cathedral, which teased us with the occasional glimpse of a spire every now and then when the streets angled just right. As we entered the old city, the narrower streets funneled the crowds closer together, and Mark disappeared in the swarm. There was too much to see and take in all at once, especially since we'd once again ended up surrounded by the excitable Italians in their matching scarves.

My feet hurt. My heart was racing, and I didn't know why. I didn't have a spiritual connection to the body of James or the church built over him, and I still had my own "last hundred" to walk after this. But it was impossible to deny the energy all around me.

We turned again, past a square with imposing-looking buildings on all sides. Then down an alley and under an arch filled with the distinct sound of bagpipe music, and then past a fountain and into a square.

And then we were there.

SANTIAGO DE COMPOSTELA

Fermé.

That was my first impression of the Cathedral of Santiago de Compostela. We'd followed the swarm of pilgrims around the edges of the vast complex and into the Praza do Obradoiro, the main square on the west side of the cathedral that faced the elaborate grand entrance featured on the back of Spain's one-, two-, and five-cent coins.

This was it, I thought.

And then, *this was it?*

The famous facade didn't look like the pictures. The cathedral itself wasn't actually closed, of course, but the front of the building definitely was. It was in the middle of a major renovation, so much of it was shrouded in canvas and towers of scaffolding. Somewhere up there, a statue of Saint James looked down on the arriving pilgrims, but I doubted he could see us.

Meanwhile, all around me, arriving pilgrims hugged each other and took selfies. I didn't recognize any of them. Through coincidence or bad luck, none of our friends arrived when we did. Still, this was it. I waited to feel the surge of emotion. The pilgrims in the documentaries and memoirs always broke down at this point,

The Cathedral of Santiago de Compostela

weeping or dancing, or both. I didn't expect anything that dramatic, but I was sure that I should feel *something* as I stood there.

The only thing I felt was restless. I wanted to move again, to be somewhere other than this plaza where I was being jostled by strangers. My feet were tired after our headlong hike. Even this early in the day, it was at least eighty degrees, and there was no shade. I had arrived at the church of Saint James, and I was already looking for what to do next. I had a strong urge to get settled and "do the things," but what were "the things" in Santiago?

Eric seemed to feel the same way. We had a stranger take a couple of obligatory photos of us and the scaffolding, but we didn't linger. It was only 10:00 in the morning, much too early to check into an albergue, but still too early to go inside for the noon mass.

Radio Camino had warned us that we couldn't carry our backpacks into the cathedral, so we paid a few euros to check them in a shopfront storage facility. The man behind the counter congratulated us on our arrival, and when he realized we were American, he proudly showed us a photo of himself with the actor Martin Sheen, taken during the filming of *The Way*.

Relieved of our burdens, I set off down a narrow street to find the Pilgrim Reception Office, but the line of people waiting to receive their Compostelas already stretched out the building, across the courtyard, and into the street. We'd never get through it in an hour, I decided, so I turned around and set off again.

Eric obligingly followed me as I flitted in circles like an overexcited puppy, unable to do anything because I was distracted by what I wanted to do next. I talked about finding food or a train ticket office so that I could figure out our return tickets, but I was nervous about how much time either would take. I hadn't felt this unfocused since our first day in Le Puy, when I didn't know how to start acting like a pilgrim. Now, it seemed, I didn't know how to stop.

We found ourselves in the smaller, shaded Paterias plaza, on the south side of the cathedral. Here, behind a fountain of cool water splashing over iron horses, was a set of elaborate cathedral doors, and they were open. We entered the southern transept of the sanctuary, directly in line with the main altar, over which hung the famous *botafumeiro*. The incense burner, five feet across and weighing eighty kilograms, dwarfed the average censers that Catholic priests swing in churches around the world. It hung from a thick rope that snaked all the way to the altar dome, and swinging it required eight strong priests operating a series of pulleys. It could reach speeds of forty miles per hour, arcing from transept to transept and releasing sweet smoke throughout the whole cathedral.

The spiritual significance of the botafumeiro, according to a brochure I picked up, is twofold. Smoke from the burning incense rises to heaven, carrying with it the prayers of the people, while the sweet scent fills the space around it, just as the behavior of true Christians must spread and sweeten the outside world in which they live. The more pragmatic, widely spread story is that the giant brass urn was lit daily in medieval times to fumigate and cover the smell of thousands of unwashed pilgrims, who often slept in the balconies.

Whatever the reason, keeping the incense swinging had become a challenge. All of that priest-power and ceremony didn't come cheaply, and Spain's church struggled like everyone else in the bad economy. Radio Camino was sure that the botafumeiro only swung on certain days, but some people said it was Fridays; others said Mondays. No one knew for sure if the incense would swing on *their* Santiago day.

A related rumor was that individuals or groups could donate a thousand dollars to ensure a botafumeiro swing at the service of their choice. In fact, one of the reasons our wave of pilgrims was so interested in the American seminary students was because we'd heard they'd sponsored a botafumeiro swing. If you arrive when they do, Radio Camino said, you'll be guaranteed the chance to see it. When Eric and I asked the North Dakota–bound seminarian, Mark reported that the rumor was only half right. Their group had paid for a special incense swing, but it was for a private mass of consecration happening later in the day.

I still wasn't sure if this was a lucky pilgrim mass day or not, but the presence of the incense hanging dead center in front of the gaudy Baroque altar was a good sign. The pews were already filling up, so I staked out two seats on an aisle halfway toward the back and happily sat to hold our places while Eric explored the chapels and corners of the enormous cathedral.

The whole experience felt hazy to me, as if the censer had already been swung. I'd been on my feet for five hours, after barely more sleep than that. The crowds of people swarming in every direction, greeting one another and taking pictures, left my senses overloaded. It was only when I looked up into the soaring Romanesque arches and watched the rays of light angle through the windows high above us that I felt like I could breathe normally.

The cathedral filled with more and more people, pilgrims and tourists alike, as noon drew closer. There were seats for a thousand, and that morning every inch of bench space was filled, with a few hundred more observers standing around the edges.

A middle-aged man squeezed beside me into the last seat in our pew, and we began the typical pilgrim conversation: Where did you start? Where are you from? He was French and had also started in Le Puy. He was one of us! I told him I was surprised I'd never seen him on the road over the past eleven weeks. Surely we would have overlapped somewhere. Ah, but that was the difference. He was a bicycle pilgrim, with a support car carrying his belongings. He'd started his Camino ten days earlier and averaged 150 kilometers per day.

There had been some *weeks* I hadn't traveled 150 kilometers.

I tried to imagine what a blur it would be to see everything I'd seen in ten days, but then the mass began. The service was in Spanish, and the acoustics of the beautiful stone structure, not to mention the restless crowd, made it hard to follow. At one point priests came down the aisles and offered wafers to all those who desired communion. Hundreds crowded around them, and I understood why wine was impractical.

My attention wandered to the main altar. Dozens of feet above the action on the floor was a life-sized statue of Saint James, shimmering with Baroque flourishes and New World gold. This wasn't James the Moor Slayer or even James the pilgrim. This was a regal James, covered in jewels. Even his staff was made of gold.

He almost blended into all of the ornamentation around him, but something about him caught my eye. As I watched, there was a movement in the shadows behind him. And then, without warning, a human arm, and then a head, appeared just for a second before disappearing.

That's when I remembered that the cathedral was about more than swinging incense and crowded masses. There was also the tradition of hugging Saint James. Behind the altar of the cathedral of Santiago is a set of stairs that leads to a *camarín*, or small room, behind the statue of Saint James. For centuries, pilgrims have climbed those stairs to directly offer the saint thanks for a safe journey—and then they hug the statue. The line can stretch for hours, so the camarín is always open when the cathedral is open, even during services.

My interest was ignited. This was exactly the quirky, hands-on, personal kind of thing that could make me fall in love with this city and its thousand-year-old story all over again.

It turned out that we were there on a lucky pilgrim mass day after all. At the end of the service, eight men in red robes came out and swung the botafumeiro. The effect was logistically amazing, but anticlimactic, as our view was blocked by the sea of iPhones thrust into the air, recording the moment instead of experiencing it.

As soon as the mass was over, I explained to Eric that all I wanted to do in Santiago—my very reason for being in this city—was to hug Saint James. He was less enthusiastic. The line stretched all the way around the ambulatory, and he was hungry. Plus, he pointed out, thanking a statue was silly. We compromised and agreed to eat first, but to come back to the cathedral and explore later. I'd have a better moment with James, I reasoned, on a full stomach.

So we ventured back into the bright sunlight and crowded streets, found a low-ceilinged stone bar, cool even in the heat of the afternoon, and revived ourselves with thick cheese and sausage bocadillos. By the time we emerged, the city felt a little quieter, so we went to the Pilgrim Office for a second try at our Compostelas.

For as long as pilgrims have traveled to Santiago, there have been those who try to claim the benefits of pilgrimage without doing the work. In response, the Pilgrim Office of Santiago established, and continues to update, their guidelines for Compostelas. It's not enough for a person to arrive and claim to have walked at least one hundred kilometers. They must show their credential, issued by one of the officially recognized national Camino associations or confraternities (to dissuade entrepreneurs who try to sell "credentials" for profit). The credential must bear at least two stamps per day, from different locations along the way, over the last one hundred kilometers. This prevents, or at least makes it more difficult for, people like the blue-scarved Italians to arrive by car or bus and claim a Compostela.

I don't know how uniformly enforced this is. When it was my turn to step up to the Pilgrim Office counter, the volunteer behind the desk was polite but harried. He barely looked at my two full, colorfully stamped credentials, certainly not long enough to see specifically where I'd been three days earlier. He asked whether I had walked for religious, cultural, or recreational reasons (I said cultural), and then he gave me the fancy certificate that said I had completed the Camino. It was written in Latin, with my name translated to an awkward-sounding and probably not historically accurate *Elizabetham.*

For an extra five euros, he would also give me a certificate with the specific distance I had walked. I declined that; my muscles and bruises knew how far I'd come.

When we went back to the cathedral, it was quieter. I took a half-hearted loop around the chapels, not really taking much in, and then dragged Eric toward the narrow stairs behind the altar—me giddy and bouncing, Eric embarrassed and hanging back. The short line moved quickly, guided by a volunteer who made sure no one lingered with James too long.

The man just in front of me in line was, in polite terms, a big guy. I waited in the doorway of the camarín while he went to the statue to have his moment. Everyone else was behind me on the stairs, so I was the only witness when he bumped James's gilded staff as he tried to reach around the golden shoulders. The jeweled ornament wobbled and jangled precariously.

Did the pilgrim in front of me break Saint James? He backed away quickly, and I stepped forward. Everything seemed to be all right. James was tougher than he looked.

I leaned out of the shadows and into the bright spotlights from the cathedral floor below and reached out.

And there, away from the crowds and the noise, I had my Santiago Moment.

It was one of those rare experiences where I was entirely present for something I knew would never happen again. I laid my head on the shiny gold and said *gracias* to the guy who started it all.

Thanks for a thousand miles without serious injury.

Thanks for the millions of people who trekked this way before me, and the hundreds who walked with me.

Thanks for the story you left behind.

Thanks for letting me be a part of it.

It was a short moment, and as the line pressed forward behind me, I stepped away and continued down a second set of stairs, a tingle of happy tears in my eyes.

I didn't see Eric's moment with James. He said it wasn't all that special.

The line continued down to the sepulcher, where a box held the remains of a man presumed for centuries to be the disciple of Christ. This, for me, was less engaging, but we paid our respects before going back into the city, hoping to find a few familiar faces and share the experience.

We saw the lovely Italian couple and had a final drink with them. When we parted ways, they wished us a "buona vita," a good life. We did the same. They were the only friends we saw that night. The city was big and crowded, and our pilgrim family was well dispersed. Eric and I ate a mediocre dinner at an outdoor cafe table and watched noisy, rambunctious groups wandering by. They all seemed happy.

When we were done, it felt like there was nothing else to see, so we wandered back to our albergue in the growing twilight. The lost sleep and long day caught up with us almost as soon as we got to our beds, and we were asleep before the sun went down.

In hindsight, there's a lot that I wish I could change about that day in Santiago. I wish I could have stopped being disappointed that my reaction didn't mirror what I saw in everyone else. I wish that I'd taken more time to see the city. I wish I'd taken the tour of the cathedral grounds, including the rooftops and the cloisters, to understand more of the symbolism and culture. I wish I'd made more effort to find our friends.

But I know I didn't do any of those things because I was exhausted in a way I didn't understand yet. Even as I gloated about how walking had become my natural state, it was taking its toll. My body was stronger than it probably had ever been, but I could feel the strain of the past seventy-five days in my hips and in my mind.

There was a reason I'd shied away from exploring the towns we passed through in that last week, seeking quiet corners instead. I'd taken in about as much "new" as I could. New places. New people. New scenery. New feelings. I desperately needed to rest and to give my memories a chance to settle.

But I couldn't let go in Santiago, because I wasn't done yet. Santiago de Compostela was a significant milestone, but it wasn't our destination. We were still ninety kilometers from the end of the world. And the sooner I got there, the sooner I could really stop.

Santiago was quiet the next morning when Eric and I passed the cathedral one last time, once again heading west. Even the plaza was deserted, and there were no cafes open so early. Later, I learned that the Parador Hotel, just across the street from the cathedral in the grand former Royal Hospital, offers free food to the first ten pilgrims who arrive for each meal, Compostela in hand. The line for breakfast starts at 6:00 a.m., which is about when we passed by.

But we were ready to walk again, and I felt no desire to linger in this anticlimactic city. Surely there would be a cafe open in one of the villages ahead.

I didn't yet know about the Feast of Saint John the Baptist.

BUT WAIT, THERE'S MORE

As we walked out of the city and into the western foothills of Santiago, urban neighborhoods faded into rural lanes and then wooded paths. The hazy sunrise turned the spires of the cathedral behind us into a postcard-perfect silhouette, scaffolding and all, against the orange sunrise.

For the first time, we were walking *away* from Santiago. The Camino trail to Finisterre was still well marked with Galicia's familiar concrete bollards, emblazoned with the scallop shell and yellow arrows. But the kilometers now counted down to the end of the world.

Something else was different. It was quiet. We didn't see another pilgrim for twelve long kilometers that morning. We barely saw another person.

Most pilgrims finish their pilgrimage in Santiago, either because they're limited by time or because they don't see a reason to continue. Santiago is the historic destination after all, and where they get their Compostela. This is the Camino de Santiago, not the Camino de Finisterre. Why keep walking?

I could see their point. But for me, the coast had always been the goal. And it isn't quite accurate to say that Santiago is *the*

The bronze boot at Cape Finisterre

historic destination. After all, people made spiritual journeys to Finisterre for hundreds of years before Pelayo unearthed a grave under a star.

The Santiago pilgrimage, like many Christian traditions, borrowed heavily from the cultures in place before it. Celtic pagans had journeyed west to make sacrifices at the Ara Solis temple on the point of Cape Finisterre for centuries before the Romans left the Italian peninsula, and so the local population had a long history and familiarity with the tradition of traveling toward "the place where the sun died."

Not that I was walking to Finisterre because of the pagans, any more than I walked to Santiago because of the Catholics. I was here because it seemed like an epic journey west should end with my feet in the ocean. I was going to walk until I couldn't walk anymore.

But on that first morning, I wasn't thinking about epic journeys. I was thinking about my missing breakfast. Our faith that we would find a cafe had been misplaced. Our trail mostly followed dirt tracks across fields and behind farms, and when we did pass through a village, the bars we saw were cerrado. By midmorning, long past the time I needed my café con leche, the delay made me hangry.

It seemed that I was going to end this Camino journey much the way I'd started it three months before, sulking over a lack of a sandwich.

When we caught up to a middle-aged American couple limping along the side of the road, I had to concentrate on not taking my annoyance out on them. The wife looked ready to break already, anyway. They were from Arkansas, and this was their very first day of their very first Camino.

"You started in Santiago?" I asked. "That's unusual." They agreed, but said they weren't used to walking, especially not distances like this, and the thought of going for weeks intimidated them. They would test the Camino by walking to Finisterre. If they enjoyed it, they'd consider coming back and doing a longer stretch another time.

New as they were, they'd still picked up information that we didn't have. "We almost didn't start today," the husband said. "It's a holiday, something about Saint John the Baptist, and we were worried things would be closed." All of those cerrado signs started to make sense, and I had a sinking suspicion that I would have to starve all the way to Negreira.

We chatted for a few minutes, but I was never going to get to food at their pace, so Eric and I wished them "buen Camino" and picked up to our normal speed.

Finally, twelve kilometers into our day, our luck turned, and we came across a single open cafe. It was filled with *peregrinos* digging into giant slices of empanada and sipping coffee, and I half-heartedly wondered where they'd all come from, since I hadn't seen any of them walking earlier.

I collapsed into the first chair I saw, and Eric brought me a huge plate of food. With each bite my attitude improved.

Just as we finished, a familiar face appeared in the doorway, and the day brightened a little more. Arjan was the young Dutch police officer we'd met two weeks earlier in Mazarife, where we shared pitchers of sangria while the town paraded behind a man shooting fireworks. He'd gotten ahead of us after that, but he'd lingered in Santiago for a few days after his arrival, and now here we all were again.

We chatted while Arjan ate and then set out together for Negreira. The next three kilometers were a steep climb, and even in the shade it was uncomfortably hot. We distracted ourselves by swapping stories. Arjan was friendly and open, eager to describe his dream of giving up his desk job to travel the world—especially the parts of the world where there were beautiful women.

We were laughing and sweating when we reached the bridge over the Río Tambre. If we hadn't noticed the kids on the rocks below, we might have kept walking. If we hadn't been so hot from the climb, maybe the sight of teenagers diving into cool water wouldn't have been so appealing. But we did notice, and we were hot.

I thought about Heather's love of river swimming. I thought about the shallow stream in Ribadiso and how good it felt on tired muscles. Eric clearly had the same idea. "Wanna swim?"

I was the first to agree. If there was ever a place or a time in my life for a wild swim, this was it. A perfect river, a hot afternoon, and strangers I'd never see again.

Arjan hesitated. "I don't have a suit," he said.

"Neither do we." His eyes grew wide. "No," I assured him. "We're not going to skinny dip." Backpacking clothes, I'd accepted long ago, were not sexy. Every day I wore modest black underwear and a sports bra that covered more than the average bikini. Eric, too, had black boxer briefs that could pass for trunks from a distance. We had travel towels in our bags, and our clothes were all quick-dry.

I wiggled my eyebrows. "C'mon, you know you want to . . . "

Arjan finally said yes, and we scrambled down the bank into an open, grassy area that I assumed was a public park. We dropped our packs, and then our clothes, on rocks in the sun, and jumped into the river.

It was blissful. The water was cold but not freezing, deep enough to swim, with only a gentle current. The guys swam across the river and dove off half-submerged rocks while I floated close to our packs on the shore. A few pilgrims hooted and waved as they crossed the bridge above us, but no one joined us. The river was ours.

Camino surprises can turn around even the hardest days.

We eventually climbed out and dried off most of the river water and then let the sun do the rest as we ambled the final few kilometers to Negreira. We stopped at the first albergue we found, a generic place without much going for it except convenience. Still feeling relaxed and playful, we rushed through the daily washing and headed out to find the closest bar.

For the next six hours, the bartender poured drinks, and we talked about everything from politics to sex to gossip about other pilgrims. And as we talked, other familiar faces showed up. Dennis was there, and we got to introduce our two favorite Dutch officers of the peace. Neither of them, unfortunately, knew an older man named Jan, with a guttural voice, who lived near Aachen.

Roy, the American I'd first met in Astorga, was there, too. And there were new friends—a brother and sister from Austin and a couple from Spain. Others dropped in and left as the afternoon wore on.

Here, in this uninspiring Spanish town, I found the reunion I had missed in Santiago. My weariness disappeared.

The next morning—after a hearty breakfast, because I'd learned my lesson—we walked with Arjan through the farms of Galicia, with their horreos and fields of sheep. Arjan was good company, but when we reached the tiny town of Santa Marina, which was really just a row of businesses along a busy road, I stuck to our original plan and announced I was done for the day.

It is possible to walk from Santiago to Finisterre in three days, but because of where the towns and albergues are located, it requires walking two thirty-five-kilometer days in a row. I had no interest in pushing that hard at the very end, and we were in no rush. I'd planned a more sedate, four-day approach.

Arjan, Dennis, and all of our new friends were on the three-day plan. They looked skeptical when they left us, but I'd learned by then that "walk your own Camino" meant not trying to keep up with the younger, fitter, faster crowd. If we were meant to see them again, we would.

The small Santa Marina albergue was owned by the same woman who owned the local bar, where we lingered and watched others trickle in through the afternoon, often looking as tired and worn as I felt. We were well into dinner, and it was well past 8:00, when the final couple staggered in. They'd left Santiago that morning and had, ill advisedly, walked past Negreira, thinking that this would be like the Camino Francés, with lodging available every five or ten kilometers. Instead, they'd trudged all the way here, making it a forty-five-kilometer day. They were exhausted, but our albergue was full.

Our hospitalera didn't seem surprised. Perhaps things like this happened often on the path to Finisterre. She settled them at the table with food while she made some calls and eventually found a guesthouse a few kilometers away that would come to pick them up, give them a place to sleep, and take them back to the Camino the next morning.

Our attic room that night was full and stuffy. The Spanish couple near the window closed it, and the air smelled like middle-aged sweat. I was happy to get back on the road the next morning.

I was determined to slow down and appreciate this last thirty-kilometer day, which would mostly cross open scrubland. The moody gray sky kept the heat away, and the farms gave way to land that reminded me of the coastal sand dunes and marshes where I grew up.

Long before it was reasonable, I looked for signs of the ocean. It had to be so close by now. Finally, just after noon, I caught the faintest glimpse through the haze of a brighter space between two hills. Was that water?

It was, but to get there we needed to navigate a final steep, sandy descent into Cee, a seaside industrial town that was more function than form. At the foot of the hill was an albergue—a private place owned by a man who cared for the people who came through and took pride in his establishment. There were real sheets and blankets on the beds, colorful rugs on the floor, and modern, sparkling clean bathrooms. An album on the coffee table was full of photos of past guests, and an elaborate guest book recorded their stories and artwork.

It was the best place I could imagine for my last night in a bunk bed.

On our final day we followed the saltwater bay west, past harbors full of fishing boats and weathered, salt-sprayed buildings in pastel colors. We'd come a long way from the black-rock volcanic mountains where we'd begun.

I wanted to be quiet, to soak in these final hours. I wanted a chance to reflect. But real life doesn't work out as neatly as that. At the edge of Cee we met Mike, an American from the Midwest, and he shadowed us all morning, keeping up a steady stream of stories in which he was always the hero. When we stopped for breakfast, he stopped too. When we sped up, he kept up. The Camino had decided Mike was going to be part of my arrival, so I didn't fight it.

The trail took us over one last ridge, where on a clear day we would have been able to see the lighthouse of Finisterre, framed in the iron gateway arch of one final chapel dedicated to San Roque. But real life wasn't going to give me that either. It was hazy and gray, and the lighthouse point was shrouded in fog.

We descended back to the sea and along wooden boardwalks through salt marshes and then to a white sand beach. I still couldn't see the ocean, but the tang of salt was in the air, and there were scallop shells on the beach.

Finally, the mist cleared, and a patch of blue sky emerged just over Finisterre. Sometimes real life saves the best surprise for last.

I loved Finisterre—"Fisterra" in the Galician language Gallego—the second I saw it. It was small and modest, historic but not fancy, rising from a steep bank in the sheltered east-facing cove.

At the edge of town Mike finally went his own way, and Eric and I climbed to the guesthouse where we had a reservation for *three nights*. The last time we'd slept three nights in the same bed was in our own apartment in Seattle, before we left. This made it official. We weren't pilgrims anymore.

Relieved of our packs and hiking shoes, we wandered back into town and toward the waterfront. We saw several albergues and plenty of guesthouses, and the open plaza on the waterfront was lined with restaurants, but beyond that, Finisterre didn't seem interested in their Camino tourists. This was a working fishing town, where the day's catch was auctioned every afternoon to restaurants, wholesalers, and the occasional local resident. The huge, modern commercial fish market, with its sharp steel and polished marble, was the center of the town, not a cathedral or pilgrim statue.

Just past the fish market was a tiny cove with a public beach, and it was here that I stripped off my sandals and made my symbolic walk into the Atlantic Ocean. Eric rolled his eyes and stayed on shore but obligingly took a few photos as saltwater swirled around my feet. When that was done I walked along the beach, which was littered with beach glass. I collected it by the handful, knowing that I no longer had to worry about the weight of what I carried.

We lingered in the plaza beside the marina, watching schools of fish swim in the rising tide, until the afternoon shadows lengthened and it was time for the final leg. We collected our supplies—a bottle of wine and a bag of snacks—put our walking shoes back on, and set out.

There were still three kilometers to go.

Eric and I followed the road that wound up and south through open parkland to the point of the peninsula, where a lighthouse protected the sharp, rocky cliffs from the boats that were drawn to them. Here was the actual point of Finisterre, the end of the known world a thousand years ago.

Just beside the lighthouse was the final Camino marker.

It read 0.00 K.M.

There was nowhere else to go.

Eric and I sat on the rocks, opened the wine, and watched the sun . . . well, not exactly set, but disappear into the bank of clouds on the horizon. It was a gentle end to a momentous day.

We didn't talk much, and I didn't have much of an appetite. All around us there were clusters of people, most of them obviously Camino pilgrims, also watching the sun. Some were quiet. Others were rowdy and celebratory. They built small bonfires among the rocks to burn things that they'd worn or carried across Spain—another Camino tradition that probably evolved from a pagan practice of sacrificing to the sun, or perhaps from a medieval custom to protect from the plague.

This was it. The end of the journey. The end of the world.

We couldn't go farther, but I couldn't imagine going back just yet. We returned to our fancy private room in the gathering twilight, passing through the already-quiet town. With no albergue curfew or need to put in early morning kilometers, Eric and I could finally stay up as late as we wanted, but Finisterre was asleep at 10:00 p.m. Fishing villages wake up early.

The next morning we lingered over a leisurely breakfast on the patio of our guesthouse and then split up to explore. Eric went to a cemetery we'd seen on the road to the lighthouse. I went back to the beach we'd crossed when we first arrived and found it littered with shells of every color, including perfect scallop shells.

Eric and I were both back in the plaza when Arjan arrived, fresh from the trail and in the company of a pretty young woman. After he left us in Santa Marina he'd gone to Muxía, another seaside town with ties to the Camino, and spent a day there before winding down to Finisterre. Along the way he'd met Sara, a Spanish scientist who'd walked a different Camino trail in northern Spain called the Camino Primitivo. That evening, the four of us bought more wine and snacks and once again walked to the lighthouse to watch the sunset.

If the first night was reflective and quiet, the second night was a celebration. We all posed for photos on the cliffs, and told stories, and watched the bright sun disappear into a bank of clouds above the horizon. I felt myself let go of another little piece of the Camino, but I still wasn't ready to go back.

The third day we ventured to the western side of the peninsula and what Radio Camino called "the wild beach," where the Atlantic Ocean crashed directly onto soft white sand. This was where James's body supposedly washed ashore. The place was almost deserted, and once again we swam in our underwear, splashing in the waves and fighting a powerful undertow. I joked that the ocean wanted us to keep going west.

We returned to town to find that more of our Camino family had arrived. Rory and Lis had shaken most of their entourage in Santiago and now had the chance for a few relaxing days on the coast to decompress and celebrate. Rory, it turned out, had been carrying an engagement ring all the way across Spain, and he'd popped the question in the shadow of the Santiago cathedral the day they arrived. The six of us feasted on fresh seafood and then bought bottles of wine and set out for the lighthouse. It seemed we couldn't stay away.

If the first night was reflective, and the second night was a celebration, the third night was an all-out party. Our group kept growing—Rory and Lis knew everyone in Spain, it seemed—and together we laughed and toasted and cheered the sun as it, again, shyly slipped behind cloud banks before dropping into the ocean. Eric made a fire and burned his straw hat. Arjan did impressive handstands on the edge of the world.

I leaned back against a rock and soaked it all in.

I wanted to spend another three nights here. I wanted to spend a month here. But as we joked and skipped down the hill that night back toward town, I was finally ready.

It was time to go back. Not just because I wanted to sleep in my own bed and enjoy a drawer full of underwear I didn't have to wash in a sink every day, although those pieces would definitely be nice. But I also knew, intuitively, that I had soaked in as much as I could for now.

A pilgrimage is designed to be a temporary stage in a human's life, and mine, for now, was over.

The next morning, Eric and I got up, packed our backpacks, said goodbye to the Atlantic Ocean and our lovely three-night room, and boarded a crowded bus to Santiago. We still had a week before our flight left Paris, and I would have gladly extended our stay in Finisterre, greeting pilgrims and eating seafood for another few days, except for this one thing.

The Dane was in Santiago.

We'd gotten a couple of emails from her since we'd left her at the chapel near Pamplona. She'd volunteered there for a week and then sidetracked again near Rabanal, spending a few days in a collective community that ground their own flour and lived off the land. But when she did walk, she covered a lot of kilometers, so she arrived in Santiago just three days after we did. She was there now, waiting for us.

We'd practically started our Camino with The Dane, and we ended it with her as well, eating tapas in Santiago and marveling at how much can happen in eleven weeks. She would leave the next day for her final walk to Muxía and Finisterre. We would leave too, on a train bound east.

That night, Eric and The Dane and I didn't talk much about the future. For one last night we were simply pilgrims of the Camino, sharing stories as the summer sun went down.

I think we may have even sung a round of "Ultreia."

Onward.

EPILOGUE
HOME

It was time to go home.

Our train from Santiago sped east, blending the hills of Galicia and then the plains of the Meseta into a blur of landscapes. This was the only way I'd seen the world for years, I realized—from moving metal boxes that were climate controlled, comfortable, and going too fast for me to notice the details. But for seventy-nine days, my only climate control had been a sun hat and a rain jacket. I was rarely comfortable, and I moved so slowly that I could watch the seasons changing day by day and make solemn eye contact with cows. A person can't spend seventy-nine days making eye contact with cows and not see the world in a slightly different way.

I felt it as I sat on that train. We'd done something Big. Something we would talk about for the rest of our lives. In some ways, we would never be the same.

Sure, we came home to the same apartment, the same high-maintenance cat, the same smartphones and jobs and busy routines. We settled back into many of our habits, both good and bad. Another one of Eric's mantras is "wherever you go, there you are," and that was true. We'd brought our quirks and weak points to France, carried them all the way to the Spanish coast, and brought them home again.

But on a deeper level, our perspectives had changed. The normal annoyances of modern life seemed smaller. When faced with a car that arbitrarily died on the side of a highway, or a challenging person at work, Eric and I would look at each other. "Practice acceptance," one of us would say. Or his favorite: "Sometimes you win, sometimes you lose."

When our screens lit up with breaking news about a terrorist attack in Paris or a flood in Australia, we paid attention. We had friends there. When the latest manufactured crisis or scandal swamped social media, we looked at it through the lens of a thousand years of history.

Walking the Way of Saint James made me stronger, not just in my hamstrings but also in my heart. It taught me stamina and the importance of finding delight in something new and beautiful every day, despite trials of pain and weather. It showed me how to push past myself to forge connections that breach culture and language barriers. It taught me to be content with myself and my place in a bigger story.

The Camino de Santiago wasn't an extreme experience. I never feared for my life or went without the daily necessities. But the Camino was never easy. A thousand-year-old path had tested my body and my mind, and I'd persevered. Me, who wasn't "the type" to spend sixteen hours a day outside, or climb mountains, or sleep in rooms full of strangers. Me, who'd once shunned the word "pilgrim" and everything it stood for. Me, now a long-distance hiker.

But those were the particular gifts the Camino gave *me*, and as they say in the commercials, "results may vary." A quarter of a million people walk some part of the Way of Saint James every year, and they all bring home their own gifts, stories, and memories.

Some walk for just a week, and some walk for a year. It rains on some of them more often, and on others not at all. Many of them barely remember the towns that imprinted on my heart, and their life-changing moments happen in places that I breezed through without noticing.

Camino pilgrims come home energized, or contemplative, or nostalgic, or relieved.

But I've never met anyone who came home unchanged.

APPENDIX I.
OUR CAMINO CALENDAR

Day 1.   Le Puy-en-Velay to Saint-Privat-d'Allier (24 kilometers)
Day 2.   Saint-Privat-d'Allier to Saugues (18 kilometers)
Day 3.   Saugues to Chanaleilles (14 kilometers)
Day 4.   Chanaleilles to Les Estrets (26 kilometers)
Day 5.   Les Estrets to Finieyrols (23 kilometers)
Day 6.   Finieyrols to Saint-Chely-d'Aubrac (30 kilometers)
Day 7.   Saint-Chely-d'Aubrac to Saint-Côme d'Olt (14 kilometers)
Day 8.   Saint-Côme d'Olt to Estaing (19 kilometers)
Day 9.   Estaing to Espeyrac (22 kilometers)
Day 10.   Espeyrac to Conques (15 kilometers)
Day 11.   Conques to Livinhac-le-Haut (23 kilometers)
Day 12.   Livinhac-le-Haut to Figeac (26 kilometers)
Day 13.   Figeac to La Cassagnole (5 kilometers)
Day 14.   La Cassagnole to Cajarc (29 kilometers)
Day 15.   Cajarc to Varaire (25 kilometers)
Day 16.   Varaire to Cahors (32 kilometers)
Day 17.   Cahors to Lascabanes (22 kilometers[1])
Day 18.   Lascabanes to Lauzerte (23 kilometers)
Day 19.   Rest day in Lauzerte
Day 20.   Lauzerte to Moissac (24 kilometers)
Day 21.   Moissac to Auvillar (21 kilometers)
Day 22.   Auvillar to Castet-Arrouy (22 kilometers)
Day 23.   Castet-Arrouy to La Romieu (30 kilometers)
Day 24.   La Romieu to Larressingle (20 kilometers)
Day 25.   Larressingle to Eauze (28 kilometers)
Day 26.   Eauze to Nogaro (20 kilometers)
Day 27.   Nogaro to Barcelonne-du-Gers (26 kilometers)
Day 28.   Barcelonne-du-Gers to Miramont Sensacq
           (18 kilometers)
Day 29.   Miramont Sensacq to Larreule (27 kilometers)

[1] Not including the 10-kilometer detour to Hospitalet.

Day 30. Larreule to Arthez-de-Béarn (18 kilometers)

Day 31. Rest day in Arthez-de-Béarn

Day 32. Arthez-de-Béarn to Navarrenx (31 kilometers)

Day 33. Navarrenx to Aroue (20 kilometers)

Day 34. Aroue to Ostabat (24 kilometers)

Day 35. Ostabat to Saint-Jean-Pied-de-Port (23 kilometers)

Day 36. Saint-Jean-Pied-de-Port to Roncesvalles (26 kilometers)

Day 37. Roncesvalles to Zubiri (22 kilometers)

Day 38. Zubiri to Pamplona (21 kilometers)

Day 39. Rest day in Pamplona

Day 40. Pamplona to Uterga (16 kilometers)

Day 41. Uterga to Puente la Reina (12 kilometers, including side trip to Eunate)

Day 42. Puente la Reina to Estella (22 kilometers)

Day 43. Estella to Los Arcos (22 kilometers)

Day 44. Sick day in Los Arcos

Day 45. Los Arcos to Viana (19 kilometers)

Day 46. Sick day in Viana

Day 47. Viana to Nájera (40 kilometers, by car)

Day 48. Nájera to Santo Domingo de la Calzada (22 kilometers)

Day 49. Santo Domingo de la Calzada to Villafranca de Montes d'Oca (35 kilometers)

Day 50. Villafranca de Montes d'Oca to Cardeñuela Riopico (24 kilometers)

Day 51. Cardeñuela Riopico to Burgos (13 kilometers)

Day 52. Burgos to Hornillos del Camino (19 kilometers)

Day 53. Hornillos del Camino to Castrojeriz (20 kilometers)

Day 54. Castrojeriz to Fromista (25 kilometers)

Day 55. Fromista to Carrion de los Condes (19 kilometers)

Day 56. Carrion de los Condes to Terradillos de los Templarios (27 kilometers)

Day 57. Terradillos de los Templarios to Bercianos del Real Camino (23 kilometers)

Day 58. Bercianos del Real Camino to Mansilla de Mulas (27 kilometers)

Day 59. Mansilla de Mulas to León (18 kilometers)

Day 60. Rest day in León

Day 61. León to Mazarif (22 kilometers)

Day 62. Mazarif to Hospital de Órbigo (12 kilometers)
Day 63. Hospital de Órbigo to Astorga (14 kilometers)
Day 64. Astorga to Rabanal (20 kilometers)
Day 65. Rabanal to Molinaseca (25 kilometers)
Day 66. Molinaseca to Ponferrada (7 kilometers)
Day 67. Ponferrada to Villafranca del Bierzo (23 kilometers)
Day 68. Villafranca del Bierzo to La Faba (28 kilometers)
Day 69. La Faba to Biduedo (18 kilometers)
Day 70. Biduedo to Sarria (25 kilometers)
Day 71. Sarria to Portomarín (23 kilometers)
Day 72. Portomarín to Palas de Reí (25 kilometers)
Day 73. Palas de Reí to Ribadiso (25 kilometers)
Day 74. Ribadiso to O Pino (of many names) (23 kilometers)
Day 75. O Pino to Santiago de Compostela (20 kilometers)
Day 76. Santiago de Compostela to Negreira (21 kilometers)
Day 77. Negreira to Santa Marina (21 kilometers)
Day 78. Santa Marina to Cee (32 kilometers)
Day 79. Cee to Finisterre (15 kilometers)

APPENDIX II.
CAMINO ROUTES

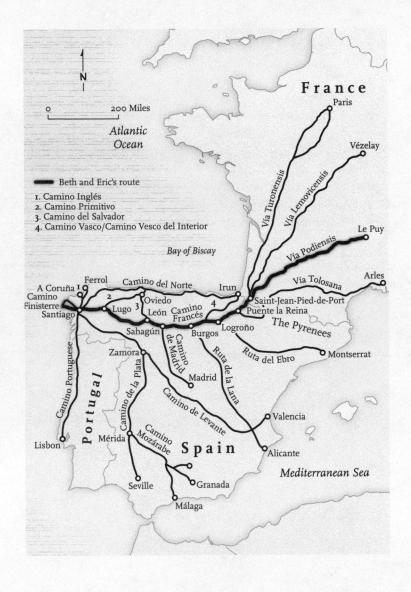

N

200 Miles

*Atlantic
Ocean*

France
Paris

Vézelay

━━ Beth and Eric's route
1. Camino Inglés
2. Camino Primitivo
3. Camino del Salvador
4. Camino Vasco/Camino Vesco del Interior

Vía Turonensis

Vía Lemovicensis

Vía Podiensis

Le Puy

Bay of Biscay

Vía Tolosana

Arles

Ferrol   Camino del Norte   Irun
A Coruña 1
Camino   2   Oviedo   Saint-Jean-Pied-de-Port
Finisterre   Lugo 3   León   Camino   4   Puente la Reina
Santiago   Francés   The Pyrenees

Sahagún   Logroño
                Burgos
Zamora   Camino
            de Madrid
                    Ruta de la Lana   Ruta del Ebro   Montserrat

Camino Portuguese

Portugal

Camino de la Plata

Madrid

Camino de Levante

Valencia

Lisbon   Mérida   Camino
                    Mozárabe   **Spain**
                                        Alicante

Seville   Granada   *Mediterranean Sea*

Málaga

APPENDIX III.
PACKING LIST

What does one carry on a three-month walk across Europe? When I look at the list, it seems like a lot. And by some standards, it was. According to a scale of questionable accuracy in France, my pack, including a full water bottle, weighed about ten kilograms, or twenty-two pounds. That's more than what many "experts" would recommend, but it was still light enough that I could carry it daily.

I certainly don't claim this is the *right* packing list for anyone else. There are things I'd change (which I note here), and everyone's priorities are different. For example, not many Camino walkers carry a pillow, but for me, a side sleeper, it was worth the extra seven ounces.

I sometimes sacrificed weight for thrift. I lusted after a thirteen-ounce sleeping bag but saved $140 and bought one that was a full pound heavier. And finally, I needed to pack for all seasons. Eric and I set out when there was still snow on the ground in France's high country and arrived on the coast during a heat wave. Two years later, when I returned to the Camino Francés for a couple of weeks in the heat of summer, I brought only half the clothes listed here.

So with those caveats, here's what I ended up carrying:

Supplies
- 38-liter backpack
- Sleeping bag, 55-degree Fahrenheit rating
- Travel pillow
- Travel towel, 24 by 48 inches
- .75-liter water bottle (Eric carried 1.25 liters, so between us we had plenty.)
- 3 mesh laundry-style bags for organizing clothes
- Walking poles (bought in France; lost three weeks later in Spain)
- Headlamp

Guidebooks

- Alison Raju's *The Way of St. James Vol 1: Le Puy to the Pyrenees*
- *Miam Miam Dodo GR65*
- John Brierley's *A Pilgrim's Guide to the Camino de Santiago* and *A Pilgrim's Guide to the Camino Finisterre*

Clothing

- Lightweight trail runners, traded midtrip for midweight hiking shoes and high-arch inserts
- Nylon sandals
- Merino wool jacket
- Merino wool vest (probably a luxury but the perfect layer in early spring)
- Long-sleeved merino-blend half-zip shirt
- Sleeveless quick-dry hiking shirt
- Short-sleeved merino-blend T-shirt
- Tank top (intended to be a base layer; instead became my sleep shirt)
- 2 pair hiking pants (sturdier pair with pockets for daily hiking; thinner pair for evenings)
- Merino wool leggings
- Travel skirt (a luxury but nice for hot summer afternoons)
- 2 pair thin merino socks
- 2 pair thick merino socks (lost one pair after two weeks)
- 3 pair underwear
- 2 sports bras
- Rain shell
- Nylon hat for sun and rain protection
- Straw sun hat (bought in Spain—definitely a luxury)
- Merino wool tube scarf
- UV-protection headband
- Sunglasses (and case)
- Digital watch with alarm

Toiletries
- Shower bag with hook (Many shower stalls didn't have a way to keep clothes or supplies off the floor.)
- Bar soap in a quick-dry mesh bag (for cleaning bodies and clothes; the mesh bag helped with laundry scrubbing)
- Travel-sized folding toothbrush
- 3-ounce travel-sized toothpaste
- 3 cheap, disposable razors
- Travel-sized hairbrush
- 3-ounce deodorant
- 2-ounce conditioner (I used bar soap to wash my hair but wasn't willing to deal with frizz unless I put product into my curls. Don't judge.)
- 2-ounce hair styling lotion (See above about judging.)
- Safety pins (Not a luxury! We used safety pins for everything: on clotheslines, for attaching still-wet clothes or other gear to our packs, to fix damaged clothes, etc.)
- A few spare hair elastics
- Eyeliner pencil (a luxury, yes, but does this even weigh enough to register?)
- Nail file
- Toenail clippers
- Q-Tips
- Ibuprofen tablets
- Feminine products
- Lotion (bought in France—I tried to live without but my dry skin cracked)

Other
- Passport
- Camino credentials
- Small billfold to carry cash and debit card
- Small nylon cross-body purse to keep cash, passport, credentials (I left this in my backpack when

walking, and it was easy to pull out when we stopped in cafes or for afternoon sightseeing.)
- Camera (small, fit in a pocket)
- Titanium travel silverware (used once—could have gone without)
- Cell phone
- Journal and pen
- Books (I brought paperbacks of Ernest Hemingway's *The Sun Also Rises* and *The Fifth Column,* and Paul Harding's *Tinkers.* When I finished, I left them in gîtes. In hindsight, I should have used my phone's Kindle app.)
- Charging cords for the phone and camera, plus a European outlet adapter
- Various sizes of resealable plastic bags (for storing food, keeping books and electronics dry in the rain, etc.)
- 2 tall kitchen trash bags (Used to line the inside of my backpack on rainy days. Between this and the rain cover on the outside of my pack, everything stayed dry even in the worst downpours.)

Eric's packing list was similar to mine, except without the luxuries. That man has figured minimalism out: two pairs of pants, three T-shirts, sweater, rain jacket, some socks and underwear. A tube scarf. Sunglasses. Minimal sneakers. Minimal sandals. A bar of soap and a toothbrush. A book. I think that's it. He carried most of our food as well as some of our shared supplies:

- First-aid kit: adhesive bandages (which we hardly used), moleskin bandages (which we did), antibiotic ointment, tweezers, needles and thread (for puncturing blisters), disposable lighter (for sterilizing needles; in hindsight, alcohol wipes would have been better), athletic tape

- Parachute cord (we only used this once as an indoor laundry line and could have left it at home)
- Pocket knife (bought in France, since airlines wouldn't allow it)

ACKNOWLEDGMENTS

First and foremost, I wouldn't have much of a story to tell without my Camino family. To Jean Claude, the Brothers Grim, the Eight Walkers, Virginie, Eugene, Gwen, Jan, the Black-Eyed B's, Stephanie, The Dane (known to most as Amanda), Marieke, Guy, Jean-Francois, Wolfgang and Margarete, Caroline, Chris, Lis, Rory, Mette, Ian, Nic, Emily, Heather, Arjan, Roy, Dennis, Sarah and Kim, Hans and Gertrude, the lovely Italian couple whose names I never learned, and Sara: more than the weather, more than the steep climbs, more than the fairy-tale villages, you each shaped my experience and made it better.

To Dora Machado, the writer whose blog about walking to Santiago first inspired this trip: you could not have imagined what you were starting, but I'm so glad you did.

To Chris Matthias and Emily DenBleyker, who kept the home fires burning and the cat alive for three long months: I could turn off the outside world only because I knew you had it all under control.

To my blog readers at Camino Times Two: your "likes" and comments have encouraged me and pushed me forward more often than I can tell you.

To the American Pilgrims of the Camino community, and especially the Facebook group: your steady stream of questions, inspiration, and honesty have kept my passion burning.

To my writing support team, including my colleagues at Monkey Barrel Media, the best and cheapest co-op office a writer could ask for; the staff at Chautauqua Lodge in Long Beach, Washington, where much of this book was written in week-long sprints; and the staff at Chocolati Cafe in Seattle's Greenwood neighborhood, where much of this book was revised: your Pacific Northwest kindness infuses these pages.

To my beta readers: Emily Scherb, Elsa Bowman, Melinda Brovelli, Charley Brozina, Bill Charters, Nancy Frye, and Jane Ryder: you freely gave your time and opinions in order to make this book better. I hope you each find an unexpected adventure of your own.

To the team at Mountaineers Books: Kate Rogers, Mary Metz, Jen Grable, Linda Gunnarson, Amy Smith Bell, Julie Briselden, and everyone I haven't met yet: when I first dreamed up this book, you were my first choice of publisher, and I'm so honored by your enthusiasm and support. Thanks for taking in a writer who doesn't mountaineer in any traditional sense.

And finally, of course, to Eric. This book begins and ends with you. It wouldn't have happened without you. I'm thankful every day that you're with me on this great adventure called marriage, pushing me when I need pushing and carrying my *sac* when it needs to be carried. I love your warm brown eyes, your gorgeous-shaped toes, and your pathological helpfulness. Thank you for volunteering your journals, tolerating two years of writing, offering cautious but honest feedback on the early drafts, and sharing a piece of our story with the world.

ABOUT THE AUTHOR

Beth Jusino is an active member of the American Pilgrims on the Camino and offers workshops and talks about the Way of Saint James as often as anyone lets her. She has returned to the Camino twice (so far): she walked part of the Camino Francés with a friend in 2017, and she and Eric walked part of the Camino del Norte in 2018. You can find photos and read much more about her Camino obsession at caminotimestwo.com.

When she's not carrying a backpack across Europe, Beth is a writer, editor, and publishing consultant in Seattle. She is the author of the award-winning *The Author's Guide to Marketing* and has ghostwritten and collaborated on half a dozen additional titles. She regularly teaches classes about writing, publishing, and marketing at conferences and libraries. Find out more about Beth's day job at bethjusino.com.

The Barbara Savage *Miles from Nowhere* Memorial Award

The Barbara Savage *Miles From Nowhere* Memorial Award supports the publication of previously unpublished works that meet Mountaineers Books' specific criteria for nonfiction adventure narratives. We look for compelling accounts of personal journeys, typically experienced through a muscle-powered outdoor adventure. Award winners vividly convey a sense of the risks, joys, hardships, triumphs, humor, and accidents of fate that are inevitably part of any such journey, as well as describe the wilderness landscapes through which they navigate. Titles chosen are frequently by first-time authors or writers working in the nonfiction adventure genre for the first time.

> **"Over 300 pages of the most delightful travel literature I have ever read."**
> –Santa Barbara News Press, on *Miles from Nowhere*

This memorial award, initiated in 1990, commemorates the late Barbara Savage, author of the bestselling book *Miles from Nowhere: A Round-the-World Bicycle Adventure*, published in 1983. Tragically, Barbara was killed in a cycling accident shortly before the book's publication. The story of her and her husband's two-year, 25,000-mile biking journey, however, continues to inspire a wide readership and to generate letters from readers who have come to know Barbara through her book. Larry Savage created an award fund in cooperation with Mountaineers Books by donating the royalties from *Miles from Nowhere* to encourage personal adventure and writing in its spirit. Authors of the selected titles receive an advance or expanded marketing efforts made possible by this fund.

Barbara Savage *Miles from Nowhere* Memorial Award titles include:

- *Himalayan Passage: Seven Months in the High Country of Tibet, Nepal, China, India, and Pakistan* by Jeremy Schmidt
- *Where the Pavement Ends: One Woman's Bicycle Trip through Mongolia, China, and Vietnam* by Erika Warmbrunn
- *Spirited Waters: Soloing South through the Inside Passage* by Jennifer Hahn
- *A Blistered Kind of Love: One Couple's Trial by Trail* by Angela and Duffy Ballard
- *Faith of Cranes: Finding Hope and Family in Alaska* by Hank Lentfer
- *I Promise Not to Suffer: A Fool for Love Hikes the Pacific Crest Trail* by Gail D. Storey

To find these titles and more, visit Mountaineers Books at
www.mountaineersbooks.org.